CAPITAL AS ORGANIC UNITY

Philosophical Studies in Contemporary Culture

VOLUME 9

The titles published in this series are listed at the end of this volume.

CAPITAL AS ORGANIC UNITY

The Role of Hegel's Science of Logic *in Marx's* Grundrisse

by

MARK E. MEANEY, Ph.D.

Executive Director,
Institut for Clinical and Corporate Ethics,
Liberty, MO, U.S.A.

KLUWER ACADEMIC PUBLISHERS
DORDRECHT / BOSTON / LONDON

A C.I.P. Catalogue record for this book is available from the Library of Congress.

ISBN 1-4020-1037-0

Published by Kluwer Academic Publishers,
P.O. Box 17, 3300 AA Dordrecht, The Netherlands.

Sold and distributed in North, Central and South America
by Kluwer Academic Publishers,
101 Philip Drive, Norwell, MA 02061, U.S.A.

In all other countries, sold and distributed
by Kluwer Academic Publishers,
P.O. Box 322, 3300 AH Dordrecht, The Netherlands.

Printed on acid-free paper

Printed in the Netherlands.

Für Elyse, Paul Martin, und Annabeth Gleason

CONTENTS

PREFACE

This book is a work of historical critical exegesis. It aims to establish the influence of G.W.F. Hegel's *Science of Logic* (SL) on the *Grundrisse* of Karl Marx. I demonstrate that the Hegelian logic guided Marx's doctrinal development, and that the ordering of economic categories in the *Grundrisse* reflects the ordering of the logical categories in the SL.

A historical critical exegesis can establish the influences on an author only in terms of probability. The exegesis can establish a particular influence with varying degrees of probability, but rarely with certitude. Thus, historical critical exegeses are limited in scope. This fact has advantages and disadvantages. Historical critical exegesis confines us to the particular texts under consideration and avoids the complexity often associated with other forms of textual exegesis, for example, structural exegesis. It must on occasion rely on such dubious evidence as phraseology.

Moreover, when one text is allegedly found in another as a subtext, the exegesis focuses on the subtext prescinding from all other content. This narrow focus poses a danger, because such an exercise is naturally reductive. It can appear to reduce the entire work under consideration to the subtext. This particular danger is heightened when the work under consideration was not published by the author, but is a series of manuscripts—a kind of laboratory. Because my exegesis focuses on the subtext, the *Grundrisse* appears smoother and more complete than it actually is. These manuscripts are more complete than is sometimes supposed, but they are nevertheless manuscripts.

The charge of reductionism, however, cannot be entirely avoided. Readers may think on the basis of this method that Marx simply deduced the content of the *Grundrisse* from the categories of Hegel's logic. But this impression is misguided. It does not do justice to my exegesis, or to Marx. It is simplistic to suppose that Marx sat at his desk with a copy of the SL and simply translated logical categories into economic ones; I do not make such a claim. The *Grundrisse* manuscripts are a critique of political economy, and a critical appropriation of Hegel's SL.

The relationship of the *Grundrisse* to the SL is thus subtle and complex. Nevertheless, my exegesis does focus on Hegel's SL as a subtext. Though I prescind from the rich content of the *Grundrisse*, and sometimes give the impression that the text is smooth; in fact, the ordering of the economic categories often proceeds in fits and starts. Marx begins the exposition of a particular aspect of capital at one place, and picks it up later at another. He interrupts the logical development of a particular category when the content leads him to a consideration of its historical instantiation, or for reasons that we cannot readily discern and may never fully understand.

Readers familiar with the *Grundrisse* will know that I abstract from very rich content indeed to focus on the subtext of logical form. I do not intend to reduce the content of the *Grundrisse* to logical form, but the nature of the exegesis guides the selectivity of the study.

This particular form of historical critical exegesis relies on "concept exegesis" (*Begriffsexegese*). Concept exegesis demonstrates that the ideas found in one text are related to ideas in another; and, in this instance, that the logical form of a work is indebted to the logical form of another. The method is empirical. I begin by breaking the *Grundrisse* into its component parts, and further subdivide the text. I then isolate the logical form of each argument and compare it to the logical form of Hegel's SL for purposes of establishing indebtedness.

The logical forms of argument are expressed in language. Concept exegesis relies, therefore, on phraseology. I not only expose the form of an argument, but I also link developments in the *Grundrisse* to the SL based on similar terminology. Though I focus primarily on logical form, concept exegesis nevertheless depends on philological study to establish a relation of one text on another. Philological evidence must be accumulated until support for the conclusion is overwhelming.

Needless to say, the result is a complex and dense exposition. I have tried to alleviate some of the difficulty but not all difficulties associated with this methodology can be avoided. Some difficulties arise in the nature of history itself. The more the exact details of a particular historic event are told, the less the meaning of the event as historic is communicated. Similarly, the more I focus on the details of logical form and phraseology, the less I convey the meaning of the *Grundrisse* as a whole, its relative importance in the development of Marx's thought, and the context within which he wrote the manuscripts. My hope is that readers will see that Marx was keenly aware of the reciprocal relation between form and content in Hegel's presentation of the logical development of the categories of science. Marx sought the complete exposition of capital as an organic unity. Because he recognized the scientific nature of such an exposition, Marx respected Hegel's ordering of the logical categories in the SL.

Over the long course of writing and preparing this book, I have benefited from the support of many persons and institutions. The book would not have been possible without the encouragement and support of Professor Joseph O'Malley. I had the privilege of preparing the first version under his supervision. Professor O'Malley's erudition rooted me in the text; his comprehension inspired me to learn; and his tolerance encouraged me to experiment. I am also grateful to him for introducing me to his friend and colleague Professor Burkhard Tuschling. I completed the first period of research for this book at the Institute for Philosophy in Marburg as Professor Tuschling's guest. My work has benefited enormously from his gentle criticisms and kind suggestions. A Smith Family Fellowship made possible my research in Marburg. I am grateful to Thaddeus Burch, S.J., for his administration of the fellowship. The Smith Family Fellowship also allowed me to spend time at the International Institute for Social History in Amsterdam; I am grateful to this Institute and to Jurgen Rojahn for his kind attention and interest.

While in Marburg, I made a lasting friendship with Dieter Huning, with whom I spent many hours debating the premises and conclusions of this work. As a consequence, the work is so much the better for those discussions. I am grateful to Dieter for his comments and his friendship.

I am indebted to many people who read parts or all of various versions of this book and offered suggestions and encouragement over the years. Professor Howard Kainz has been unwavering in his support of my work. Professor Kainz read a number of versions, and offered numerous suggestions. George Khushf read a final draft and generously advocated on behalf of publication. For his friendship, financial support and warm encouragement, I am especially grateful to Anthony Boswell.

I would also like to thank the following people for their support and encouragement over the years: Gyorgy Andrassy, Curtis Carter, Terrell Carver, Robert Cohen, David Duquette, Laszlo Kiss, Jan Heller, Franz Hespe, David McClellan, Patrick Murray, Rachel Reeder, Michael Vater and Mehdi Zamani. Above all, I want to thank my wife, Elyse, for her patient support of my work, and for her friendship and love throughout the completion of this book.

LIST OF ABBREVIATIONS

(STW-II) *Wissenschaft der Logik*, vol. I-II. Frankfurt: Suhrkamp Taschenbuch Wissenschaft, 1969.

(SL) *Science of Logic.* trans. A. V. Miller. London: George Allen and Unwin, 1965.

(N) *Grundrisse: Foundations of the Critique of Political Economy (Rough Draft).* trans. Martin Nicolaus. New York: Penguin Books, 1973.

(MEW) *Grundrisse der Kritik der politischen Ökonomie, (Rohentwurf) Werke,* vol. 42. Berlin: Dietz Verlag, 1983.

CHAPTER 1

INTRODUCTION

This work seeks to demonstrate that the doctrinal content of Marx's *Grundrisse der Kritik der politischen Ökonomie (Rohentwurf 1857/58)* is indebted for its logical form to Hegel's exposition of logical categories as found in the *Wissenschaft der Logik.*[1] The *Grundrisse* are a series of manuscripts in notebook form that Marx composed from August 1857 to June 1858. As Marx stated in a letter to the German socialist Ferdinand Lassalle (February 1858), the work represents the culmination of fifteen years of research into the origins and nature of political economy.[2] It is a "synthesis" of the wealth of empirical data that Marx had gathered in his study of economics.[3] It was in fact Marx's first, large scale attempt to set out his critique of the capitalist mode of production.

Marx drafted the *Grundrisse* at the end of a period of transition in his intellectual development.[4] In his Preface to *A Contribution to the Critique of Political Economy* (1859), a work written immediately after completing the *Grundrisse,* Marx referred to an early pivotal point in his life.[5] While working in 1842-1843 as editor of the *Rheinische Zeitung,* Marx found himself having to discuss issues related to political economy. Recognizing his ignorance of the subject, he undertook an intensive study of the literature of political economy. This study led him to the conclusion that legal relations and political forms are rooted in the economic conditions of life.[6] From that point on, Marx devoted himself to the comprehension of the economic conditions of modern, bourgeois society.

Many years of research followed, and Marx produced writings that were in large measure a process of "self-clarification."[7] But it was not until August 1857 that he felt obliged to undertake a large scale critique of bourgeois society. He lived in London at the time, and it became apparent to him that Britain was about to be thrown into a deep, economic crisis. He perceived that this crisis would be of much greater magnitude than those that had occurred before. He refers in his correspondence to the added pressure he felt to quickly provide a critique of capitalism that would lay bare its contradictions for all to see. In a letter to Engels dated 8 December, he wrote that he was working quite frequently through the night on a synthesis of his studies in political economy. Given the impending crisis, "before the deluge" he wanted to have clear "at least the outlines" of an exposition on why capitalism suffered such upheavals.[8] His studies of economics in the 1840s and 1850s would now bear fruit, and in one relatively short, feverish burst of energy he produced a complex manuscript of some 800 pages.

Although the crisis was not of the proportion that Marx anticipated, he nonetheless proceeded to publish the "preliminary chapters" of his critical theory as *A Contribution to a Critique of Political Economy.* In the Preface to this work, he again referred to the *Grundrisse* manuscripts when he announced to his readers that he intended to produce a six-part *magnum opus,* the entire material for which lay before him in "the form of monographs" that he would put into publishable form as circumstances permitted. Many authors refer to this remark when they conclude that the *Grundrisse* served as a foundation piece for Marx's *Das Kapital.*[9]

The discovery of the *Grundrisse* manuscripts among Marx's literary remains was first announced in 1923; but they were published only in 1939, by the Marx-Engels-Lenin Institute in Moscow, under the title *Grundrisse der Kritik der politischen Ökonomie (Rohentwurf 1857/58).*[10] They were again published in 1953 in East Berlin, but remained largely unknown in the West until the 1960s. The first complete translation into English was in 1973 by Martin Nicolaus.[11]

Upon its translation into English, the *Grundrisse* quickly became the subject of study and commentary.[12] For example, Carol Gould and George McCarthy have provided full-length studies that consider the text in depth.[13] My project, however, is not an exposition of the "social ontology," the "social ethic," or the history of modes of production or theories of surplus value that are contained within the *Grundrisse.* Instead, as stated at the outset, I seek to demonstrate that the *Grundrisse* are indebted for their logical form to Hegel's SL. I do not intend, however, to reduce the content of the *Grundrisse* to its logical form, but rather to show how the Hegelian logic governs Marx's doctrinal development in the *Grundrisse,* something quite different from such a reduction, and also quite different from a mere application of Hegel's categories to economic data.[14]

1. THE METHOD OF POLITICAL ECONOMY

We have from Marx's own hand a testimony to his indebtedness to Hegel's SL in his ordering of the materials that appear in the 1857/1858 manuscripts. In a letter to Engels in January 1858, Marx stated that a rereading of the SL afforded him the conceptual tools that allowed him to unlock the secrets of profit.[15] He also expressed the desire to "make accessible to the ordinary human intelligence . . . what is rational in the method which Hegel discovered but at the same time enveloped in mysticism."[16] Elsewhere he lamented that he wished he had had time to extract and make accessible the "rational kernel" that is contained in Hegel's treatment of scientific method. The expression of such a desire is, in fact, in keeping with a central motif that may be found in his earlier work. Hegel is notable for having conceived a "proper logic," or a "principle of movement," or a "pure logical formula of movement in general."[17] Yet he is to be blamed for his mystification. Marx wished to extricate this "proper logic" from its mystical trappings.

What, in brief, did Marx take to be the "rational kernel" in Hegel's scientific method? In the section entitled "The Method of Political Economy," Marx gives an account of the proper method of procedure in his exposition of a "mode of production."[18] While he does not explicitly credit Hegel for having discovered this method, it is clear in his criticisms here that he is indeed indebted to Hegel for it.[19] The following brief sketch will serve as a springboard to a general discussion in the next section of the nature of Hegel's scientific method—the "rational kernel," if you will. I return in the conclusion to a more thoroughgoing consideration of the logical structure and content of the "Introduction" to the *Grundrisse*, and Marx's characterization of scientific method.

Marx states in the "Introduction" that scientific method includes both analysis and synthesis. One naturally begins with what is given in experience. But what is given in experience are complicated ("concrete") things. Because any concrete thing is a "concentration of many determinations," an investigator's initial conception of it is chaotic. Investigation consists in moving analytically from this chaotic conception of the whole to the simple determinations that are constitutive of it. Once having arrived at the simplest determinations of the whole, the investigator then proceeds to order these determinations in reconstructing in the mind precisely what the whole is.

We can see in Marx's short exposition of the nature of scientific method, an elaboration of what had only been hinted at in earlier works. He reiterates what had been stated in *The German Ideology* as the premise of the true scientific exposition. The subject is society: real men acting together to create and reproduce their conditions of existence.[20] The real remains after theoretical exposition as before, independent of the thoughts of the scientist. Nevertheless, the real is said to be comprised of a system of hierarchically ordered relations. The nature of the subject matter, therefore, is not given to sense. Since the whole is a functioning system of hierarchically ordered relations, the reconstruction of the real in thought must be accomplished in a systematic manner.

It is important to note that for Marx the term "concrete" denotes two realities.[21] It is on the one hand the ontologically prior real. The concrete is, in the language of the *Critique*, an "organism."[22] As stated in the GI in the language of the idealists, it is "substance," or "society as subject," or a "totality."[23] The concrete is represented in the *Poverty of Philosophy* as a self-moving, self-reproducing whole that is comprised of hierarchically ordered, dialectically related forms of existence.[24]

The term "concrete" also denotes the complex. In this sense it describes both things like existing social systems, and our scientifically adequate concepts of them. What is required to arrive at the knowledge of that which is complex is to move from simple or abstract determinations of the whole to a complete elaboration of the system of relations that comprise it. The achievement of such a result in a "totality of thoughts" is a "mirroring" of the concrete that is the ontologically prior real.[25] Now since the concrete as ontologically prior is an "organism," the method that one uses in reconstructing the real in thought must be adequate to the object. Such a method must be based on the exposition of what in earlier works Marx called an "organic development." In fact, as Marx here states, this method is the only way that the mind can appropriate the real, i.e., as a "totality of thoughts." In saying as much, Marx echoed what he had said concerning Hegel's scientific method in the *Poverty of Philosophy*: "he [Hegel] is merely reconstructing systematically and classifying by the absolute method the thoughts which are in the minds of all."[26]

In contending that the real is a system of hierarchically ordered and dialectically related "parts," which must be appropriated by the mind in and through the use of a scientific method that is based on the exposition of "organic development," Marx is committed to the claim that the real can only be known through what Hegel terms *Wissenshaft*. A brief, general overview of Hegel's scientific method—the "rational kernel"—will give us a better understanding of the essential nature of Marx's "holistic" approach.

2. THE RATIONAL KERNEL

The proper object of Hegel's SL is at once subjective, or epistemological, and objective, or ontological. Hegel's SL is on one level an exposition of the relationship between, and development of, categories of thought. It is a "thinking study of thought." Yet, on another level, the SL is also an exposition of the relationship between, and development of, the various characteristics of inorganic, organic, and mental existence. It is at the same time a "thinking study of things."[27] The categories of the SL, therefore, have both a subjective and an objective foundation. In effect, Hegel, on the one hand, sides with Aristotle and against Kant, when he contends that the categories that are developed by the human mind adequately reflect reality.

At the same time, however, he sides with Kant, when he maintains that the categories or principles of knowing, the determinations of thought, are likewise the principles of reality. Hegel is committed, therefore, to an identity of thought and being, subject and object. It cannot be said of him, however, that he has a correspondence theory of truth in the usual sense of that term. Indeed, the identity of thought and being is not established until the very end of the SL. The entire SL is then a demonstration of this thesis. Truth is not merely a function of the identity of concept and object, or propositions and facts. In fact, no concept or proposition can be true apart from its relation to other concepts or propositions, or, indeed, apart from a system of concepts or propositions that link them all to form a systematic whole.

The above follows precisely because Hegel is committed to conceiving of the real in the particular fashion of his own unique discovery. The real is conceived of as a systematic or organic whole. That is, it is comprised of hierarchically ordered, interrelated forms of existence.[28] He views the real as a progression from the simplest and most abstract forms of existence to the most complex. The highest, most complex form of existence on the evolutionary scale is Spirit. No adequate treatment of the nature of reality can do without an exposition of the development of Spirit. Hegel reasons that Spirit is the end that evolution tends toward and produces. As the goal of the evolution of life-forms, it must in some fashion be present even within the incipient or abstract forms of existence. Hegel does not say that Spirit exists as such at the level of the inorganic, but that it is immanent in every stage, and serves as the foundation for further development. The process of the development of Spirit is not solely a physical or biological evolution. Hegel's theory differs in this sense from contemporary evolutionary theory, since he contends that the process is also a dialectical one. Dialectic is said to be the principle of movement and of all activity in the world.[29] The definition of "dialectic" is a difficult and complex one. Keep in mind, however, that Hegel views the real as a systematic or organic whole of hierarchically ordered, interrelated forms of existence, and that the end or outcome of evolution is in some sense present even in the most elemental forms.

As we have seen, Hegel defines the real as an organic whole. Since it is an organic whole, it is not merely a simple unity, but different elements comprising an integrated whole. An organic whole, then, must be seen as a unity of distinct or different elements. These different elements combine to form a unity precisely because their integration is a function of the organizing principle of the whole. The latter, while present in the particular elements, is not reducible to them. It must therefore be a universal organizing principle of the whole. Because each particular element contained within the whole is determined by the universal organizing principle, each contains this principle of the whole within itself. Each particular element is, therefore, an expression or representation of the whole. But since it is only a part of the whole, it expresses or represents the whole only in a partial manner. The fullest realization of the universal organizing principle awaits the complete elaboration of the system of relations that orders and organizes the integration of the many elements, in hierarchical fashion.

As each form of existence is only part of the whole, it is incomplete within itself and requires for its very existence the other elements that comprise the whole. Hegel would say that what each element or form of existence excludes from itself, it requires in order to exist as a part. In this way each element is "contradictory" within itself, when taken in isolation from the other parts. It excludes from itself "other" forms of existence, yet requires them for its very existence. It therefore contains within its very existence reference to what it excludes. In other words, since the universal organizing principle of the whole is immanent in each part, each part is determined by that which is external to it, i.e., its opposite. Thus, each part is both different from, or in opposition to, every other part. Yet each is at one and the same time in identity with every other, as parts of a whole. The higher, more complex form of existence that emerges from the contradictory nature of partial manifestations of the whole does not abolish these lower forms when it emerges. Rather it includes and preserves within itself the less complex, less adequate forms. Hegel terms this special relation *Aufhebung.*[30] It is the core concept of dialectic.

To repeat, for Hegel anything less than the complete elaboration of the whole is a partial, and therefore, inadequate manifestation of it. When a higher, more complex form of existence emerges, it cancels out the inadequacies of the less complex. But this cancellation does not mean that it annihilates the less developed forms of existence. These less developed forms are in fact transformed, since they are now parts of, or elements in, a greater whole. They are included and preserved within it, since the whole is dependent upon the different forms of existence which unite to produce it.

The dialectical process or what is sometimes called "thesis, antithesis, and synthesis" continues up to the complete elaboration of the universal organizing principle. In Hegel's system the systematic or organic whole as a unity of different elements is complete with the development of the most complex stage or form of existence, i.e., Spirit. As the highest, most complete manifestation of the whole, it is the aforementioned universal organizing principle. Spirit has, in this sense, been present since the outset of the evolutionary process. But it only achieves fruition or completion in and through the development of that being capable of self-consciousness, i.e., a human being; and, indeed, its evolution continues in the full actualization of human potentiality. With the development of Spirit all the contradictions present in the partial manifestations of the whole are resolved. The result is a complete organic unity that is comprised of a system of relations of different forms of existence.

The self-development of Spirit is the foundation of the SL. As Hegel states, it is the ground of the entire development. Thus, it is presupposed at the beginning of the SL that the existence of the real is a function of hierarchically ordered, dialectically related elements. The beginning originates from this organic unity and is, in fact, the most abstract characteristic of it. The movement of the SL starts from this abstract beginning and, moving through the exposition of progressively more complete or concrete determinations, finally arrives at the knowledge of the totality that is organic unity. The latter, whose logical expression is "the Idea," is therefore as much the result as the foundation of the development. In this way scientific methods circular in nature. [31] It is by no means circular in a spurious sense, since it is only as a result that we know the subject matter as a concrete unity of many determinations.

We see, therefore, that the logical development is determined by the subject matter itself, the content, and the thought of it, the form. In and through correct inferences we see that the particular subject matter under consideration is not the organic whole that we are seeking to know, but merely part of it. These partial insights are superseded until we arrive at an insight into the whole. As this insight is, of course, constantly developing, the exposition is open-ended. Hegel repeatedly emphasizes that the form and content are reciprocally related, and indeed determine one another.[32] Thus, at each level of the exposition of a subject matter the form of thinking determines the nature of the content. But likewise, the nature of the content determines the form of thinking. Since the form and content are inseparable, the nature of the development of the categories of the SL is absolutely necessary. Each transition is inexorably linked to the prior development, and, in turn, form and content determine subsequent developments.

We are now better prepared to take a closer look at what Marx terms the "scientifically correct method." As we have seen, Marx distinguishes between two meanings of the term "concrete." In the first meaning, the term denotes the ontologically prior real: real men acting together to create and reproduce their conditions of existence. Since, in the *Grundrisse*, Marx seeks to explicate the system of relations that comprise capitalist production, the ontologically prior real is the organic unity of capital. In fact, as Marx himself states, the organic unity that is the proper object of exposition is a world market founded on capital. This market is the organic whole that serves as the foundation for the entire development of the *Grundrisse*.

The second meaning of the term "concrete" included the reconstruction of this organic whole in the mind, its complete exposition of it. According to this meaning, the "concrete" is not the starting point, but the end result. This somewhat confusing way of stating the matter may now be clarified by appeal to Hegel's presentation of the nature of scientific method. Recall that the real is characterized as an organic system comprised of hierarchically ordered, dialectically related forms of existence, or "parts." This organic unity is the ground of the entire development of the categories of the SL. Since this whole is a systematic unity, it requires a systematic exposition to be reconstructed in the mind. It cannot be known all at once, as it were. The beginning of the SL, then, originates from this concrete organic unity in its most simple or abstract determination. The development of the categories, in turn, starts from this abstract beginning and by analyzing progressively more concrete determinations, finally arrives at the knowledge of the totality that is the concrete or complete, organic whole.

This method or procedure is precisely the one that Marx deems scientifically correct. The exposition of the capitalist mode of production is grounded in the ontologically prior "concrete." But since this concrete is an organic or systematic whole, it can only be known through a systematic exposition. This method entails beginning the exposition with the simple, most abstract determination of the whole. The exposition starts from this abstract determination and by analyzing progressively more concrete determinations, finally arrives at the knowledge of the totality that is the concrete organic system of capital. In this way, scientific exposition is for Marx, as it is for Hegel, circular in nature.

For Hegel the universal organizing principle, whose logical reality is "the Idea," is present even in the most abstract and simple of relations. These partial manifestations of the whole are superseded or transformed, yet preserved and included in the further development of the exposition. "The Idea," then, is the ground of the entire development though we do not know the complete nature of this universal organizing principle until the end of the development. Likewise for Marx, capital is latent or immanent even in the least developed form of simple circulation. While the latter is, of course, an incomplete or partial manifestation of capital, it nevertheless must be taken as one form of its existence: it is capital as it appears. The organic system of capital, therefore, is the ground or foundation of the entire development contained in the *Grundrisse,* and the logical development of the exposition is determined by a reciprocal relation between form and content. But our knowledge of the nature of this "living-whole" must await the complete elaboration of the entire system of relations that comprise it. Thus, scientific exposition is not circular in a spurious sense because it is only as a result that we know the organic whole that is capital.

3. FORM AND CONTENT IN MARX'S CRITIQUE

There exist some one hundred terms or phrases in the *Grundrisse* taken directly from the SL. In an important and provocative work, Hiroshi Uchida sets out to demonstrate that Marx's use of Hegel's SL is indeed systematic.[33] Uchida also makes the claim that the "rational kernel" contained in Hegel's SL is exemplified in Marx's precise ordering of the economic categories in his outline of a critical presentation of capital. Uchida not only takes note of the similarity in terminology between the two works; he also attempts to locate a term from the *Grundrisse* in the precise context within which it appears in the SL. The employment of a term in the SL is a function of its placement within a dialectical whole and its role in the development of the whole. Uchida therefore attempts to link the development of the *Grundrisse* directly to the development of the entire SL. In short, he makes the claim that one cannot understand Marx's exposition of particular aspects of capital, and the positioning of each particular development within the context of the whole of the Grundrisse, without comprehending in detail the dialectical development of Hegel's SL. He demonstrates that Marx's use of the SL is systematic; that Marx employed the categories of "Being" in his critique both of the SL, and of simple circulation; that he employed the categories of "Essence" in a critical presentation of the dialectical structure of production based on capital; and finally, that Marx employed the categories of the "Concept" in a critical presentation of capital as a dialectical unity of opposed extremes.

Uchida's work is, however, open to some major objections, particularly his interpretation of Hegel's SL. Uchida fails to give an adequate account of the nature of dialectic and the method that it entails, as both Hegel and Marx conceived it. I shall focus on this objection regarding to his interpretation of Hegel's SL, because it leads to difficulties in his demonstration of how the doctrinal content of Marx's *Grundrisse* is indebted for its logical form to Hegel's exposition of logical categories.

The logical development of Hegel's SL is determined by the subject matter itself, the content, and the thought of it, the form. In and through correct inferences we realize that the subject matter under consideration is not the whole we are seeking to know, but part of it. These partial insights are superseded until we arrive at an insight into the whole. Thus, at each level of the exposition the form of thinking determines the nature of the content; likewise, the nature of the content determines the form of thinking. Since the form and content are inseparable, the nature of the development is absolutely necessary, and therefore scientific. Each transition is inexorably linked to the prior development, and, in turn, form and content determine subsequent developments. One cannot, therefore, as with formal logic, simply extricate forms of thought from the SL and apply them to some externally given content. Each category appears within the systematic whole. It depends on the development that precedes it and on the categories that follow. Indeed it requires the whole to have any sense at all. The employment of any category, therefore, commits one to the use of all. But this necessity Uchida fails to comprehend.

The same objection threatens Uchida's claim that the doctrinal content of Marx's *Grundrisse* is indebted for its logical form to Hegel's SL. There can be no question, and Uchida makes it clear, that Marx had intimate knowledge of the SL. Since Marx viewed capital as an organic system comprised of hierarchically ordered, dialectically related forms of existence, he would quite naturally see in Hegel's SL a scientific method (albeit in "mystical trappings") that could be used in the exposition of the system. Uchida documents that Marx handles with aplomb the most difficult of Hegel's categories. This, in itself, implies an acute comprehension of the SL in its entirety.

If this is the case, and surely it is, the question then arises: would Marx apply the categories in a manner that Uchida suggests? For example, Uchida claims that Marx began his exposition of capital using the categories of "Identity," "Difference," "Opposition," and "Contradiction," as Hegel presented them in "Essence." Yet, if Marx knew the SL intimately, would he have disregarded the absolute necessity of the development, that very element that makes Hegel's method scientific? That is, would he simply extricate from the middle of the SL, categories that require a great deal of development, and use them in the piecemeal fashion that Uchida suggests? Unless he did so in some metalogical sense, a sense in no way intended by Uchida, it simply cannot be the case.

This work proposes to show that Marx was keenly aware of the intimate relation between form and content in the SL. Because Marx sought the complete exposition of the entire nature of capital, and, to be more specific, of capital in general in the *Grundrisse,* he did not treat Hegel's ordering of the categories lightly; rather, he saw the absolute necessity of the ordering of the categories, and therefore, he saw the scientific nature of a dialectical exposition of capital as organic unity based on Hegel's method. He therefore respected that ordering.

As suggested at the outset of this chapter, the purpose of this work is to make explicit the deep, logical structure of the *Grundrisse.* Each economic category, or group of economic categories in a single exposition of a specific aspect of capital, contains a relation to the whole of the organic system. My aim is to make explicit the Hegelian logical content of this system.

This work may be divided into three sections for the following reason. A tripartite division of the *Grundrisse* neatly follows that of Hegel's SL, which can be demonstrated only through the exposition of the concept of capital. Hegel begins his exposition of the Concept with what he terms the immediate content of knowledge, and with thought in its merely conceptual phase. Reflection upon this immediate content reveals an inner essence in terms of which the appearance of immediate being is to be explained. This inner essence is then dissected and its various "moments" analyzed. In the final part, or "The Doctrine of the Concept," Hegel shows that the subject matter under consideration is actually a unity of Being and Essence.

The various moments that are presupposed in its "becoming" are superseded in this concrete unity. It is thereby shown how this concrete unity transforms these "moments" to accommodate the "end-in-itself" of the Concept.

In his exposition of the concept of capital, Marx uses scientific method to show that monetary circulation is merely a "moment," in fact the most abstract moment, of the system of capitalist production. Thus, as I will demonstrate, a dialectical exposition of capital must begin with commodity and money circulation, - the immediate being of capital (chapter 2). This reflection on the nature of simple circulation will then reveal an inner essence in terms of which the appearance, or surface layer, of capital can be explained (chapters 3 and 4). This inner essence of capital can then be dissected, and its various "moments" analyzed.

In the final section, Marx demonstrates that capital is a unity of its different moments of circulation and production (chapters 5 and 6). Capital must appear on the surface as simple circulation, in which case, it is shown to have adapted to its own "self-movement" what had been the presuppositions of its "becoming." Thus, it is shown how both circulation and production are transformed to accommodate the "end-in-itself" of capital.

---

[1] Karl Marx, *Grundrisse der Kritik der politischen oekonomie (Rohentwurf 1857/58)*, Marx-Engels Werke, vol. 42 (Berlin: Dietz Verlag, 1983); G.W.F. Hegel, Werke 5-6, *Wissenschaft der Logik* (Frankfurt: Suhrkamp, 1986).

[2] Marx-Engels Werke, vol. 29 (East Berlin: Dietz Verlag, 1963) (hereafter MEW), p. 263

[3] Ibid., p. 263; see also Allen Oakley, *Marx's Critique of Political Economy*, Volume 1, (London: Routledge & Kegan Paul, Inc., 1984), pp. 135-36.

[4] For a detailed exposition of the evolution of Marx's intellectual development, both before and after the *Grundrisse*, see "A History of Marx's Economics," by Maximilien Rubel in *Rubel on Karl Marx*, ed. by Joseph O'Malley and Keith Algozin (Cambridge: Cambridge University Press, 1981), pp. 82-190.

[5] Karl Marx, *A Contribution to the Critique of Political Economy*, trans. by S.W. Ryazanskayz (Moscow: Progress Publishers, 1977) (hereafter Contribution); see also Allen Oakley, *The Making of Marx's Critical Theory* (London: Routledge and Kegan Paul, 1983), esp. pp. 52-53.

[6] Contribution, p. 20.

[7] Ibid., p. 22.

[8] MEW, vol. 29, p. 258; see also Allen Oakley, *The Making of Marx's Critical Theory*, p. 52.

[9] See for example, Roman Rosdolsky, *The Making of Marx's "Capital,"* trans. by Pete Burgess (London: Pluto Press Limited, 1977), esp. pp. 1-10; see also Allen Oakley, *The Making of Marx's Critical Theory*, pp. 52-80; and Rubel, "A History of Marx's 'Economics,'" and "The Plan and Method of the 'Economics'," in *Rubel on Karl Marx*.

[10] See Rosdolsky in *The Making of Marx's "Kapital"*, for a brief history of the manuscripts, esp. pp. 1-10.

[11] Karl Marx, *Grundrisse: Foundations of the Critique of Political Economy (Rough Draft)*, trans. and ed., with a Foreward by M. Nicolaus (London: Allen Lane, 1973) (hereafter N); see also Karl Marx, *The Grundrisse*, trans. and ed. by David McLellan (New York: Harper and Row, 1971) for the translation of selected parts of the *Grundrisse*.

[12] See bibliography below.

[13] See Carol Gould, *Marx's Social Ontology: Individuality and Community in Marx's Theory of Social Reality* (Cambridge, Mass: MIT Press, 1978); and George E. McCarthy, *Marx and the Ancients: Classical Ethics, Social Justice, and Nineteenth Century Political Economy* (Maryland: Rowan and Littlefield Publishers, Inc., 1990); and Georg Lukas, *History and Class Consciousness: Studies in Marxian Dialectics*; for the consideration of the underlying philosophy of human nature that serves as a foundation for the *Grundrisse*; cf. *Pre-capitalist Economic Formations*, trans. by Jack Cohen, ed. with an intro, by E.J. Hobsbawn (London: Lawrence and Wishart, 1964); for the consideration of the history of modes of production as outlined by Marx in the *Grundrisse*.

[14] I am indebted to Professor Burkhard Tuschling of the Philipps-Universität in Marburg, Germany, for helping me clarify the nature and aim of this work. Professor Tuschling cautioned me to make explicit to the reader that this work, though about logical form, does not reduce the content of the *Grundrisse* to logical form. There is much more at work in the *Grundrisse* than the sequence of economic categories, as the works of Lukas, Gould, McCarthy, Hobsbawn, et al., make abundantly clear.

[15] See Marx-Engels Werke (Berlin: Dietz Verlag, 1963-65), vol. 29, p. 260.

[16] Ibid., p. 260.

[17] See Karl Marx, *Critique of Hegel's "Philosophy of Right"*, trans. by Annette John and Joseph O'Malley, ed. By Joseph O'Malley (Cambridge: Cambridge University Press, 1970), p. 3. Cf. Karl Marx, *Economic and Philosophic Manuscripts of 1844*, trans. by Martin Milligan, ed. by Dirk J. Struik (New York: International Publishers, 1964), pp. 188-89; and Karl Marx, *The Poverty of Philosophy* (New York: International Publishers, 1936), pp. 163-164.

[18] See Karl Marx, "Introduction," *Grundrisse*, p. 100ff; *"Einleitung,"* *Grundrisse der Kritik der politischen Okonomie*, Marx-Engels Werke (Berlin: Dietz Verlag, 1983), vol. 42, p. 19ff.

[19] See Terrell Carver, "Introduction," in *Karl Marx: Texts on Method* (Oxford: Basil Blackwell, 1975), for a general consideration of the Hegelian origins of Marx's discussion of method in the "Introduction."

[20] Karl Marx and Frederick Engels, *The German Ideology*: Part 1 (hereafter GI) (New York: International Publishers, 1986), ed., with an introduction by C.J. Arthur, p. 42ff.

[21] See David A. Duquette, "Methodology and Development in Marx and Hegel," *The Owl of Minerva* 19 (Spring 1988): 131-148, for a seminal discussion of the term "concrete" in Marx; Tony Smith, *The Logic of Marx's Capital: Replies to Hegelian Criticisms* (New York: SUNY Press, 1990).

[22] See Marx, *Critique*, p. 3, for an example of the early Marx's commendation of Hegel for having conceived of the real as an organism.

[23] See Marx, GI, pp. 48-60.

[24] See Marx, *The Poverty of Philosophy*, pp. 163-64.

[25] See Tony Smith, *The Logic of Marx's Capital*, esp. pp. 19-21, for a discussion of Marx's account of how the method of presentation ideally reflects the life of the subject matter.

[26] Ibid., pp. 163-64.

[27] Errol E. Harris, *An Interpretation of the Logic of Hegel* (London: University Press of America, 1983), p.9; cf. chapters 1 and 2 for a discussion of the proper object of Hegel's logic. This section is indebted in the main to Harris's eminent work on Hegel's logic; see also Justus Hartnack, *An Introduction to Hegel's Logic*, trans. by Lars Aagaard-Mogensen (New York: Hackett, 1998) (hereafter Introduction), intro., for a discussion of the subject and objective foundation of the categories of Hegel's SL.

[28] Cf. Harris, *An Interpretation*, esp. chapters 1 and 2.

[29] Ibid., 29-34.

[30] Ibid., pp. 40-45, and also Hartnack, Introduction, pp. 4-6, for two short, concise discussions on the nature of *Aufhebung*.

[31] Cf. Harris, "Introduction," for a consideration of the circular nature of Hegel's scientific method; see also Tony Smith, *The Logic of Marx's Capital*, pp. 3-18.

[32] See Eric Weil, "The Hegelian Dialectic," in *The Legacy of Hegel: Proceedings of the Marquette Hegel Symposium*, 1970, ed. by J.J. O'Malley, K.W. Algozin, H.P. Kainz, and L.C. Rice for an interesting discussion on the absolute necessity of the development of categories in the SL. See also Professor Findlay's "Comments on Weil's "The Hegelian Dialectic," for an alternative view to that of both Weil and Harris.

[33] Hiroshi Uchida, Marx's *Grundrisse and Hegel's Logic*, ed. by Terrell Carver (London: Routledge, 1988), esp. "Preface;" see also H. Uchida, "The money of Spirit: the Young Marx's analysis of the homology between political economy and Hegel's philosophy," *Monthly Report of the Institute for Social Sciences of Senshu University* (Tokyo, 1986), 272:2-30.

CHAPTER 2

MONEY AS A MEASURE, MONETARY CRISES AND THE DOCTRINE OF BEING

A dialectical exposition must begin with the way in which a subject matter first appears to consciousness. It must begin with the immediate content of knowledge, that is, the most simple, and therefore the most abstract determination of what is. Hegel calls the categories of "Being" the categories of perceptual thinking.[1] These categories are the principles of the real existence of its object. They are the ways in which an "organic system" first appears to consciousness. They are its immediate forms of existence. Thus, "Quality," "Quantity," and "Measure" are the determining principles of real determinate beings, and they are the concepts without which perception would be blind.[2]

1. THE ECONOMIC QUALITY OF THE IMMEDIATE PRODUCT

Marx begins his exposition of capital in the precise manner that is recommended by Hegel. He begins with capital as it first appears to consciousness. He begins with the immediate content of knowledge, that is, the most simple, and therefore the most abstract determinations of capital. He tells us here in the *Grundrisse* as elsewhere that capital first appears, and is perceived as, a mass of exchanges of commodities.[3] A commodity is brought to market and exchanged for money, and the money is in turn exchanged for a commodity, which is exchanged for money, in a virtual "infinite series" of exchanges of commodities mediated by money. Marx terms the appearance of capital, or capital as first perceived, "simple circulation."

The first section of the *Grundrisse,* the "Chapter on Money," is concerned to make explicit the form and content of "simple circulation," or what is commonly known as the monetary system. It is both the historical and the logical presupposition of capital. In what follows it will be shown how Marx had organized the economic data that was to be used in the presentation of the monetary system by employing the categories of quality, quantity, and measure as taken from the SL. It will be shown that not only was Marx aided by these concepts in his understanding of money as a measure and the monetary system, but that he was also aided in his understanding of the potentiality for crises at the level of simple circulation.

Simple circulation presupposes that money has emerged not only as a measure of the exchange value of products, but also as a medium of exchange. Money as a measure and as a medium of exchange is to be distinguished from its final determination when it emerges from simple circulation as the universal material representative of wealth. It is the latter that is both the historical and, as we will see, the logical presupposition of capital. An understanding of money in its developed form, however, presupposes an understanding of money as a measure and as a medium of exchange.

Money as a measure of exchange value presupposes the commodity form of the product. It is the commodity form of the product therefore that is the root source of simple circulation. In order to be able to understand simple circulation, one must first understand the origin of the commodity form.

Prior to Marx, no one in the history of classical political economy had completely succeeded in understanding the origins of the commodity form. No one had succeeded in deriving money as a measure of value from the particular products of human labor. Although they had recognized the problem and sought a solution, their efforts ended in failure. The classical political economists simply did not possess a scientific method that would enable them properly to address the issue. Their "crass materialism" simply prevented them from being able to grasp that which is the result of both internal and external relations.[4] The problem of the origin of the commodity form may be stated as follows: How is it possible that a qualitatively unique product of a naturally specified kind of labor could become quantitatively equivalent to every other like determined product? In short, what are the conditions of the possibility of the quantification of what is qualitatively unique?

Surely this is no mean task. It requires a conceptual schema that would allow one to move from the concept of quality to the concept of quantity; and, in a way that does not merely set them side by side, so to speak, but one that derives quantity from quality. Marx finds just such a conceptual schema in Hegel's treatment of the relationship between quality and quantity.

The problem of the origin of the commodity form may also be stated in terms of what Marx calls the "double existence" (*doppelte Existenz)* of the commodity.[5] How can a product/commodity be both qualitatively unique, yet quantitatively equivalent? The "immediate product" (*unmittelbare Produkt)* is the "specific result of a specific, of a naturally specified kind of labor which differs qualitatively from other kinds" (N 143, MEW 78).[6] Each product possesses certain "natural qualities" and/or "natural properties" (*natürlichen Eigenschaften)* that are unique to itself (N 142, MEW 77). It's qualities are immanent in its "natural determinate being," (natürliche Dasein) in its "identity with itself" *(Gleichheit mit sich).* The set of unique, qualitative characteristics that distinguish each product from one another, make them "incommensurable" (*inkommensurabel*) (N 141, MEW 76). Each is a "measure for itself" (*Mas für sich*)(N 613, MEW 514). He states: "In its natural determinate being, with its natural qualities, in natural identity with itself, the commodity is neither constantly exchangeable nor exchangeable against every other commodity; this it is only as something different from itself, something distinct from itself, as exchange value" (N 143).[7]

In beginning with the qualitative determination of the "immediate product," Marx is beginning precisely where Hegel contends a dialectical exposition must begin. Quality is that without which a thing could not be what it is.[8] It is the most simple and therefore the most abstract determination of what is. It must be treated first. In fact, Marx's characterization of the "natural qualities" or the "natural determinate being" of the "immediate product" echo Hegel's consideration of the qualitative nature of determinate being.

Of prime importance here is the recognition that the quality of any immediate, determinate being distinguishes this being from every other. For Marx as for Hegel an "immediate, determinate being" is the result of activity. Insofar as it is the result of a qualitatively distinct activity, it possesses "qualities" and/or "properties" that are immanent to its existence.[9] As such, it is wholly unique and incommensurable, i.e., it is in "identity with itself." It is its own measure. But the process or activity that leads to a qualitatively unique, determinate being is also the foundation of the possibility of the quantification of this existent.

For Marx, what had been defined by its own unique qualities, acquires a quantitative determination in a process of exchange (N 143, MEW 78). It is within the exchange process that the "immediate product" realizes its exchange value. When it realizes an exchange value, and in the process becomes a commodity, it becomes what Marx terms an "equivalent" *(Äquivalent)* (N 141, MEW 76). As an "equivalent" the product no longer stands in a special, qualitative relationship toward other products. Rather, all its natural properties are extinguished (N 141, MEW 76). Once they have acquired an "exchange value," all commodities are "qualitatively equal" and differ only quantitatively (N 141-143, MEW 76-78). How it acquires this quantitative determination is indeed a complex issue; one that is resolved with the aid of Hegel's consideration of the relationship between quality and quantity.

The possibility of the quantification of the immediate product is first of all a function of the laboring activity itself. While the product is in possession of certain natural qualities that make it unique, it is also a specific "objectification of a given amount of labour time" *(Vergengenständlichung einer bestimmten Arbeitszeit)* (N 140, MEW 75). It is "materialized labor time, labor time not in the form of motion but at rest; not in the form of the process, but of the result" (N 143).[10] In short, it is the "realization of a specific amount of labor time," a "quantity of labor time," i.e., a "magnitude of labor time" (*bestimmte Arbeitsgroße*).[11] As his exposition unfolds, Marx moves from a consideration of the quality of the immediate product to the foundation of its quantifiability. The fact that it may later on acquire an external, quantitative determination as an exchange value is first of all a function of the fact that it is already quantitatively determined.[12] The question then becomes how are we to understand the fact that a qualitative unity can at the same time be quantitatively determined?

The product is a "quantity of time." In so far as it is potentially quantifiable, it must be perceived as containing within itself the duration of time that it took to produce it. It embodies within itself the discrete moments that went into its creation. As a "quantity," it must be perceived as a continuous unity of discrete moments, or, a plurality in a simple unity.[13] As such it is a continuous and discrete magnitude.

This logical progression in the presentation of the appearance of capital from quality to quantity is precisely one that is developed by Hegel. The final result of Hegel's exposition of qualitative change is an "immediate being-for-itself" wholly unique in its qualitative determination (SL 157-8, STW 174-76). Hegel labels this simple unity "the one" (SL 163, STW 182). Nevertheless and despite the fact that it is a qualitative, simple unity, it is the result of activity and/or movement. It contains in itself a quantitative determination.[14] The process that is the becoming of this simple unity entails the unity of discrete moments (SL 177, STW 198-99). It is a continuity of such moments. In short, it is a continuous unity of discrete moments, or a "plurality" (SL 187-88, STW 209-10). The fact that it is a continuous unity is the basis of its quantitative determination. Hegel defines quantity as "simply the omnipresent real possibility within itself of the one" *(schlechthin in ihr allenthalben die reale Möglichkeit des Eins ist)* or discreteness (SL 188, STW 213). This simple unity must therefore also be defined as a continuous and discrete magnitude.[15]

Marx employs these categories when he contends that the quantitative determination of the "immediate product" is a function of the real possibility of conceiving of it as an "amount of time." Since it is "measurable only in time," or in terms of duration, it is comprised of both continuous and discrete moments. Marx calls a product at this juncture a "quantum of labor time" *(Quantum Arbeitszeit) (N* 143, MEW 78). It is a unity as a continuous and discrete magnitude.

Insofar as it possesses these quantitative determinations, the product is capable of acquiring "a number" *(eine Zahl)* (N 143, MEW 78). In its "becoming an exchange value," it must be transformed into a "denominated number" *(benannte Zahl)* (N 144, MEW 78). When it acquires its numerical value, it is a "specific quantum of labor time" *(bestimmtes Quantum Arbeitszeit)* (N 143, MEW 78).

Once the product acquires the determination of number, it is now "a number which expresses the quantity of other commodities which equal it which are its equivalent" (*eine Zahl, die ausdrückt, welche Quantität von andren Waren ihm gleich ist, sein Äquivalent, oder in welchem Verhältnis es das Äquivalent andrer Waren ist*) (N 143, MEW 78). As such, all its "natural properties" are extinguished, and it is equivalent, or it is comparable to, each and every other so quantitatively determined product.[16] In so far as they acquire a quantitative determination or a numerical value, each product now stands in relation to every other. Marx states: "Exchange value is their social relation, their economic quality" (*Der Wert ist ihr gesellschaftliches Verhältnis, ihre ökonomische Qualität*)(N 141, MEW 76). In short, rather than qualitatively unique, as numbered they are qualitatively equivalent, and differ only quantitatively.[17]

The terminology used in the above passages and the logical progression from a treatment of the product as a continuous and discrete magnitude, to its transformation into a denominated number," and finally to its treatment as a "specific quantum" as an expression of its economic quality, recalls Hegel's treatment of the transition from "quantity" to "specific quantum." In fact, Hegel's treatment of this logical progression provided Marx with a conceptual schema that allows him to understand what had been misunderstood by the classical political economists. It permits Marx to see how the qualitatively determined, "immediate product" of the laboring activity could acquire a quantitative determination that is the logical presupposition of the emergence of money as a measure of value.

For Hegel, the qualitative, simple unity that is the result of activity or movement must also be defined as continuous and discrete magnitude. As both a unity and a continuous and discrete magnitude, it is defined as a quantum.[18] A quantum may be numbered and is an "amount"(*Anzahl*) (SL 203, STW 232). As numbered, and therefore as an "amount," this determinate being is said to be a "specific quantum" (*bestimmtes Quantum*).[19] The number that expresses the amount of a specific quantum is not only the determination of this quantum, but also expresses the relation this specific quantum has to other quanta that exist external to itself (SL 219, STW 252-53). In short, the numerical value of each specific quantum relates it as a certain amount to other quanta. Hegel calls this relation a quantitatively determined quality (SL 219-20, STW 252-53).

If we follow carefully the logical progression and transitions made in Marx's account of the quantitatively determined "economic quality," we see that he follows Hegel's exposition of the emergence of "specific quantum." Hegel had provided the concepts that were necessary in determining the way in which what had been incommensurable, immediate products could be seen to have become related through quantitative determination. Hegel in effect shows Marx the conditions for the possibility of the quantification of what is qualitatively unique. Where they had once been simply qualitatively unique, they are now seen to have become qualitatively equivalent, through having become quantitatively determined.

2. FROM INFINITE COMPUTATIONS TO MONEY AS MEASURE

Once the "immediate product" has been quantitatively determined, it has acquired a "double existence" (N 145). This "double existence" denotes a contradiction which has emerged within the product itself. The product possesses an "economic quality." This economic quality, or number, expresses the specific amount of labor time that is materialized in the product, and it relates it to all other like determined products. Its economic quality makes it an "equivalent." It nevertheless remains a qualitatively unique, "immediate product." It is therefore not immediately related to every other commodity. It is not really or actually equivalent, but merely potentially so.[20]

Thus, despite the fact that each product possesses an exchange value, because each is qualitatively unique it is not immediately exchangeable. To make a product actually an "equivalent," one would have to compare it against every other product in order to determine it as general exchange value. Since exchange value is ultimately a function of labor time, in order to establish it as general exchange value, one would have to determine the labor time that is materialized in every other product in comparing them to the amount which is materialized in the one product (N 143, MEW 78).

Furthermore, one would have to perform this operation with every product in order to determine it as general exchange value, as "equivalent." Marx contends that the contradiction within the product between its qualitative and quantitative determinations would entail an infinite number of computations, in order to determine the "economic quality" of each product.[21]

The product, then, acquires its exchange value, its economic quality, only in relation to all other products. Insofar as it is a quantity of labor time, a "denominated number," and a specific materialization of labor time, a "specific quantum," its exchange value is a function of its relation to all other "magnitudes of labor" (*Arbeitsgroßen*), i.e., the determinateness of each consists in its relation to the other.

Exchange value relates the product not to any other particular commodity, but "expresses it as an equivalent, the ratio of its exchangeability to all other commodities" (N 143). When a product becomes exchange value, it is "transformed into a particular quantitative ratio, a numerical ratio" *(in eine bestimmtes quantitatives Verhältnis verwandelt, eine Verhältniszahl)* (N 143, MEW 78). This numerical ratio is an exponent of the relation between quantitatively determined products. The exponent determines the economic quality of the one in its relation to all others.

When Marx concludes that the "double existence" of the product, or the contradiction between its qualitative and quantitative determinations, results in a ratio or an exponent of the relation between quantitatively determined products, he is recalling Hegel's formulation of the nature of quantitative ratio. Hegel demonstrates that the derivation of a quantitatively determined quality entails a contradiction between a qualitative substrate and its quantitative determinations. The specific quantum is so determined that it exists in a "double form" (*gedoppelte Form*), or in a "dual determination" (*gedoppelte Eestimmungen*), as both a "qualitative something" (*qualitative Etwas*), and as that which may be expressed in number (SL 221, 222-3). As such, it is "internally self-contradictory."[22]

The contradiction that arises within the quantum results in the "quantitative infinite." Since the determination of each is a function of its relation to every other, the quantum is finite "as impelled beyond itself, as being determined in an other" (*als das Hinausschicken über sich selbst, als das Bestimmtsein in einem Anderen*) (SL 226, STW 260). This infinite progress is therefore an expression of contradiction.

The quantitative infinite progress results in a relation between specific quanta, because each is what it is solely in relation to every other.[23] This relation is a quantitative ratio, or an exponent that expresses the relation between all quanta.

When Marx uses the logical categories in Hegel's development of the quantitative ratio, he proves that the numerical value of exchange value must achieve a separate existence from the product. The end of exchange is the exchange of one particular product for another. In the act of exchange two specific magnitudes of labor are brought into relation. If they are to be exchanged, they must "become (or be reduced to—MM) magnitudes of the same kind, of the same unit, i.e., commensurable" (*benannte Großen werden, mit derselben Einheit, also kommensurabel*)(N 143, MEW 78).

The relation of the two magnitudes (the exponent of the ratio of the one to the other) must be a magnitude that is distinguished from the related magnitudes (N 143).[24] The two quantitatively determined products are related to each other through this third magnitude that expresses their quantitative ratio. Only then do the two magnitudes stand in relation, i.e., only then may it be said of them that they are magnitudes of the same kind.

Thus the contradiction that emerges in exchange within the product between itself as qualitatively determined magnitude and itself as a denominated number is resolved only when it is related to, or determined by, this exponent taken as unit of comparison. This exponent of the ratio, this unit of comparison, expresses and/or determines the economic quality, or social relation, of the one toward the other.[25]

Here it may be seen that the "third magnitude" in fact measures the exchange value embodied in specific magnitudes of labor time, in order to determine their exchangeability vis-á-vis all other commodities.[26] It serves as the standard for the measure of specific amounts of labor time, precisely because it represents labor time in general.

Money emerges as a result of the quantitatively determined economic quality that exists between related magnitudes. The quantitative ratio that exists at first only in the head, attains a real separate existence from related products. It, in turn, serves as the measure—the unit of comparison—of the exchange value of specific magnitudes of labor time. It is not simply another particular commodity, because then it would not represent a relation. Rather, the "third magnitude" must be a symbol of the relation between commodities as exchange values. It represents labor time as such. In money is unified both a quantitatively determined amount of labor time, and the social relations or economic quality of all commodities. Money as a measure is a unity of quality and quantity, i.e., it is a qualitative quantum.

In this progression Marx moves from the consideration of the quantitative ratio, that is, the exponent of the relation between specific magnitudes of labor time, to the separate existence of measure. Here again in doing so, he remains logically consistent in following the logical progression of categories as found in the SL. In the chapter entitled "The Quantitative Relation or Quantitative Ratio," Hegel demonstrates that the quantitative ratio necessarily achieves a separate existence from related quanta, and becomes a unit of comparison. The related quanta are now determined by this exponent. Each no longer has significance as a determinate quantum. Rather, the exponent of the ratio determines the value of the related quanta. This "third magnitude" expresses and/or determines the two related quanta as the same magnitude (SL 323, STW 382-83). It embodies within itself the relation between the two. This self-relation of quantum to itself as expressed by the exponent is the quality of quantum (SL 323-33, STW 381-94). It is the qualitative quantum, and as such it is measure.as a standard or a unit of comparison—it symbolizes the quality that is the result of relation.

3. PRICE AS THE REALIZATION OF MEASURE

Because exchange value must attain an existence alongside commodities as the measure of their exchangeability, its existence must appear as "a certain definite sum of money" (*eine bestimmte Summe Geld*) (N 165, MEW 98). It must become a particular commodity alongside others, but one that is the universal commodity or general exchange value, i.e., the objectification of labor time in general.[27]

Prior to the initial exchange of the commodity for money, the commodity "latently contains" (*latent enthalt*) or "ideally contains" (*ideell enthalt*) its exchange value (N 147, MEW 81). It realizes its exchange value when the commodity is transformed into a price. Because money has an existence independent of commodities, the commodity must first equate itself with money.[28] The commodity attains a price upon this equation.

The equation of commodity and money, or price, is to be distinguished from the actual immediate exchange value that the commodity possesses relative to all other commodities. In the instance of the realization of price, the commodity acquires a "reflected quality" (*reflektierte Bestimmtheit*), which is a function of external determination (N 190, MEW 121). Money stands opposed to the commodity as the measure of exchangeability. The commodity relates to money as something external to itself. The commodity as price becomes (ideally) money itself. The commodity with a price becomes the universal equivalent, i.e., the measure of exchangeability. It becomes a measure.[29]

What had been posited as ideal becomes real in the act of exchange. The commodity, having been transformed into money—having acquired a price—first in the mind, becomes really transformed into money in exchange. In so far as it really becomes a measure of exchange value—is exchanged for money—it may then be exchanged for any other like, quantitatively determined commodity (N 193, MEW 123-24).

That Marx's treatment of the nature of price closely follows Hegel's exposition of measure is most apparent when Marx contends that while the commodity initially stands opposed to money, it then becomes a measure in the equation. In the sections entitled "The Specific Quantum" and "Specified Measure," Hegel details the way in which the specific quantum that had emerged as a measure relates to, and determines, the related quanta.

Measure is at first an "immediate quantum" (*unmittelbares Quantum*) i.e., "just some specific quantum or other" (*irgendein bestimmtes Quantum*) (SL 333, STW 394). It is an intrinsically determinate unit that stands external to that for which it is a standard. It stands opposed to quantum having a particular existence (SL 337, STW 399). This latter is measured by the rule, or it is determined as an amount of said unit. The comparison is an external act (SL 337, STW 399).

The something that stands opposed to the measure acquires the quality of the measurable as a consequence of its relatedness to the standard. This quality is initially external to the something, since it possesses it relative to the standard.[30] What then occurs is the transformation of the, what was, external quantum. The latter assimilates the new quality imposed on it by the formerly opposed qualitative quantum. The measurable something thereby itself becomes a qualitative quantum—it becomes a measure (SL 339, STW 402). This specification of measure is, in turn, expressed in an exponent. The exponent expresses the relation between the original measure and the newly determined measures. It is only when measure appears as realized in the measurable something that it is a real measure. It is a real measure only when the measurable something becomes a measure (SL 347, STW 411).

This opposition between measure and the measurable something, and the supersession of opposition in the generation of an exponent, is the logical schema that precisely demonstrates how money is realized as a measure. The commodity first stands opposed to money, and then acquires a "reflected quality" that is expressed in an exponent. The latter is of course the price of the commodity. The commodity ideally becomes a measure in price, and then becomes a real measure in the act of exchange.

4. NODAL LINES, LEAPS IN NATURE, AND MONETARY CRISIS

In further characterizing the relation that now obtains between the commodity as exchange value and money in price, Marx demonstrates that a new kind of relation emerges between commodities with the attribute of price. He does so with the aid of Hegel's exposition of "self-subsistent measure."

The commodity is ideally transformed into money when it acquires a price. Each commodity is taken as equal to a specific amount of money. In so far as each commodity has been transposed into a specific quantity of money as priced, they are all actually identified with each other. Money reacts back on the commodities and transforms each of them into an expression of money—a measure. They are now all brought into relation with each other, because each exemplifies the relations between all commodities in its attribute of price. Where prior to the emergence of money as measure, they were theoretically related to each other, each is now really related to the other in price. Money serves as the foundation for the interrelation between all commodities, because it is that through which a commodity becomes an equivalent when priced.[31]

A commodity may be ideally transformed into money only within a context wherein there exists a "circle of exchange, a totality of the same, in constant flux, proceeding more or less over the entire surface of society; a system of acts of exchange" (*ein Umkreis von Austauschen, eine Totalität derselben, in beständigem Flusse und mehr oder minder auf der ganzen Oberfläche der Gesellschaft vorgehend; ein System von Tauschakten*) (N 188, MEW 119). Exchange begins at an "infinite number of points, and to an infinite number of points it returns" (*unendlich vielen Punkten,und kehrt an unendlich viele züruck*)(N 195, MEW 125).

Thus, the actualization of the equivalence of the commodity as price—the realization of its relatedness to all others—entails a series of acts of exchange. Commodity A at such and such a price actually realizes itself as an equivalent when it is exchanged for the universal equivalent—money. It now actually exists in a form where relation to all other commodities. Only then may it be subsequently brought into relation with another. The transformation from the commodity into itself as measure—as price—entails a series or a circle of exchanges that begin at an infinity of different points, and to an infinity of different points it returns. Circulation is the first economic category that is called a totality.

When Marx describes the consequence of the realization of measure as a "circle of exchange, a totality of the same," or as an "infinite series," he remains logically consistent in recalling Hegel's exposition of the realization of self-subsistent measures.

What had been an immediate measure that had been opposed by external quanta, transforms the latter into measures themselves. This generates an exponent—a number—which is a function of the direct ratio between the original, immediate measure taken as unit and the, what have become, self-subsistent measures. The emergence of this exponent, in turn, leads to a series of relations between measures—equivalents (SL 352, STW 417). What had been the immediate measure now serves as the basis (the unit) of comparison between the generated series of relations. Hegel describes such a series as indefinite—infinite. There are, in effect, series upon series of relations. This infinite series entails a "circle of combinations" (*Kreise von Verbindungen*) of measured relations (N 354, STW 421).

It thus appears that Marx's presentation not only of money as a measure but also as a medium of exchange is indebted in its logical form to this section of the SL. In keeping with the necessary and/or scientific development of dialectical exposition, he moves from a consideration of measure to a resultant indefinite, or, as Marx states, an "infinite" series of acts of purchase and sale, a "circle of combinations."

Upon closer consideration, however, circulation is not a "spurious infinite process" (*schlecht unendlicher Prozeß*) (N 197, MEW 127). Though commodity is exchanged for money, and money is exchanged for commodity in an endless process, there is a "return of the point of departure into itself" (*der Rückkehr des Ausgangspunkts in sich*) (N 197, MEW 127). The exchange of commodity for commodity is a mediated one. The purchaser must again become seller, and the seller must again become a purchaser. The acts of purchase and sale appear therefore as "two mutually indifferent acts" (*zwei gegeneinander gleichgültige Akte*)(N 197, MEW 128). Each is "posited in the double and the antithetical aspects, and hence in the living unity of both aspects" (*in der doppelten und entgegengesetzten Bestimmung gesetzt, und so die ledendige Einheit beider Bestimmungen*)(N 197, MEW 127).

Since in order to realize itself as a universal equivalent a commodity must be exchanged for money, the relation between particular commodities is split into two distinct acts, purchase and sale. Money serves as the mediating element in the exchange between two commodities. In order for the price of one to be realized, and thereby exchanged for the price of the other, it must now be realized and it must be sold. The act of exchange is thereby complete as a unity of purchase and sale.

The exchangeability of a commodity is thus a function of whether it can realize its price. This quality, property, or attribute of the commodity is a function of a specific quantitative determination. Should it be the case that this numerical determination fluctuates to such a level that its quality as price cannot be realized, then the commodity would have effectively ceased to be a product. In short, a quantitative alteration may at a specific point extinguish the quality of the relatedness of the commodity to all others.[32]

It is the case, then, that with the emergence of money as a measure, and the transformation of the commodity into price, the exchange between commodities entails two separate acts: C-M-M-C. As a consequence, the further possibility arises that since the first act could fail to be completed, i.e., the commodity effectively ceases to be a commodity (becomes depriced and/or measureless), the exchange between commodities or the completion of the circle, might altogether collapse. The gradual alteration of price may suddenly develop into a fortification of purchase as against sale, whereupon commodities may not be exchanged for each other in the event of monetary crisis.[33]

If we follow carefully here the logical progression of Marx's treatment of the potentiality for crisis at the level of simple circulation, we will see his indebtedness to Hegel's exposition of the "nodal line of measured relations." Recall that the relation between the immediate measure and the self-subsistent measures produced an exponent. The latter entails an infinite series of relations, or a "circle of combinations" of measured relations. This latter infinite series is to be distinguished from the merely quantitative infinite progression. The quantitative infinite progression had entailed a negation of quantum upon further determination. In the infinite series that is generated in measured relations, each self-subsistent measure plays an integral role in the series (SL 352-55, STW 417-18). It is not simply negated or extinguished when we pass over into the next member of the series. The one must maintain its integrity against the other, if the relation is to be sustained. The fact that the measured relation as a series is comprised of self-subsistent measures—each is exclusive in its own right—entails that the series is, in effect, separable into the moments which united to produce it.[34]

Each moment of the series, because its quality or relation to the others is based on quantity, is subject to alteration. As a qualitative quantum, its variation in number may not affect its relation to the others within the series. There is a range within which it may vary without affecting its quality, i.e., its relation to or comparison with the others (SL 366-67, STW 436-37). On the other hand, if it should exceed this quantitatively determined range, a change in the quality, or relatedness, would ensue.[35] When this occurs the series is interrupted. Because a moment of the series has undergone a quantitative change beyond the range that is acceptable to the series, the relation between the members of the series is severed.[36]

Water, for example, is a unity of separable, specified measures that may be expressed in terms of an exponent. This quantitatively determined qualitative whole is subject to alteration. Should it be the case that this numerical determination fluctuates to such a level that its quality (or relatedness) as liquid can no longer be sustained, it will have effectively ceased to be water in this form. In short, a quantitative alteration may at a specific point extinguish the quality or relatedness of the separable, specified measures that combine to make water. Their relative independence may develop into a complete separation that is brought about by this quantitative alteration. What had been a unified whole is suddenly interrupted, and the result is the existence of two quantitatively distinct, but more important, qualitatively different forms of water. The one form may no longer be brought into relation with the other, given the fact that they are no longer measured according to the same exponent.[37]

In Marx's studies of political economy, and in particular in his analysis of the nature of price and simple circulation, he noted that the determination of price and also the subsequent development of simple circulation, could be conceived and presented according to the logical progression of categories that had been developed by Hegel in the SL—the latter is an ideal expression of the former. Furthermore, Hegel's exposition of the development of measured relations could lend insight into the foundation of the possibility of monetary crisis at the level of simple circulation.

Marx was able to discern that, while money may resolve the contradiction that exists between the qualitative and quantitative determinations of the "immediate product," it nevertheless generalizes the contradiction. Once money mediates the exchange of commodities, the exchange is separable into two distinct acts of purchase and sale. The one must realize its price in the form of money, in order then to result in the exchange of money for the other. The possibility arises that the one could fail to realize its price, or become depriced, and could not be exchanged for money. In which case, the commodities again have no basis of comparison, and cannot be exchanged. They cannot be exchanged precisely because the contradiction between their qualitative determination as "immediate products" and their quantitative determination as exchange values again reemerges. They are no longer measured according to the same measure, and there is no basis of comparison for purposes of exchange.

5. MONEY AS THE UNIVERSAL MATERIAL REPRESENTATIVE OF WEALTH AND MEASURE AS MATERIAL SUBSTRATE

The process of circulation has been characterized as a series of acts of purchase and sale, i.e., a "circle of combinations" (N 188, MEW 119). First the commodity becomes a universal equivalent in and though its exchange with money. It may then be exchanged for another like determined commodity, because it has attained a form that actually expresses its relatedness to every other commodity. Circulation is defined in the first instance as the exchange of one commodity for another through the medium of money (N 186-191, MEW 117-123).

In the process of circulation, money acquires a property that is distinguished from its existence as the measure of exchange value. As a measure, its quality as the universal equivalent is what is essential to it. Where gold has emerged as the universal equivalent, its property as gold serves as the basis of its function as a measure.

In the process of circulation, money serves two purposes: (1) It serves as that which realizes the price of commodities; and (2) it serves as the medium through which commodities realize their relations to each other. When it serves as medium of circulation, it only serves as medium of circulation. It realizes the price of the commodity and then is exchanged for another commodity. As such, money "appears only fleetingly, or its existence consists only in this constant appearance as disappearance, as this vehicle of mediation" (*erscheint das Geld nur verschwindend, und seine Substanz besteht nur darin, daß es fortwährend als dies Verschwinden erscheint, als dieser Träger der Vermittlung*) (N 209, MEW 138). It is a reality destined "constantly to disappear, to be superseded, not to count as a definitive realization, but always only as an intermediate, mediating realization" (*beständig zu verschwinden, aufgehoben zu werden, nicht als definitive Realisation zu gelten, sondern fortwährend nur als intermediäre, vermittelnde*)(N 211, MEW 141).

Money as a medium of circulation has negated, or is the contradiction of, itself as measure (N 210-11, EW 140-41). When it acts as a measure, its quality as gold is the foundation of its function. When it serves as a medium, its quality is no longer of importance. Rather, it must appear as a definite quantity of some material—a mere symbol of itself.[38]

If money as medium of circulation is the "wheel of circulation," it has at the same time a circulation of its own (N 193, MEW 124). Marx states: "If not as a constant alternation, but motions which it describes within itself, then this circular path appears as a double one: C-M-M-C; and in the other direction M-C-C-M; i.e., if I sell in order to buy, then I can also buy in order to sell."[39] Where money is exchanged for money, "money is mediated with itself by the commodity, and appears as the unity which joins with itself in its circular course" (*das Geld durch die Ware mit sich selbst vermittelt wird and als die sich mit selbst in seinem Umlauf zusammengehnde Einheit erscheint*) (N 201, MEW 131). Money has become the aim of circulation. It steps outside of circulation as a definite quantity of itself."

The existence of money as a definite amount of itself is to be distinguished from the appearance of a definite sum of some commodity or other. In the case of gold, while it is a particular commodity, it is also the universal equivalent. It embodies the relations, or economic quality, of all commodities. It is just as much a presupposition of circulation as it is a result. Marx states: "When money in its independent existence is derived from circulation, it appears in itself as a result of circulation; by way of circulation, it closes the circle with itself" (*Sofern das Geld in seiner selbständigen Existenz aus der Zirkulation herkommt, erscheint es in ihr selbst als Resultat der Zirkulation; es schließt sich mit sich selbst durch die Zirkulation zusammen*)(N 216, MEW 145).

As both presupposition and result, it is the universal material representative of wealth (N 216-17, MEW 145-46). It is not a measure which exists as ideal, nor is it a mere quantity of material that is needed in the exchange of commodities. Rather, with its withdrawal from circulation, it is "the negation (negative unity) of its character as medium of exchange and measure" (*die Negation [*negative *Einheit] seiner Bestimmung als Zirkulationsmittel und Maß*)(N 228, MEW 154). Money in its third attribute is the unity of its qualitative and quantitative aspects.[40]

Marx's characterization of money in its third attribute as a "negative unity" that is both presupposition and result of simple circulation—general wealth as both form and content—recalls Hegel's derivation of the third and final determination of measure as a material substrate.

Measure had first emerged as a standard and/or a rule. It was at first a quantum with a qualitative significance, i.e., a quantum that had not been a mere quantitative determination, but one that embodied the relations between quanta. It then became a ratio that expressed the relation between specific quanta that had the form of self-subsistent measures. But with the transition to a nodal series of measured relations, measure as such disappears in an "infinite series" or a "circle of combinations." Its determination as a qualitative quantum is negated in the context of the infinite quantitatively determined qualitative alternations. In short, in this negation of measure as such, measure disappears into a constant "alternation of specific existences with one another" (*die Abwechslung von spezifischen Existenzen miteinander*) (SL 371, STW 442).

It is the case, however, that the infinite nodal series of measures is to be distinguished from both the merely qualitative and the merely quantitative infinite.[41] The infinite nodal series is not a mere quantitative infinite that "points beyond itself." This infinite series is the unity of measure posited. Measure in this instance is the result of the generation of an infinite series that it itself had posited. It emerges as the negative unity of qualitative and quantitative determinations (SL 371, STW 442).

The final conclusion of this circular motion of measure is the unity of a self-subsistent material substance or thing.[42] It possesses three characteristics. The unity of this material thing is posited as "the perennial substrate of its differentiations." It "contains directly in its own self the determination of affirmative infinity."[43] And finally, the meaning of the process is "only to show or to posit the determinate being of such a substrate underlying the process, a substrate which is their unity (i.e., of quality and quantity—MM)" (*nur das Dasein, das Zeigen oder Setzen, daß demselben ein solches Substrat zugrunde liegt*) (SL 373, STW 445).

We see, then, that Marx's exposition of money as a medium seems to have benefited in its logical form, or in the organization of the pertinent data, from Hegel's exposition of the quantitatively determined qualitative infinite of measured relations. Hegel had demonstrated how measure as such is negated in this its immediate quality. It then disappears into the "constant alternation" of the specific existences that it had originally determined. This supersession of measure results in an "infinite process" of the passage of one self-subsistent measure into the next.

Marx likewise contends that as a medium of circulation, money is "negated" as a measure. It had already played its role as measure prior to circulation, and now is "superseded" in the "constant alternation" or "infinite process" of the exchange of commodity for commodity. Yet exchange is not only a mediation of commodities through money, but also the mediation of money with itself through commodities. Money posits the relation between "equivalents," thereby negating itself in their relations, only to return to itself as a "negative unity," as the result of the process that it had initiated. Money is "mediated with itself," and is the "unity which joins itself with itself in its circular course." It is both presupposition and result and now stands as the "universal material representative of wealth." It is the "general form of wealth, while the totality of these particularities form its substance. . . . Money is therefore the god among commodities."

Though money in its completed development emerges from circulation and stands opposed to it, its independence does not end its relation to circulation.[44] Its independence from its particular manifestations is a mere semblance (N 234, MEW 160).[45] Its very existence as such is reducible to the exchange of commodities. The latter forms its "content."

If money is to prove itself to be the real material representative of wealth, it must be negated in its "purely objective form, as a form of wealth external and accidental to individuals" (*rein dinglichen Form, den Individuen gegenüber außerlichen und zufälligen Form des Reichtums*) (N 234-35, MEW 161). In its realized form it must produce wealth. Its entry into circulation must prove to be a moment of its own determination.

Here again, we see that it appears that Marx was aided in his formulation and organization of this exposition by Hegel's exposition of the circle that measure describes within itself. Though measure as such disappears into the "constant alternation of specific existences," it nevertheless reemerges as a unity of quality and quantity. It posits itself as specific measures, supersedes itself in their relations, and returns-into-itself as a negative unity. The whole process is the mediation of measure with itself, a "circular course."

Yet the unity and independence of posited, real measure as a material substrate is merely a function of quantitative determinations that result in qualitative change. It is a mere arrangement that remains external. The unity of the substrate is ultimately reducible to, or co-extensive with, these measured relations that it produces within itself. It is not as yet the "free Concept which alone gives its differences an immanent determination" (SL 373, STW 445).

---

[1] Georg Friedrich Hegel, *Science of Logic* (SL), trans. by A.V. Miller (London: Allen and Unwin, 1969), pp. 67-80; (STWI), pp. 65-82; cf. Errol E. Harris, *An Interpretation of the Logic of Hegel* (London, U.K.: University Press of America, 1983), pp. 85 93.

[2] See Harris, *An Interpretation*, esp. "Introduction," for a thorough discussion of the objective and subjective foundations of Hegel's concept of scientific method; cf. "With What Must a Science Begin," in Harris, *An Interpretation*, for a consideration of the foundations of the beginning of science according to Hegel.

[3] N 140, MEW 75.

[4] See George E. McCarthy, *Marx's Critique of Science and Positivism: The Methodological Foundations of Political Economy* (London: Kluwer Academic Publishers, 1988); Patrick Murray, *Marx's Theory of Scientific Knowledge* (New Jersey: Humanities Press International, Inc., 1988); and, Tony Smith, *The Logic of Marx's Capital* (New York: State University of New York Press, 1990) for Marx's critique of positivism.

[5] Marx, N 145, MEW 80.

[6] ". . . *bestimmte Resultat einer bestimmten, natürlich bestimmten, von andren Arbeiten qualitativ verschiednen Arbeit ist. . .*" (MEW 78).

[7] "*Die Ware ist in ihren natürlichen Eigenschaften weder beständig austauschbar noch mit jeder andren Ware austauschbar, nicht in ihrer natürlichen Gleichheit mit sich; sondern*

also noch selbst ungleich, als etwas von sich ungleiches, als Tauschwert gesetzt" (MEW 77).

[8] Hegel, SL, p. 111; Cf. Harris, *An Interpretation*, pp. 93-123, for an exposition of Hegel's consideration of Quality.

[9] Hegel, SL, p.116. Cf. Harris, *An Interpretation*, 100-115 for a discussion of Hegel's consideration of the unique, qualitied nature of determinate being.

[10] "*. . . materialisierte Arbeitszeit; Arbeitszeit nicht in der Form der Bewegung, sondern der Ruhe; nicht des Prozesses, sondern des Resultats ist. . .*" (MEW 78).

[11] Marx also refers to the product as simply "particular labour time" (*bestimmte Arbeitszeit*)(N 168, MEW 101). It is the "static presence of the force which created it" (*ruhndes Dasein der Kraft, die es geschaffen*)(N 613, MEW 514). Marx goes so far as to say that labor is the "temporality" of the product.

[12] See Dieter Wolf, *Ware und Geld*, for an excellent consideration of the quantitative content of the "immediate product," esp. chap. 1-3; compare with Richard Winfield, "The Logic of Marx's Capital," *Telos* 32 (1976): 111-139. Though Winfield's criticisms of Henrich, Hans-Jurgen Krahl, and Helmut Reichelt are, I think, well taken, he fails to comprehend the most fundamental relation in the determination of the "immediate product." Winfield associates the qualitative determination of the product with need and makes value a function of will. As Wolf demonstrates, this is an egregious error that leads to obfuscation, and ultimately renders Marx's exposition of money contradictory. In addition, it leads to a misidentification of the Hegelian logical categories that are at work in Marx's organization and presentation of the economic categories of capital, e.g., cf. Tony Smith's criticisms of Winfield in *The Logic of Marx's Capital*, esp. pp. 74-78.

[13] Marx states: ". . . the labour time objectified in the product—or amount of labour (expressed passively, the magnitude of labour appears as an amount of space; but expressed in motion, it is measurable only in time) . . ." (*. . . die im Produkt vergegenständlichte Arbeitszeit—oder Quantum Arbeit [ruhend ausgedrückt, erscheint die Grosse der Arbeit als Raumquantum, aber bewegt ausgedrückt, ist sie nur durch die Zeit messbar] . . .*) (N 321, MEW 240).

[14] Cf. Harris, *An Interpretation*, pp.115-124, for a discussion of the transition from Quality to Quantity.

[15] Being-for-self, then, is seen to be an "uninterrupted continuity" that is at the same time a "plurality." Yet despite the fact that it is both continuous and discrete, being-for-self nevertheless remains a "self-identical immediacy" (*sichselbstgleicher Unmittelbarkeit*)(SL 187-88, STW 211-12).

[16] Marx states: "As a value, the commodity is an equivalent; as an equivalent, all its natural properties are extinguished, it no longer takes up a special qualitative relationship towards the other commodities" (*Als Wert ist die Ware Äquivalent; als Äquivalent sind alle ihre natürlichen Eigneschaften in ihr ausgeloscht; steht sie in keinem qualitätiven besondren Verhältnis mehr zu den andren Waren*)(N 140, MEW 76).

[17] Marx states: "What does a solely quantitative difference between things presuppose? The identity of their qualities. Hence, the quantitative measure of labour presupposes the equivalence, the identity of their quality" (*Was setzt der nur quantitative Unterschied von Dingen voraus? Die Dieselbigkeit ihrer Qualität. Also das quantitative Messen der Arbeiten die Ebenbürtigkeit, die Dieselbigkeit ihre Qualität*)(N 173, MEW 105).

[18] Insofar as it is a unity as both a continuous and discrete magnitude, it is said to possess "the enclosing, encompassing limit" (*umschliessende, befassende Grenze*) (SL 201,

STW 230). Hegel states: "Real discrete quantity is thus a quantity, or quantum — quantity as a determinate being or a something" (*Die reale diskrete Quantität ist so eine Quantität oder Quantum—die Quantität als ein Dasein und Etwas*) (SL 201, STW 230).

[19] Hegel, SL, pp. 217-19. As a "specific quantum," it is not merely a plurality, but exists as an "intensive magnitude." Hegel states: "The degree is thus a specific magnitude, a quantum; but at the same time it is not an aggregate or plural within itself; it is a plurality only in principle, for plurality has been brought together into a simple, unitary determination, determinate being has returned into being-for-self" (*Der Grad ist also bestimmte Grösse, Quantum, aber nicht zugleich Menge oder Mehreres innerhalb seiner selbst; er ist nur eine Mehrheit; die Mehrheit ist das Mehrere in die einfache Bestimmung zusammengenommen, das Dasein in das Fürsichsein zurückgegangen*) (SL 218, STW 252).

[20] Marx states: "As a value, the commodity is general; as a real commodity it is particular. As a value it is always exchangeable; in real exchange it is exchangeable only if it fulfills particular conditions. As a value, the measure of its exchangeability is determined by itself, exchange value expresses precisely the relation in which it replaces other commodities; in real exchange it is exchangeable only in quantities which correspond to the needs to the participants in exchange" (*Als Wert is sie allgemein, als wirkliche Ware eine Besonderheit. Als Wert ist sie stets austauschbar; in dem wirklichen Austausch ist sie es nur, wenn sie besondre Bedingungen erfüllt. Also Wert ist das Maß ihrer Austauschbarkeit durch sie selbst bestimmt; der Tauschwert drückt eben das Verhältnis aus, in dem sie andre Waren ersetzt; im wirklichen Austausch ist sie nur austauschbar in Quantitäten, die mit ihren natürlichen Eigenschaften zusammenhängen und den Bedürfnissen der Austauschenden entsprechen*) (N 142, MEW 76-77).

[21] This logical transition is also clearly stated in the *Contribution;* cf. pp. 39ff.

[22] Hegel states: "This difference, as internally self-contradictory, is posited as being the simple, self-related determinateness which is the negation of itself, having its determinateness not within itself but in another quantum" (*Er ist als sein Widerspruch in sich selbst gesetzt, die einfache sich auf sich beziehende Bestimmtheit zu sein, welche die Negation ihrer selbst ist, ihre Bestimmtheit nicht an ihr, sondern in einem anderen Quantum zu haben*) (SL 225, STW 259).

[23] Hegel states: ". . . quantum is posited as having its determinateness in another quantum by means of its non-being, of infinity; that is, it is qualitatively that which it is" (*. . . das Quantum so, dass es vermittels seines Nichtseins, der Unendlichkeit, in einem anderen Quantum seine Bestimmtheit habe, d.i. qualitativ das ist, was es ist.*) (SL 239, STW 278).

[24] Marx states: "The commodity first has to be transposed into labour time, into something, qualitatively different from itself (qualitatively different (1) because it is not labour time as labour time, but materialized labour time; labour time not in the form of motion, but at rest; not in the form of the process, but of the result; (2) because it is not the objectification of labour time in general, which exists only as a conception (it is only a conception of labour separated from its quality, subject merely to quantitative variations), but rather the specific result of a specific, of a naturally specified, kind of labour which differs qualitatively from other kinds), in order then to be compared as a specific amount of labour time, as a certain magnitude of labour, with other amounts of labour time, other magnitudes of labour" (*Die Ware muß erst in Arbeitszeit, also etwas von ihr qualitativ Verschiednes, umgesezt werden (qualitativ verschieden; 1. weil sie nicht Arbeitszeit als Arbeitszeit, sondern materialisierte Arbeitszeit; Arbeitszeit nicht in der Form der Bewegung, sondern der Ruhe; nicht des Prozesses, sondern des Resultats ist; 2. weil sie nicht die*

Vergegenständlichung der Arbeitszeit im allgemeinen, die nur in der Vorstellung existiert [selbst nur die von ihrer Qualität getrennt, nur quantitativ verschiedne Arbeit ist], sondern das bestimmte Resultat einer bestimmten, natürlich bestimmten, von andren Arbeiten qualitative verschieden Arbeit ist, um dann als bestimmtes Quantum Arbeitszeit, bestimmte Arbeitsgröße, mit andren Quantis Arbeitszeit, andren Arbeitsgrößen verglichen zu werden)(N 143, MEW 78).

[25] Marx states: "[Exchange] Value is at the same time the exponent of the relation in which the commodity is exchanged with other commodities . . ." (*Er ist zugleich der Exponent des Verhältnesses, worin sie sich austauscht mit andren Waren . . .*)(N 140, MEW 76).

[26] Marx states: "Because the product becomes a commodity, and the commodity becomes an exchange value, it obtains, at first only in the head, a double existence. This doubling in the idea proceeds (and must proceed) to the point where the commodity appears double in real exchange: as a natural product on one side, as exchange value on the other; i.e., the commodity's exchange value obtains a material existence separate from the commodity" (*Dadurch, dass das Produkt Ware and die Ware Tauschwert wird, erhält es erst im Kopfe eine doppelte Existenz. Diese ideell Verdopplung geht (und muß dazu fortgehn), daß die Ware im wirklichen Austausch doppelt erscheint: als natürliches Produkt auf der einen Seite, als Tauschwert auf der andren. D.h., ihr Tauschwert erhält eine materiell von ihr getrennte Existenz*) (N 145, MEW 79-80).

[27] The following is in substantial agreement with both Winfield and Uchida. In "The Logic of Marx's Capital," Winfield correctly identifies the Hegelian logical categories that are at work in Marx's exposition of the nature of price. His analysis is, however, flawed for the reasons given above. While Uchida sees that Marx's exposition of the nature of money is related to Hegel's exposition of Quantum and Measure, he develops the relationship in a haphazard manner; cf. Winfield, "The Logic of Marx's Capital", esp. pp. 123-27; and, Uchida, *Marx's Grundrisse and Hegel's Logic*, esp. pp. 45-64.

[28] Marx states: "After money has been posited as independent exchange value, separated from commodities, then the individual commodity, the particular exchange value, is again equated to money, i.e., is posited as equal to a given quantity of money, expressed as money, translated into money" (*Nachdem das Geld als der von den Waren selbständige, getrennte Tauschwert gesetzt worden, wird nun die einzelne Ware, der besonder Tauschwert, dem Geld wieder gleichgesetzt, d.h. gleich einem bestimmten Quantum Geld gesetzt, als Geld ausgedrückt, in Geld übersetzt*) (N 189, MEW 120).

[29] Marx states: "Thus, just as originally money expressed exchange value, so does the commodity as price, as ideally posited, mentally realized exchange value, now express a sum of money: money in a definite proportion. As prices, all commodities in their different forms are representative of money, whereas earlier it was money, as the independent form of exchange value, which was the representative of all commodities. After money is posited as a commodity in reality, the commodity is posited as money in the mind" (*Wenn also ursprünglich das Geld den Tauschwert, so drückt jetzt die Ware als Preis, als ideell gesetzter, im Kopf realisierter Tauschwert, eine Summe Geldes aus: Geld in einer bestimmten Proportion. Als Preise sind alle Waren unter verschiednen Formen Repräsentanten des Geldes, während früher das Geld, also der verselbständigte Tauschwert, der Repräsentant aller Waren war. Nachdem das Geld reell als Ware, wind die Ware ideell als Geld gesetzt) (N 191*, MEW 122).

[30] Hegel states: "Measure is a specific determining of the external, i.e., indifferent magnitude which is now posited by some other existence in general in the measurable something . . ." (*Das Maß ist spezifisches Bestimmen der äusserlichen Große, d.i. der*

gleichgültigen, die nun von einer anderen Existenz überhaupt an dem Etwas des Maßes gesetzt wird. . .) (SL 337, STW 399).

[31] Marx states: "Money as price shows first of all the identity of all exchange values; secondly, it shows the unit of which they all contain a given number, so that the equation with money expresses the quantitative specificity of exchange values, their quantitative relation to one another. . . . By being equated to money, they again become related to one another as they were, conceptually, as exchange values: they balance and equate themselves with one another in given proportions. . . . Thus, just as originally money expressed exchange value, so does the commodity as price, as ideally posited, mentally realized exchange value, now express a sum of money: money in a definite proportion. As prices, all commodities in their different forms are representatives of money, whereas earlier it was money, as the independent form of exchange value, which was the representative of all commodities. After money is posited as a commodity in reality, the commodity is posited as money in the mind" (*Im Preise erscheint das Geld erstens als die Einheit aller Tauschwerte; zweitens als die Einheit, von der sie eine bestimmte Anzahl enthalten, so daß durch die Vergleichung mit ihm ihre quantitative Bestimmtheit, ihr quantitatives Verhältnis zueinander ausgedruckt ist. . . Dadurch, daß sie dem Geld gleichgesetzt sind, sind sie wieder aufeinander bezogen, wie sie es dem Begriff nach als Tauschwerte waren: Dass sie sich in bestimmten Verhältnissen decken and vergleichen. . . Wenn also ursprünglich das Geld den Tauschwert, so drückt jetzt die Ware als Preis, als ideell gesetzter, im Kopf realisiterter Tauschwert, eine Summe Geld aus: Geld in einer bestimmten Proportion. Als Preise sind alle Waren unter verschiednen Formen Repräsentanten des Geldes, während früher das Geld, als der verselbständigte Tauschwert, der Repräsentant aller Waren war. Nachdem das Geld reell als Ware, wird die Ware ideell als Geld gesetzt*)(N 189, MEW 120).

[32] Marx states: "If the commodity cannot be realized in money, it ceases to be capable of circulating, and its price becomes merely imaginary; just as originally the product which has become transformed into exchange value, if it is not really exchanged, ceases to be a product" (*Wenn sie nicht in Geld realisiert werden kann, hört sie auf, zirkulationsfähig zu sein, and ihr Preis wird nur imaginär; wie ursprünglich das in Tauschwert verwandelte Produkt, wenn es nicht wirklich ausgetauscht wird, aufhört, Produkt zu sein*) (N 198, MEW 128-29).

[33] Marx states: "In so far as purchase and sale, the two essential moments of circulation, are indifferent to one another and separated in place and time, they by no means need to coincide. Their independence can develop into the fortification and apparent independence of the one against the other. But in so far as they are both essential moments of a single whole, there must come a moment when the independent form is violently broken and when the inner unity is established externally through a violent explosion. Thus already in the quality of money as medium, in the splitting of exchange into two acts, there lies the germ of crises, or at least their possibility, which cannot be realized, except where the fundamental preconditions of classically developed, conceptually adequate circulation are present" (*Insofern Kauf und Verkauf, die beiden wesentlichen Momente der Zirkulation, gleichgültig gegeneinander sind, in Raum and Zeit getrennt, brauchen sie keineswegs zusammenzufallen. Ihre Gleichgültigkeit kann zur Befestigung und scheinbaren Selbständigkeit des einen gegen das andre fortgehn. Insofern sie aber beide wesentlich Momente eines Ganzen bilden, muß ein Moment eintreten, wo die selbständige Gestalt gewaltsam gebrochen and die innre Einheit äußerlich durch eine gewaltsame Explosion hergestellt wird. So liegt schon in der Bestimmung des Geldes als Mittler, in dem*

Auseinanderfallen des Austauschs in zwei Akte, der Keim der Krisen, wenigstens ihre Möglichkeit, die nicht realisiert werden kann als da, wo die Grundbedingungen der klassisch ausgebildeten, ihrem Begriff entsprechenden Zirkulation vorhanden sind) (N 198, MEW 128).

Furthermore, he states: "Sometimes it becomes evident that what appeared to be an essentially divided act is in reality an essentially unified one; then again, sometimes, that what was thought to be an essentially unified act is in reality essentially divided. At moments when purchasing and selling assert themselves as essentially different acts, a general depreciation of all commodities takes place. At moments where it turns out that money is only a medium of exchange, a depreciation of money comes about. General fall or rise of prices" (*Bald zeigt es sich, dass, was also ein wesentlich getrennter Akt erschien, ein wesentlich Zusammengehöriges ist; bald, daß, was als ein wesentlich zusammengehöriger Akt gedacht wurde, in der Wirklichkeit wesentlich getrennt ist. In Momenten, wo das Kaufen and Verkaufen sich als Wesentlich verschiedne Akte behaupten, findet die allgemeine Depreziation aller Waren statt. In Momenten, wo es hervortritt, dass das Geld nur Mittel des Austauschs, findet die Depreziation des Geldes statt, Allgemeines Fallen oder Steigen der* Preise) (N 200, MEW 130).

[34] Hegel states: "This measure, based on such a relation, is thus infected with its own indifference (i.e., of each element, within the whole, to the other); it is in its own self something external and alterable in its relation to itself" (*Dadurch ist dies Maß, daß auf einem solchen Verhältnisse in ihm selbst beruht, mit eigener Gleichgültigkeit behaftet; es ist ein an ihm selbst Äußerliches and in seiner Beziehung auf sich ein Veränderliches*) (SL 367, STW 436).

[35] Hegel states: "But there enters a point in this quantitative alteration at which the quality is changed and the quantum shows itself as specifying, so that the altered quantitative relation is converted into measure, and thus into a new quality, a new something. But because the difference falls into this quantitative aspect, the relation between the new something and its predecessor is one of indifference; their difference is the external one of quantum" (*Aber es tritt ein Punkt dieser Änderung des Quantitativen ein, auf welchem die Qualität geändert wird, das Quantum sich als spezifizierend erweist, so daß das veränderte quantitative Verhältnis in ein Maß und damit in eine neue Qualität, ein neues Etwas, umgeschlagen ist. . . Aber indem der Unterschied in dieses Quantitative fällt, verhält sich das neue Etwas gleichgültig gegen das vorhergehende; ihr Unterschied ist der äußerliche des Quantums*) (SL 367, STW 437).

[36] Hegel states: "On the quantitative side, therefore, the gradual, merely quantitative progress which is not in itself a limit, is absolutely interrupted; the new quality in its merely quantitative relationship is, relative to the vanishing quality, an indifferent, indeterminate other, and the transition is therefore a leap; both are posited as completely external to each other" (*Nach der qualitativen Seite wird daher das bloß quantitative Fortgehen der Allmählichkeit, das keine Grenze an sich selbst ist, absolut abgebrochen; indem die neu eintretende Qualität nach ihrer bloß quantitativen Beziehung eine gegen die verschwindende unbestimmt andere, eine gleichgültige ist, ist der Übergang ein Sprung; beide sind als völlig äußerliche gegeneinander gestezt*) (SL 368, STW 438).

Hegel provides us with a concrete example of such an occurrence. He states: "Again, water when its temperature is altered does not merely get more or less hot but passes through from the liquid into either the solid or gaseous states; these states do not appear gradually, on the contrary, each new state appears as a leap, suddenly interrupting and checking the gradual succession of temperature changes at these points. Every birth and death, far from being a progressive gradualness, is an interruption of it and is the leap from quantitative into a qualitative alteration" (*Oder das Wasser, indem es seine Temperatur ändert, wird damit nicht bloß mehr oder weniger warm, sondern geht durch die Zustände der Härte, der tropfbaren Flüssigkeit und der elastischen Flüssigkeit hindurch; diese verschiedenen Zustände treten nicht allmählich ein, sondern eben das bloß allmähliche Fortgehen der Temperaturänderung wird durch these Punkte mit einem Male unterbrochen ungehemmt, und der Eintritt eines anderen Zustandes ist ein Sprung. Alle Geburt und Tod sind, statt eine fortgesetzte Allmählichkeit zu sein, vielmehr ein Abbrechen derselben und der Sprung aus quantitativer Veränderung in qualitative*) (SL 369, STW 440).

[37] Hegel further demonstrates that upon the quantitative alteration and the subsequent emergence of two qualitatively distinct "somethings," the one becomes, as it were, "measureless" with respect to the other. In other words, when it is the case that what is a unity of separable, specified measures exceeds the quantitative limit that binds them together, they are no longer related in terms of the same measure, or, they become "measureless" (SL 371, STW 442).

[38] Marx states: "As a mere medium of circulation, in its role in the constant flow of the circulatory process, money is neither the measure of prices, because it is already posited as such in the prices themselves; nor is it the means for the realization of prices for it exists as such in one single moment of circulation, but disappears as such in the totality of its moments; but is, rather, the mere representative of the price in relation to all other commodities, and serves only as a means to the end that all commodities are to be exchanged at equivalent prices" (*Als bloßes Zirkulationsmittel, in seiner Rolle im Prozeß der Zirkulation als beständigem Floß, ist das Geld weder Maß der Preise, denn als solches ist es schon in den Preisen selbst gesetzt; noch Mittel der Realisation der Preise, denn als solches existiert dies in dem einen Moment der Zirkulation, verschwindet es aber in der Totalität ihrer Momente; sondern ist bloßer Repräsentant des Preises gegen alle Waren und dient nur als Mittel, dass Waren zu gleichen Preisen ausgetauscht werden*) (N 211, MEW 140-41).

[39] *Wenn die Zirkulation nicht nur als ein beständiges Abwechseln betrachtet wird, sondern in den Dreislaufen, die sie in sich selbst beschreibt, so erscheint dieser Kreislauf doppelt: Ware-Geld-Geld-Ware; andererseits Geld-Ware-Ware-Geld; d.h. wenn ich verkaufe um zu kaufen; so kann ich ebenso kaufen, um zu verkaufen* (N 201, MEW 131).

[40] Money as the result of circulation is said to be: ". . . the "prècis de toutes les chose," in which their particular character is erased; it is general wealth in the form of a concise compendium, as opposed to its diffusion and fragmentation in the world of commodities. While wealth in the form of the particular commodity appears as one of the moments of same, or the commodity as one of the moments of wealth; in the form of gold and silver general wealth itself appears concentrated in a particular substance" (*der "prècis de toutes les chose," worin ihr besondrer Charakter verwischt; der allgemeine Reichtum als kurzgefaßtes Kompendium gegenüber seiner Ausbreitung and Zersplitterung in der Welt der Waren. Während in der besondren Ware der Reichtum als ein Moment derselben erscheint oder sie als ein besondres Moment des Reichtums, erscheint im Gold und Silber der allgemeine Reichtum selbst konzentriert in einer besondern Materie*) (N *218*, MEW *147)*.

Furthermore, Marx states: "With money, general wealth is not only a form, but at the same time the content itself" (*Im Geld ist der allgemeine Reichtum nicht nur eine Form, sondern zugleich der Inhalt selbst*)(N 218, MEW 147).

[41] Hegel states: "But this infinity of the specification of measure posits both the qualitative and the quantitative as sublating themselves in each other, and hence posits their first, immediate unity, which is measure as such, as returned into itself and therefore as itself posited" (*Aber diese Unendlichkeit der Spezifikation des Masses setzt ebensowohl das*

Qualitative wie das Quantitative als sich ineinander aufhebend und damit die erste, unmittelbare Einheit derselben, welche das Maß überhaupt ist, als in sich zurückgekehrt und damit selbst als gesetzt) (SL 372, STW 443).

[42] Hegel states: "This unity which thus constitutes itself into itself in its alternating measures is the truly persisting, self-subsistent material substance or thing" (*Diese so sich in ihrem Wechsel der* Maße *in sich selbst kontinuierende Einheit ist die wahrhaft bestehenbleibende, selbstandige Materie, Sache*) (SL 372, STW 443).

[43] Hegel states: "This self-sameness of the substrate is posited in the fact that the qualitative self-subsistent measures into which the specifying unity is dispersed consist only of quantitative differences, so that the substrate continues itself into this differentiation of itself" (*Diese Dieselbigkeit des Substrats ist darin gesetzt, daß die qualitativen Selbständigkeiten, in welche die Maßbestimmende Einheit abgestoßen ist, nur in quantitativen Unterschieden bestehen, so daß das Substrats sich in dies sein Unterschieden kontinuiert*) (SL 372, STW 443).

[44] Marx states: ". . . it stands independent of circulation, but this independence is only its own process. It derives from it just as it returns to it again. Cut off from all relation to it, it would not be money, but merely a simple natural object, gold or silver" (. . . *es steht ihr selbständig gegenuber, aber these seine Selbständigkeit ist nur ihr eigner Prozeß. Es kommt ebenso aus ihr her, wie es wieder in sie eingeht. Außer aller Beziehung auf sie wäre es nicht Geld, sonder ein einfacher Naturgengenstand, Gold und Silber*) (N 217, MEW 146).

[45] Because it is merely the material representative of general wealth it realizes itself "only by being thrown back into circulation, to disappear in exchange for the singular, particular modes of wealth" (*indem es wieder in Zirkulation geworfen, gegen die einzelnen besondren Weisen des Reichtums verschwindet*) (N 233, MEW 160).

CHAPTER 3

THE ESSENCE OF CAPITAL

Common sense or mere perceptual thinking had led many classical political economists to identify simple circulation or the monetary system with capital. They saw only the appearance of capital. They failed to discern the inner essence that lies beneath or behind simple circulation and in terms of which the latter must be explained. A more sophisticated exposition would distinguish between capital as it appears and capital as it is in its essence. Such an exposition would employ a scientific method that would take into account the fact that the essence of capital is merely implicit in simple circulation. Simple circulation therefore presupposes the essence of capital as the ground of its existence. A dialectical exposition of capital recognizes this fact and accepts it as a basic tenet. A careful, scientific treatment of commodity and monetary circulation detects what lies behind the mere appearance of capital. What capital is essentially differs from what it appears to be. Simple circulation is the mere "immediate being" of the underlying reality of the organic system of capital.

Marx sets out to explicate the inner nature of the capitalist system of production in this part of the *Grundrisse.* He demonstrates that simple circulation is a mere *Schein* or illusion for what takes place beneath or behind it; that circulation is in fact the necessary, outward appearance of the essence of this organic system; and, finally, that circulation is a process of "actualization." Thus, he not only formulates a distinction between appearance and reality, but also shows how the essence of capital is related to this appearance.

Such a dialectical exposition begins by relating simple circulation to the essence of capital. Once the transition from simple circulation to capital is made, Marx can examine the interrelated elements that comprise its essence. This dialectical exposition of the essence of capital proceeds in turn from an examination of its abstract or simpler moments toward ever more concrete and complex relations. Finally, the exposition culminates in a demonstration of capital as a concrete whole of inseparably, correlated moments.

Three distinct steps are entailed in the exposition of a particular moment of the essence of capital. We begin with a relatively simple identity, e.g., money, the commodity, the whole of the working day, etc., and then show how this simple identity is differentiated into opposed and/or contradictory sides. The two sides are actually two phases that constitute a single whole. The two sides then serve as the basis for further development, which likewise entail two phases that are superseded in a single whole. This advance from the abstract to the concrete does not entail that the simple moments are canceled out with the emergence of a more concrete, complex whole. Rather, Marx contends that these simpler moments are superseded, i.e., transformed yet preserved in the more complex whole. Thus, the essence of capital is conceived of as a system of hierarchically ordered, dialectically related forms of existence.

This way of understanding capital relies on a conceptual schema (a "background theory") that distinguishes between appearance and reality. Yet it must not merely distinguish between the two, it must also demonstrate how they are inextricably related. It must provide a framework through which one may understand how and why reality must appear as it does. We contend that Marx found such a logical structure in Hegel's presentation of the logic of "Essence," in the SL. Hegel provided Marx with the necessary conceptual tools that would enable him to present an exposition of the essence of capital.

1. THE BECOMING OF ESSENCE AND THE EXCHANGE BETWEEN EQUALS

Marx has told us that if money is to prove itself the real material representative of wealth, it must be negated in its "purely objective form, as a form of wealth external and accidental to individuals" (*rein dinglichen Form, den Individuen gegenüber äußerlichen und zufälligen Form des Reichtums*) (N 235, MEW 161). In short, if money is to become capital, it cannot remain a mere thing, but must become a relation between individuals. The "becoming of capital" entails the transformation of money from a material substrate into the foundation of a relation between exchangers.

The exposition of such a transformation is by no means an easy one.[1] The deep, logical structure of the development is indebted to Hegel's exposition of the "becoming of essence." Hegel shows that individual quanta are brought into relation within the context that is established by the material substrate. The former are different "states" or "individuations" of the one material substrate. Because their existence is a function of quantitative determination, they are in this sense "indifferent" toward each other. Yet since they are individuations of the material substrate, they are nevertheless reciprocally related.[2] Each is itself "the unity of the two qualities into which the qualitative moment splits itself" (*jede selbst die Einheit der beiden Qualitäten ist, in welche das qualitätive Moment sich spaltet*) (SL 378, STW 449). The existence of one is a function of its being in relation to the other.

Each continues itself out of itself into the other. They therefore maintain a state of equilibrium with respect to, or are equal to, one another (SL 379, STW 450).

Marx's treatment of the relation between exchangers as mediated by money reflects this logical schema. The bourgeois notion of equality is really a function of the "indifference" (*Gleichgültige*) of exchangers toward each other. Money has been realized as a unity that embodies differentiations in the form of particular commodities. Exchangers come to the exchange process bearing commodities. When the commodity is conceived of solely in terms of exchange value, the relation in which commodities are exchanged is an equation or a balancing out of equal exchange values. As a consequence, the individuals who undertake the process of exchange are simply and solely exchangers.[3] Each then represents money, or, their existence as exchangers is a function of their having been determined by the money system. Each appears toward the other as the universal material representative of wealth.[4] Each individual is "merely the individuation of money" (*nur die Individuation von Geld*) (N247, MEW 172).

Here, then, the material substrate determines a relation between its own "individuations." The latter are in turn "indifferent" and/or equal in an equation. Yet despite their indifference, as moments of the equation they are reciprocally related. They have different needs. A exists as the owner of a use value for B, and B as owner of a use value for A. Insofar as each possesses what the other needs, they relate reciprocally to one another; they "integrate" (*integrieren sich*) with one another, have need of one another. Each sees himself as both end and means of the exchange process. Each serves the other in order to serve himself, and this fact is present in the consciousness of the two exchangers. Each individual knowingly perceives himself as the means to the end of the other's satisfaction and at the same time as the end of the exchange. Each is "reflected in himself" (*in sich reflektiert*) (N 244, MEW 170).

Equality and freedom are thus recognized precisely because of the nature of money as measure, as the universal material representative of wealth. Money renders all things equal. Since products are exchanged based on exchange value, they must first equate themselves to the universal equivalent. The exchangers approach the exchange process bearing products that have been rendered equal insofar as each has a price. One is a buyer and the other a seller. Here the difference is merely formal, the fact remains that both represent money—both are "individuations" of money and "integrate" in the equation.

2. CAPITAL IN ITS REFLECTED NATURE

A relation between individuals based on equality and freedom is a consequence of the consolidation of the money system. Money creates the context within which individuals may "integrate" based upon "indifference and equal worthiness," as well as on the "opposition" of one individual's interest to that of another. All differences between "individuations" of money are extinguished in this "social equation."

In the context of simple circulation, money in its third attribute as the general form of wealth may be withdrawn from the exchange process and accumulated. Yet if one individual decides to do so and not realize the money in particular commodities, he in no way does so at the expense of another. It is merely the case that the one enjoys wealth in its particular manifestations, while the other accumulates it in its general form.

For money to become other than the mere general form of wealth, it must be negated in this third attribute. Once it is negated as the general form of wealth, it then realizes itself in the particular substances of real wealth. Thus, money's entry into circulation is a moment of its own realization. Marx states: "This is at the same time the negation of itself as a purely objective form, as a form of wealth external and accidental to individuals" (*Es ist zugleich die Negation seiner als einer rein dinglichen Form, den Individuen gegenüber äußerlichen und zufälligen Form des Reichtums*) (N 235, MEW 161). Here the realization of wealth becomes a function of "the mutual relations among individuals in production" (*der Beziehungen der Individuen aufeinander in der Production*) (N 235, MEW 161). Furthermore, exchange value will no longer be characterized as a thing for which circulation is only an external movement, but will instead be characterized "as a relation to itself through the process of circulation" (*als Verhälten zu sich selbst durch den Prozeß der Zirkulation*) (N 235, MEW 161). This form of circulation is wholly different from that of simple circulation. Such a form of circulation itself produces exchange values.[5]

At this juncture in his exposition of the completed development of money relations, Marx maintains that within the context of simple exchange between individuals, lies the possibility of an exchange that will no longer be premised on equality and freedom. Rather, exchange will be "mediated by the deepest of antithesis" (*die tiefsten Gegensatze vermittelt sind)* (N 248, MEW 174). In short, production and exchange, as well as the concomitant division of labor, by no means stand still in this simple form that characterizes monetary circulation. Rather, it latently contains a higher mode of production, etc., which has in fact already been realized.

In every respect, money has shown itself to be a contradiction (N 233, MEW 159). As a means of circulation, it contradicts itself as measure and as money it contradicts itself in both forms. In addition, as the universal material representative of wealth money aspires to embody the totality of its manifestations. Yet it is always only a particular amount and therefore contradicts itself as universal. Marx contends that money naturally tends toward a form in which it is measureless. Individuals may bend every effort toward its accumulation, only to realize it in its completed form as a representative of particular commodities, in which case, they lose its general character to the latter. In its highest form as a system of money relations, individuals can find no way in which to secure wealth. Money relations therefore inherently possess a tendency to develop beyond simple circulation and adopt a form "mediated by the deepest of antitheses." Here, money is negated as a thing and becomes a process.

Marx's argumentation that money is both a contradiction and the foundation of a higher development is indebted for its logical structure to Hegel's exposition of the final determination of "Being." Hegel demonstrates that although indifference marks the relation between two sides of a substrate, they are not indifferent in some respect. The two quantitatively determined qualities are such only insofar as they relate reciprocally to one another. They therefore stand in a dependent, inseparable relation. Their unity is a function of their being in a state of equilibrium, or equal one to the other (SL 379, STW 450).

This unity of the substrate with itself is at first the indifference of the two qualities. Yet on further development the substrate itself is seen to be contradictory in every way.[6] When being is for itself, it is in itself or implicitly that in which every determination of being is contained.[7] It is therefore a substrate, but a substrate that contains the differences of itself in an external manner.

The substrate has developed a moment within itself that is the negation of itself as indifferent. It is precisely the determinations of the indifference that serve as the foundation for the substrate becoming other than what it is, i.e., a mere unity based on quantum. Initially, the substrate is only implicitly the negation of itself, insofar as its two sides are moments of its unity. These two sides are negatively related, and therefore latently contain the possibility of repelling themselves from themselves in an absolutely negative relation (SL 384, STW 456-57). The negation of the material substrate as such will then result in a "relation to itself," that is "mediated by the deepest of antithesis" (SL 384, STW 457). Here, the material substrate is negated as such, and has become a process.

The logical progression of Marx's treatment of the "becoming of capital" continues with the further consideration of the negation of money in its third attribute. The form that circulation had taken of M-C-C-M, and which had resulted in money as money, may be seen as the first form in which capital as such appeared.[8] It is here that exchange value realizes itself not only as a form but as the content, the purpose of circulation. It is "commercial capital," and it is as yet merely circulating capital that in no way has become the foundation of circulation.

Exchange value as both the form and content of circulation attains a higher form in the form of money capital and money interest, or usury. This form is also present in the seminal stages of capital development. Lastly, the form C-M-M-C is the presupposition of the original appearance of merchant capital. Marx makes it quite clear, however, that the aforementioned movement of exchange values as simple circulation cannot realize capital. Simple circulation cannot regenerate itself based on its own assumptions. Marx states:

> It cannot ignite itself anew through its own resources. Circulation therefore does not carry within itself the principle of self-renewal. The moments of the latter are presupposed to it, not posited by it. Commodities constantly have to be thrown into it anew from the outside, like fuel into a fire. Otherwise it flickers out in indifference.[9]

It follows therefore that circulation can renew itself only if it is constantly mediated. Marx states:

> Looked at in itself, it is the mediation of presupposed extremes. Thus, it has to be mediated not only in each of its moments, but as a whole of mediation, as a total process itself. Its immediate being is therefore pure illusion. It is the phenomenon of a process taking place behind it.[10]

Marx goes on to say that circulation is now negated in every one of its moments: as a commodity, as money, and as a relation of the two, that is, as simple circulation.

The logical content of the economic categories leads Marx from a consideration of money as in every way contradictory and as the foundation of a higher development, to the "pure illusion" of the "immediate being" of simple circulation. Hegel presents this logical content as "immediate essence." Essence has the sphere of immediate, determinate being confronting it as that from which it has become (SL 394, STWII 18). Determinate being is a negative in relation to it. Essence is a determinate negation. It first emerges as immediate in the sphere of determinate being, but it does so as an "other" of determinate being. The latter is therefore the foundation of a distinction between the essential and the unessential within determinate being. In this way determinate being is the base of essence (SL 394, STWII 18).

This distinction between the essential and the unessential is a distinction that is externally posited (SL 395, STWII 19). When essence is taken as essential relative to what is unessential, it is because essence is superseded being, or determinate being. It is the first negation, and it shows that determinate being is not simply or solely unessential. Rather immediate, determinate being is illusion (SL 395, STWII 19). It is merely the show of something that is taking place behind it.[11]

Marx saw in Hegel's exposition of the initial positing of essence, or first negation of determinate being, a logical structure by which to explicate capital as it first emerges from simple circulation—capital at first glance—or money in its completed form. Capital must at first be seen as co-extensive with the "immediate being" of simple circulation. This initial "positing of capital" involves the first negation of money as money. The initial negation of the latter is merely "the positing of capital in a particular form which already existed prior to it, as non-capital, and which makes up one of its presuppositions" (*das Setzen desselben in einer Besonderheit, die als Nicht-Kapital schon vor ihm existiert und eine seiner Voraussetzungen ausmacht*) (N 251, MEW 177). It is money that enters into circulation and at the same time "returns from it to itself" (*aus ihr in sich zurückgehende)* (N 253, MEW 178). It is money that "supersedes itself" (*sich aufhebt*). It is the "first concept of capital and the first form in which it appears" (*der erste Begriff des Kapital und die erste Erscheinungsform desselben*) (N 253, MEW 178). Thus, the first negation of simple circulation entails that a distinction emerges between capital and simple circulation, within the context of the latter.[12]

Marx contends that social production initially appeared as the positing of exchange values, and then in its completely developed form as circulation. Once simple circulation has been negated as such, however, "circulation itself returns back into the activity which posits or produces exchange value. It returns into it as into its ground" (*so geht jetzt Zirkulation selbst zurück in die Tauschwert setzende oder produzierende Tätigkeit. Sie geht darein zurück als in ihrem Grund*) (N 255, MEW 180). Circulation is the movement that circulates exchange values or commodities. Commodities are, in turn, the realization of a definite amount of labor time. Here the negation of simple circulation, therefore, reacts back upon social production, i.e., the production of commodities by labor, and their production as exchange values. Marx states: "This is their point of departure, and through its own motion it goes back into exchange-value-creating-production as its result" (*Dies ist ihr Ausgangspunkt, und durch ihre eigne Bewegung geht sie in die*

Tauschwerte schaffende Producktion als ihr Resultat zurück) (N 255, MEW 180). This initial negation of simple circulation entails that exchange-value-creating production then becomes a form of production that now presupposes that circulation has achieved such a level of development.

Hegel contends that illusory being is determinate being that has been negated by an "other." It therefore has being, but only in the "other," in the negation of itself. As such, "it is the negative returned into itself" (*in sich zurückgehende Negative*) (SL 398, STWII 23). Here then the negation of illusory being, or the "other" of illusory being, is directed against it. This negation is directed against illusory being as the negative, and the result is purely self-related negativity. As the self-coincident negative, it "returns back into itself." Yet the latter is but a moment of essence.

The process of simple circulation does not contain the principle of its own self-renewal. Its "immediate being" is dependent upon an "other" that is presupposed to it. This "other" is therefore the negation of simple circulation; it is the process of simple circulation as a "pure illusion," which as such has its being in something "other" than itself. This "other" is the process of production. Production is therefore the source of the negation of simple circulation. A dialectical exposition of the "becoming of capital" demonstrates that the negation of simple circulation—the negative—results in the "negative returned into itself," or self-related negativity. Thus, as Marx states, production now "posits circulation and constantly returns from it to itself in order to posit it anew" (*die Zirkulation setzt und aus ihr beständig in sich zurückkehrt, um sie von neuem zu setzen*) (N 255, MEW 180). Insofar as production serves to negate simple circulation, it now relates to itself through circulation as a constant return to itself. The latter is capital, but only a moment of capital, that is, capital that is merely the reflection of itself within itself.

3. CAPITAL AS POSITING REFLECTION

As Marx states: "We have therefore reached the point of departure again, production which posits, creates exchange values . . ." (*Wir sind also wieder beim Ausgangspunkt angelangt, bei der Tauschwerte setzenden, schaffenden Produktion*) (N 255, MEW 180). Marx provides an example of such a return process wherein simple circulation is negated in favor of a different form of circulation. It has its foundation in a form of circulation that merely posits exchange and exchange values in an overflow, or a surplus product.

The movement that creates exchange value now appears in a much more complex form, because it is no longer merely simple circulation. It is a "positing" that is a "presupposing," or, "no longer only the movement of presupposed exchange values, or the movement which posits them formally as prices, but which creates, brings them forth at the same time as presuppositions" (*nicht mehr nur die Bewegung der vorausgesetzten Tauschwerte oder sie formal als Preise setzend ist, sondern zugleich sie als Voraussetzungen schaffend, erzeugend*) (N 255, MEW 180).

The realization of this positing of a form of production that presupposes circulation is the "first determination of capital" (*erste Bestimmung des Kapitals*) (N 259, MEW 184). Marx says of this determination:

> That exchange value deriving from circulation and presupposing circulation preserves itself within it and by means of it; does not lose itself by entering into it; that circulation is not the movement of its disappearance, but rather the movement of its real self-positing as exchange value, its self-realization as exchange value.[13]

Moreover, capital in this incipient form is described as follows:

> Capital, as exchange value existing prior to circulation, or as presupposing and preserving itself in circulation, not only is in every moment ideally both of the moments contained in simple circulation, but alternately takes the form of the one and of the other, though no longer merely by passing out of the one into the other, as in simple circulation, but rather by being in each of these roles at the same time a relation to its opposite, i.e., containing it ideally within itself.[14]

By no means is capital as it shall become. Marx states: "If we speak here of capital, this is still merely a word" (*Wenn wir hier von Kapital sprechen, so ist das hier nur noch ein Name*) (N 262, MEW 186). The only aspect that distinguishes capital from simple circulation is that exchange value here preserves and perpetuates itself in and through circulation.

Marx's presentation of the emergence of this incipient form of capital is indebted for its logical structure to Hegel's analysis of the emergence of determinate reflection. In the sections entitled "Positing Reflection," "External Reflection," and "Determining Reflection," Hegel explicates the emergence of the negation (essence) in the negative (determinate being), and the gradual supersession of determinate being.

Determinate being is first negated insofar as it is perceived to be illusory being. Its illusoriness is a function of an "other" which is its negation. This "other" is essence, which now has a determinate being, since determinate being is the being of essence in its immediacy. This self-related negativity of essence in its immediacy is the reflection of essence within itself. This self-relation or "return into itself" is the complete supersession of determinate being. It is the "positing" of essence as immediacy.[15]

When essence posits itself as a return movement, it is then the supersession of itself as immediate. It is described as a "positing" that is a "presupposing." This reflective movement is an "absolute recoil upon itself"

(SL 402). This reflective movement or "absolute recoil" of posited reflection is as yet the first self-movement of essence. As such it is an immediacy that is merely "in-itself" superseded, and not yet the free movement of determined reflection. In determined reflection, essence is an immediacy that is an immanent reflection, or a constant return into itself. Essence here is said to "come forth from itself." It has "infinitely fixed itself through the relation to itself" (*auf sich befestigt und unendlich fixert*) (SL 407, STWII 34).

Marx maintains that simple circulation is at one point in its development an "immediate being" that is "pure illusion." This development had entailed the positing of a wholly different form of circulation. This form entails a form of exchange-value-creating production that presupposes circulation as a developed moment. In this "self-movement" of the creation of exchange values, there is a "return to the point of departure," i.e., production. Production has now posited circulation and presupposes it in its "constant return from it into itself in order to posit it anew." This new mode of production arises from, and is imposed on, an older mode, from sources external to it.

Hegel's exposition shows that determining reflection is reflection that has "come forth from itself," or is a "positing" that is a "presupposing." So with Marx, the movement of exchange value, this incipient form of capital, is now posited at this point in the exposition as a process that constantly posits and renews itself; the process creates exchange values, or it "brings them forth as presuppositions." Determinate reflection has all of its determinations within itself, so that "determinateness has established and infinitely fixed itself through the relation-to-self (407)." Capital—as exchange value that presupposes and preserves itself in circulation—"contains within itself" both money and the totality of commodities as two moments. It "alternately takes the form of the one and of the other, though no longer merely by passing out of the one into the other, as in simple circulation, but rather by being in each of these roles at the same time a relation to its opposite; i.e. containing it ideally within itself." Furthermore, Marx states that another distinction between exchange value as it existed in simple circulation and this embryonic form of capital is that here exchange value: "(1) exists in the form of objectivity; (2) arises out of circulation, hence presupposes it, but at the same time proceeds from itself as presupposition of circulation" (1. *in der Form der Gegenständlichkeit existiert;* 2. *aus der Zirkulation herkommt, sie also voraussetzt, aber zugleich von sich als Vorassetzung ihr gegenüber ausgeht)* (N 262, MEW 187).

4. LABOR AS THE CONTRADICTION OF CAPITAL: THE ESSENTIALITIES OR DETERMINATIONS OF CAPITALIST PRODUCTION

In a reciprocal relation between form and content, a logical progression leads Marx from a consideration of the emergence of capital within simple circulation, to a characterization of it as a "simple identity" that preserves itself in each of its different moments. In what follows, Marx demonstrates that although this identity appears as diverse or different things—as money and commodity—it is in reality comprised of an "opposition"; and, in a penetrating exposition of this "opposition," he demonstrates that in fact capital is at root a "contradiction." The arguments that Marx uses to prove that capital is at root a "contradiction" are complex. They are particularly difficult because they appear to be indebted in logical form to that portion of the SL that Hegel deems the most troublesome, that is, the exposition of "identity," "difference," "opposition," and "contradiction."

Marx argues that capital is the identity of a constant movement from commodity to money and back again.[16] It "preserves its identity with itself" in each of its determinations. Capital is now always money and always commodity. It is to be distinguished from simple circulation, because the latter was a "simple repetition or alternation of the role of commodity and money" (*in der einfachen Wiederholung oder Abwechslung der Bestimmung von Ware und Geld*) (N 261, MEW 185). Now capital consists of "the identity of the real point of departure and the point of return" (*der wirkliche Ausgangspunkt auch der Punkt der Rückkehr*) (N 261, MEW 185). Marx's characterization of capital as a "simple identity" that preserves itself in its different determinations reflects Hegel's exposition of "identity." Hegel is careful to distinguish "abstract identity" and the "simple identity" that issues from determinate reflection. In determinate reflection, essence had completely negated what remained of itself as illusory being. What is now present in immediacy is no longer transitory determinateness but essential determinateness. In the supersession of its mere positedness, this simple identity returns to itself as infinite self-relation.

At this particular juncture, therefore, essence is a "simple identity with itself" (*einfache Identität mit sich*) in all its determinations (SL 411, STWII 39). It is both the positing of, and the constant supersession of, its own determinations. It distinguishes itself from itself within itself, and supersedes this its own non-being. It is essential identity.

Because essence as identity contains within itself its own self-posited determinations, a distinction must be made between it and an "abstract identity," which contains no distinctions at all. A consideration of the "simple identity" of essence must therefore move from an analysis of it as an identity to the differences contained therein. The determinations of essence first appear as merely different or diverse, or merely "indifferently different" moments. Each is alike in some ways, yet unlike in others. In an immediate relation, or in what Hegel terms an "external reflection" or comparison, the diverse are like one another, but are also "alien" (*entfremdeten*) (SL 420, STWII 50).

Marx criticizes the classical political economists, and Proudon in particular, for just this sort of "external reflection."[17] In the minds of classical political economists capital is reduced to the different moments of simple circulation. It is first money, which is then exchanged for a commodity, i.e, here labor. Labor merely exchanges the product of its activity for money. Marx suggests that the primary source of such misconceptions is the lack of an adequate methodological framework that would enable theorists to conceive of capital not as a thing, but as a relation. Though it at first appears as its different moments of money and commodity, a dialectical exposition demonstrates that it is much more than this.

Hegel demonstrates that upon closer consideration the determinations that are contained in "identity" exist only in relation to one another. The foundation of the fact that one is taken as alien from the other is not a mere diversity of things, but a specific difference between them. "External reflection" perceives two merely diverse moments, but they are two sides of an opposition. What had been perceived as two alien sides, now become wholly opposed—a negative unity of opposed sides (SL 420-21, STWII 50-52).

The fact that capital appears as money had led many classical political economists to conceive of it as a relation between two things, i.e., capital (money) and labor (the product of the laboring activity).[18] Marx contends that to develop the concept of capital, we do have to begin with money. But it must be negated in its "merely abstract generality" (*bloß abstrakte Allgemeinheit*) (N 263, MEW 187). For this to occur it must "now again posit the point of circulation" (*jetzt selbst wieder den Ausgangspunkt der Zirkulation*) (N 263, MEW 187). This part of course had been labor. In this instance, however, money must yield itself to labor and become its material, so as to renew itself and begin circulating again. In its exchange with labor, capital is "no longer a simple positing of equivalents, a preservation of its identity, as in circulation: but rather diversification of itself" (*nicht mehr einfaches Gleichsetzen, Bewahren seiner Identität wie in der Zirkulation; sondern Vervielfältigen seiner selbst*) (N 263, MEW 187-88). Here money in its return to itself through circulation has lost its rigidity, and from a tangible thing has become a process, i.e., capital.

A logical progression had led Marx from a consideration of capital as a "simple identity," to what he terms the "diversification of itself." Yet a consideration of the "diversification" of capital leads to certain conclusions that put him at odds with the classical political economists. Marx's exposition of the "diversification" of capital leads him to conclude that capital (money) "stands on one side and labor on the other, both as independent forms relative to each other, both hence also alien to one another" (*auf der einen Seite das Kapital steht und auf der andren die Arbeit, beide als selbständige Gestalten gegeneinander; beide also auch fremd gegeneinander*) (N 266, MEW 190). But further, labor that is alien labor is labor that stands "opposite" capital, and capital that is alien capital is that which stands "opposite" labor. They are alien one from the other precisely because they are "extremes which stand opposite one another and therefore are specifically different" (*Die Extreme, die sich gegenüberstehn, sind spezifisch verschieden*) (N 266, MEW 190).

In this relation between capital and labor, exchange value and use value are brought into relation (N 267, MEW 193). Capital on one side initially stands opposite the other as exchange value. Labor, on the other side, stands opposite capital as use-value. Marx states: "It must now be posited that use-value as such becomes what it is through exchange value, and that exchange value mediates itself through use value" (*Daß der Gebrauchwert als solcher wird durch den Tauschwert und daß der Tauschwert sich selbst vermittelt durch den Gebrauchwert, muß nun gesetzt sein*) (N 269, MEW 195).

The error made by the classical political economists is made understandable through Hegel's explication of the relation between the diverse and external reflection. Capital and labor are mistakenly conceived of as things, and in fact appear as such. The logical form of Hegel's exposition provided Marx with a methodological framework that allows him to present the difference as a specific difference. The fact that one is different and/or alien from the other is in reality a function of opposition. Though they may at first appear as mere diverse, different things—money and commodity—they actually stand in opposition one to the other. Because they are specifically different, they are two opposed moments of one negative unity. Capital is capital only insofar as it is related to labor; exchange value is as such only in relation to use-value. Likewise, labor is labor only in relation to capital; use-value is as such only in relation to exchange value. That Marx is indebted in this portion of the text to Hegel's exposition of "identity," "difference," "opposition," and "contradiction," is most apparent in his presentation of the relation between capital (money) and labor as a "contradiction."

Hegel defines "opposition" in terms of a relation between two moments, each of which contains within itself reference to the other.[19] Each contains reference to its non-being, and is essentially connected with it. One moment, however, is considered the positive, while the other is the negative. Opposition is comprised of a positive and a negative. Closer consideration, however, shows them to be self-subsistent. Each may be considered in terms of its opposite (SL 426-27, STWII 58-59). Because the negative contains within itself the positive, it may be considered in terms of the positive. So too may the positive be taken negatively.

This exposition of "opposition" is reflected in Marx's initial consideration of the relation between capital (money) and living-labor. He argues that the only thing distinct from exchange value as objectified labor (money) is "non-objectified labor, or labor which is still objectifying itself, labor as subjectivity" (*die nicht vergegenständlichte, sondern sich noch vergegenständlichende, die Arbeit als Subjektivität*) (N 272, MEW 197). The only use-value that can form the "opposite pole" *(einen Gegensatz)* to capital as money or objectified labor is living labor. Marx states: "The use-value which confronts capital as posited exchange value is labor. Capital exchanges itself, or exists in this role, only in connection with not-capital, the negation of capital, without which it is not capital; the real not-capital is labor" (*Der dem Kapital als dem gesetzten Tauschwert gegenübertretende Gebrauchswert ist Arbeit. Das Kapital tauscht sich aus oder ist in dieser Bestimmtheit nur in Beziehung auf das Nicht-Kapital, die Negation des Kapitals, bezug auf welche es allein Kapital ist; das wirkliche Nicht-Kapital ist die Arbeit*) (N 274, MEW 199).

Capital can only become as such when it posits within itself its "other," i.e., "non-capital." Likewise, labor is the living source or possibility of exchange value only when it is not capital. Each contains within itself reference to its non-being, and only then can one speak of a whole that contains capital and labor.

When considering the exchange between capital and its negative more closely, Marx demonstrates that it breaks up into two distinct processes. In the first, the worker sells his commodity at a given price and obtains a specific sum of exchange value that capital allots to him. In the second, capital receives labor itself, i.e., it receives "the productive force which maintains and multiplies capital, and which thereby becomes the productive force, the reproductive force of capital, a force belonging to capital itself" (*er tauscht die Produktivkraft ein, die das Kapital erhält und vervielfältigt und die damit zur Produktivkraft und reproduzierenden Kraft des Kapitals*) (N 274, MEW 200). The first is comprised of simple circulation (C-M-M-C), while the second is an altogether different category, and cannot even remotely be considered an exchange per se.[20] The capitalist obtains wealth and the worker a use-value that is immediately consumed.

At this point in the development of the relation, Marx no longer refers to it as an "opposition" (*Gegensatz*). The relation between capital (money) and labor is "contradiction" (*Widerspruch*); because the separation of property from labor is the necessary law of the exchange between capital and labor (N 295, MEW 216). Marx describes the contradiction in stark Hegelian terms—terms that are directly taken from Hegel's treatment of the nature of "contradiction," as presented in "Essence."[21]

Capital (money) and living labor comprise a negative unity. Each is the negation or "non-being" of the other, and each contains within itself reference to its "opposite." Living labor as the use-value for capital as exchange value receives an exchange value, and is thereby posited as the "negative" of capital. Capital as exchange value receives living labor as its use-value, and is thereby posited as such.

Further development, however, reveals that this opposition is in reality a contradiction; and, not only is capital and labor the contradiction of each other, but each is in itself contradictory. Marx reasons that labor receives coin for its use-value in the exchange with capital. Capital receives labor itself as a value-positing activity. Capital receives the productive force that will not only maintain it in existence, but also multiply it. Capital posits its opposite—its "non-being"—and in the form of money makes itself into its opposite. Only when capital is this contradiction within itself, can it maintain and multiply itself. It posits its opposite and thereby makes itself into its opposite, so that it may then posit itself anew. It is the unity of contradictory moments. Looked at positively it is itself all of the moments that it posits. Looked at negatively, it is money that posits its non-being as its own use-value, in and through which it preserves and multiplies itself.

Labor as the "negative" is the contradiction as realized. It is the negation or contradiction of capital, and it is in itself contradictory. Looked at negatively, it is the self-subsistent not-objectified labor; it is absolute poverty. Labor or "non-capital" conceived positively—"as a negativity in relation to itself"—is the non-objective or subjective possibility of wealth. It is therefore both absolute poverty as object and the general possibility of wealth as subject and as activity. As Marx states: "In this its contradictory nature it is the contradiction of capital" (N 296).

This exposition of the "contradiction" between capital and labor, along with their respective positive and negative aspects, recalls in vivid terms Hegel's treatment of the category of "contradiction," as may be found in "Essence." Hegel defines "contradiction" as a relation between the self-subsistent opposed moments of the positive and the negative. Because each is self-subsistent, each contains within itself the other. But because one moment is the positive and the other the negative, each is the contradiction of the other; or, they are related in a unity-in-negation.

Hegel's treatment of this negative unity is complex. Each is not only the contradiction of the other, but because each contains within itself the other, each is in itself contradictory. For example, the positive is the contradiction of the negative, but it also contains the negative within itself. It is therefore contradictory in itself. Hegel describes it as the positive positing itself as the negative. When it becomes the negative, it thereby unites with itself (SL 434, STWII 68-69). The negative likewise contains within itself its "non-being." It also is contradictory within itself. Because each is both itself and its other, they unite in a unity-in-negation. This unity-in-negation or negative unity is the unity of essence. Because the self-contradictory determinations are themselves seen to be the unity of essence, essence is the ground of this negative unity.[22]

When Marx describes the essence of capital as a contradiction that entails the contradictory moments of capital (money) and labor, he no less describes it as a contradiction that is for capital. While it is true that living-labor as use-value becomes what it is only in relation to capital as exchange value, it is capital as exchange value that "mediates itself" through "the negative." It posits its negative, so that it may maintain and multiply itself. Because capital's positing of labor is an act of its own multiplication, it is the ground of the contradiction that exists within itself.

5. THE GROUND OF CAPITALIST PRODUCTION

Marx presents the essence of capital as a series of relations. Each moment of the series contains a dyadic relation between what something appears to be, and what it really is. These latter moments are then superseded, and we are presented with a single whole that appears as it is. This single whole is itself differentiated, or more properly differentiates itself, into moments that comprise its reality. In this way, the reader is presented with an ever deeper, more comprehensive view of the nature of capitalist production. The deep, logical structure of this manner of exposition has its roots in the particular categorical schema that is presented by Hegel as the dialectical exposition of essence. Hegel in effect shows Marx the way in which the essence of capital may be exposed in and through the employment of this categorical structure. Marx in turn is able to see something about the economic data that had never been seen before.

The dialectical exposition of the "becoming of capital" had entailed that Marx first treat of the identity, difference, opposition, and contradiction that serves as the ground of all further determinations. Hegel had demonstrated that once essence had initially posited itself in a constant return-to-itself, it must be seen as an identity that contains within itself its own negation. This contradiction will, in turn, serve as the ground for all movement, all activity, as well as for the ensuing development of essence. Once the dialectical parameters within which all movement shall take place have been established, the exposition must proceed to the consideration of the form and content of the process of the development of essence. The general conditions or ground of all becoming has been considered, but essence is as yet "the determinateness that is undetermined."

The conclusion of the treatment of this return movement of essence to itself discloses that the initial determinations of essence are contained within its own becoming. Essence has shown itself to be self-identical in its negativity. The relation of the positive to the negative is shown to be grounded in the becoming of essence. Essence has positively determined itself in and through both the positing of itself as its own negation, and the supersession of the negation. As a "real mediation," it is the ground for all further development.[23] The result of this "real mediation" is a distinction between ground and grounded. The starting point of the determination of groundis again an immediate determinate being . But the latter has as its ground the negative self identity of essence. This distinction between the self-identical negation and its immediacy is a distinction between ground and grounded, or, between essence as against form. The latter is an "abstract form" as over and against the self-identical nature of ground (SL 447-50, STWII 84-88).

Marx's exposition of the "becoming of capital" benefited from Hegel's exposition of the "becoming of essence." This is evident in that Marx remains logically consistent when he also moves from a treatment of the "principle of all movement"—the "contradiction" between capital (money) and living-labor—to an exposition of the form and content of the development of capitalist production. Marx demonstrates that an exposition of the return movement of capital to itself discloses that the negation of capital is one that is for capital. Capital as money is the foundation or the groundof the contradiction.

Labor has emerged from the exchange process as the "possibility" (*Möglichkeit*), or the "ideal being" (*ideelles Sein*) of values. Furthermore, Marx states: "As against capital labor is the merely abstract form, the mere possibility of value-positing activity, which exists only as a capacity, as a resource in the bodilyness of the worker" (*Dem Kapital gegenüber ist sie die bloße abstrakte Form, die bloße Möglichkeit der wertsetzenden Tätigkeit, die nur als Fähigkeit, Vermögen existiert in der Leiblichkeit des Arbeiters*) (N

298, MEW 219). Labor is here "abstract" because it is at first only the possibility of values. The bodiliness of the worker is an "abstract form" precisely because he emerges as a simple identity that is founded on the contradiction between capital (money) and labor, and must now realize his capacity in the actual production process itself (N 298, MEW 219).

The worker will be transformed from an "abstract form," or possible value-positing activity, to real productive activity upon contact with capital.[24] Capital in its money form has not only posited the existence of this "abstract form," but it has also realized itself in what is a "formless matter" (*formlosen Stoffs*), or a "passive being" (*passiv*), i.e., "the mere material for the form-positing activity of labor" (*des bloßen Materials für die form-setzende, zweckmässige Tätigkeit der Arbeit*) (N 298, MEW 220). Labor then stands opposite capital in this its "objective form" (*objectiv Form*). Marx adds, however, capital as a "formless matter" is this only in relation to the worker. The worker relates to capital in its "objective form" as "formless matter," or "passive being." Raw material is as such not really "formless matter." Both raw material and the instrument of production have already been appropriated by capital through labor. They are already products, and hence have been "formed" by labor's form-giving activity; and as such, raw material and instrument of production are what Marx refers to as the "content" (*Inhalt*) of capital.

This initial presentation of the relation between capital and labor reflects Hegel's treatment of the distinction between ground and grounded, or essence and form. The distinction is one between "substrate" and "abstract form." The former is further characterized as "formless matter" (*formlose Materie*), or as "passive being" (*das Passive*) (SL 451, STWII 89). Essence then has distinguished itself into what is its "active side"—form—and its "passive side"—matter. Hegel cautions us to be aware of the fact that "formless matter" is a sheer abstraction. It nevertheless remains the "passive side" to form's "active side."

Hegel demonstrates that matter as such must be formed. This process of the formation of matter entails that form presupposes matter, and that matter presupposes form. Matter initially stands over and against form as indifferent, that is, as the "passive side" as compared to form as the "active side." The matter that stands over and against form is not a mere "formless identity." This matter is not a "sheer abstraction," but already presupposes or possesses form. As such, it is the "content" (*Inhalt*) of essence. But since it is only "passive being" as opposed to form, essence or ground is extinguished or has vanished in its "content" (SL 455, STWII 94).

Marx sees that this is precisely the case in the development of the simple production process. Capital appears in its "objective form" or as a mere "passive being." The latter is its "content," and it will enter into relation with labor's "form-positing" activity.[25] As such, all the formal characteristics that distinguish capital are extinguished in this its appearance as a passive object (N303, MEW 224).

In the process of production, capital is said to "distinguish itself as form from itself as content." It is therefore both aspects, and the relation of both to one another (N 302, MEW 223). Capital is the consumption of raw material that is formed by labor and its instruments. Labor is likewise consumed in the process, since the worker's form-giving activity entails the expenditure of energy. Labor in production is not merely consumed, but fixed, i.e., it is "converted from the form of the activity into the form of the object, materialized, as the modification of the object, it modifies its own form and changes from activity to being" (*aus der Form der Tätigkeit in der des Gegenstandes, der Ruhe fixiert, materialisiert; als Veränderung des Gegenstandes verändert sie ihre eigne Gestalt und wird aus Tätigkeit Sein*) (N 300, MEW 222).

The production process is further described as a productive consumption. Marx states:

> This consumption is not simply a consumption of the material, but rather consumption of consumption itself; in the supersession of the material it is the supersession of this supersession and hence the positing of the same. This form-giving activity consumes the given form of the object only in order to posit it in a new objective form, and it consumes itself only in its subjective form as activity. It consumes the objective character of the object—the indifference towards the form—and the subjective character of activity; forms the one, materializes the other.[26]

Again, we can see how Marx's exposition of the simple production process benefited in its logical form from Hegel's treatment of the relation of "form" to "content." Hegel shows that the "content" of determinate ground, or its "passive side," is at first "indifferent to the form" (*die Form gleichgültige*) (SL 455, STWII 95). Thus, the unity of ground entails a process, wherein an "external form" is imposed on the content. This unity is, however, a negative one. The two indifferent sides are superseded as such, and thereby form a unity (SL 455-56, STWII 95-96). The content is superseded as a mere passivity, and the form is superseded as a mere activity. The former is informed, while the latter is materialized. The form is realized as the form of an object, which is now a unity of form and content.

We can also find Hegel's exposition of "Ground" reflected in Marx's description of the end result of the production process. In the consideration of the simple process of production, capital as such is nowhere apparent. The production process—the "self-propelling content of capital"—appears as nothing more than "production in general." Marx cautions us, however, that nothing may emerge at the end of the process that is not a presupposition or precondition of the beginning. Yet on the other hand, everything must also come out.[27]

Capital as a "form" is comprised not of objects of labor and labor, but rather of values, and, more specifically, prices (N 312, MEW 232-33). It is present at the outset or point of departure as a simple sum of money. Thus, value constitutes the various substances present in the production process as value-elements. While it is true that both the material and formal elements in production are exhausted or destroyed, they have not been annihilated. They have been superseded, and have been made "into a substance with another form" (*in eine anders geformte Substanz*) (N 312, MEW 233).[28]

Value appears at the beginning, only to disperse itself into the simple process of production, which in turn results in "the product." Prior to the end result, the material and formal aspects of production appear as the "elemental, indifferent precondition" of the product; in the end, they appear *as* the product. The value of the product, therefore, can only be equal to the sum of the values of the raw material, instrument of production, and labor itself.[29] Value was then a particular sum prior to the production process, a particular sum of value-elements in the production process, and finally appears as a particular sum again as the result of production.

Here the product appears as though it were a mere combination of the elements that are combined in the simple production process. The sole "condition" so far observed for the self-preservation of value is that the process of production must be a total process; it must continue to the point of the production of a "product." Marx states: "The totality of the production process, i.e., the fact that it proceeds to the product, is here in fact the condition for the self-preservation, self-identity of value . . ." (*Die Totalität des Produktionsprozesses, d.h., daß er bis zum Produkt fortgeht, ist hier in der Tat Bedingung des Sicherhaltens, Sichgleichbleibens des Wert*) (N 313, MEW 234). The production process is for capital, in that value is preserved in the form of a "product"; hence, the statement that the necessary price of the product is equal to the sum of the prices of the costs of production is a purely analytical statement (N 315, MEW 236).

Insofar as the product is the direct result of the simple production process, capital is said to have "come into existence" (*er entstunde*) (N 312, MEW 233). That is, capital reenters circulation as a simple commodity.

Hegel demonstrates that the end result of the process of unification of form and content is "a one or a something" (*ein Eins oder Etwas*) (SL 462, STWII 103). This result appears at first as though it were a mere "external combination" of form and content. It appears to possess a mere "diversified content" (*verschiedenen Inhalts*), or a "togetherness" (*Verknüpfung*), which is a result of the process (SL 467, STWII 109). However, this "immediate togetherness" presupposes the fact that the entire process is a determination of the original, essential ground. This "one or something" or "immediate substrate," which is the result of the entire process, in fact owes both its form and content to the original, essential ground. It is the form and content of the ground as posited or materialized in another "substance and form" (SL 469, STWII 112). The ground is self-identical throughout the entire process.

When Marx contends that the end result of the production process is in fact the "condition" of the entire process, he is recalling Hegel's treatment of the "one or something" as the "condition" for the entire process. The "product" is the "condition for the self-perservation, relation of the self-identity of value." It is therefore the "presupposition" of the production and reproduction of value.

Hegel demonstrates that the immediate content or "simple ground" is a "presupposing reflection." Formal ground as the indifferent relation of form and content presupposes real ground as the positing of an "immediate togetherness." It is furthermore presupposed that this immediate togetherness is related to ground, in that it owes both its form and content to it. It is both form and content of ground posited in another substance and form. Ground is thereby self-identical in its determination. Each determination therefore presupposes its own further development, e.g., the entirety of ground-relation presupposes "the one or something" of "simple ground." The entire process is a conditioning mediation. Thus this "immediate substrate" to which ground is related as to its essential presupposition is its condition. The condition is that in which ground-relation has its self-identity. Conversely, the condition has its immediacy only insofar as it is related to ground. Its immediacy is essentially "mediated by the self-superseding process of mediation (472)." Condition therefore has within itself the entire form-determinations of ground.

Insofar as condition and ground are united in this immediate substrate, its immediacy is superseded and condition is now a substance (*eine Sache*). Ground has "come into existence" (*tritt sie in die Existenz*) (SL 477, STWII 122).

Marx states that since "the product" is the direct result and therefore the "condition" of the entire production process, capital has "come into existence." This entire development is indebted for its logical form to Hegel. Hegel demonstrates that the condition or immediate substrate that issues from ground-relation is a "substance;" and furthermore, ground has "come into existence" in and through the substance.

6. SURPLUS VALUE AS A PROPERTY OF *DIE SACHE SELBST*

Marx contends that: "Capital is the direct unity of product and money. . . Thus it itself is again something immediate, and its development consists of positing and superseding itself as this unity—which is posited as a specific and therefore simple relation. The unity at first appears in capital as something simple."[30] Capital is now in its specific character as form "a relation of production reflected into itself" (*ein in sich reflecktiertes Produktionsverhältnis*) (N 309, MEW 230). This reflection of production into itself likewise achieves its identity with itself in and through its negation or supersession, which, in turn, results in "the product."

Marx had made critical use of the logical structure of Hegel's treatment of the determination of ground in the emergence of the thing into existence, in the development of the simple production process. For Hegel, "form" and "content" are united in the formation or "the thing." Likewise for Marx, labor's "form-giving activity" is realized only in contact with the "content" of the production process. The latter are superseded in the formation of the product.

Furthermore, for Hegel, "form" and "content" as such are the form and content of ground as essence. Ground as essence presupposed the determinations of reflection, that is, the opposition and contradiction that characterizes the real mediation of essence with itself. The "thing-in-itself," which is at first said to be the condition of ground, is further determined as the essential immediate. We shall see that Marx remains logically consistent in continuing to follow Hegel in this logical progression. The "form" and "content" of the simple production process is the "self-propelling content of capital." Because the process is for capital, it presupposes the opposition and contradiction that characterized the relation between capital and wage-labor. Thus the result of the simple production process contains in its immediacy—in the product—all that has come before it, all that is presupposed to it. Though it appears as a mere sum its properties are the properties of capital.

With the supersession of ground relation and the emergence of "the thing" into existence, essence has advanced to immediacy. "The thing" contains within itself contradiction and mediation, but its negativity is at first extinguished in its immediacy (SL 479, STWII 124).[31]

When the thing-in-itself first comes into existence it appears as a mere sum of indifferent determinations. Its apparent diversity is a function of the ways in which *it is regarded by others* (SL 484, STWII 128). This diversity is the illusory being of the thing-in-itself, which is not what it appears to be, but rather diversity "falls to the ground and this itself becomes essential identity or thing-in-itself."[32] While it may at first appear as a mere sum of indifferent determinations, its appearance as such is solely a function of the negativity that is its essential identity. It appears as a manifold only because it is an identity that results from essential determinations.

Because the thing-in-itself possesses a negative self-relation within it, it relates to itself as to an other. Yet this other is a moment within it. Its own negative self-relation constitutes its determinateness, and is a property of the thing (SL 487, STWII 133). The property of the thing is therefore a reflection of the superseded mediation, or the negativity that constitutes it as an existent. Property is a function of the contradiction and mediations that are present in the thing, and presupposed in its ground. The thing-in-itself contains within it all that has come before it in the way of ground relations and the determinations of reflection. Because it presupposes, or is the result of, contradiction and mediation, "the whole is ground that in its repelling and determining, in its external immediacy, is self-related ground" (*das Ganze ist der in seinem Abstossen und Bestimmen, in seiner äußerlichen Unmittelbarkeit sich auf sich besiehende Grund*) (SL 489, STWII 135).

This exposition of the property of "the thing" is reflected in Marx's exposition of the product. He had made critical use of the logical structure of ground relation, and he remains consistent in his exposition of the properties of "the product."

In the development of the simple production process, value dispersed into value-elements. The "form" and "content" of capital unite to produce "the product." It is purely a matter for analysis that the necessary price of the product be equal to the sum of the original value.[33] No other relation is as yet apparent, but that the original sum is dispersed in the cost of production, and now recombines in its simplicity in the product, which now exists as a sum (N 314, MEW 235).[34]

The product, then, initially appears (and was so perceived by the classical political economists) as a mere sum of the costs of production. If this were the case, however, the process of production would merely preserve capital. We are reminded "nothing can emerge at the end of the process which did not appear as a presupposition and precondition at the beginning" (N 304). If the act of production is the mere reproduction of the value of capital, such a simple preservation would contradict its concept.[35] Because exchange value is thrown back into the production process, the production process is not a mere self-preservation, but the self-multiplication of capital.

The character of being a sum of value is a consequence of the division of value in production, but does not exist in the product as such. While the production process may appear as a mere sum of value, it produces a product. The product is not a mere sum, but a new use value. The question of course is this: how can the production process result in a higher exchange value as realized in the product, than had been present in the actual process?

There can be only one reason why the product as a use-value may result in a higher exchange value—may appear as a higher price—than the original sum of value. There is only one reason why the commodity is not reducible to the sum of the costs of production. The labor that is objectified in the price of labor is smaller than the living labor time that is exchanged for it.[36] In short, the surplus value that is realized in the price of the product must already presuppose the exchange that had taken place prior to the simple production process. What this entails for Marx is as follows.

The price of the product not only presupposes the mediation of the production process, but also presupposes that capital has obtained a certain amount of labor's form-giving activity for free: it presupposes the contradiction between capital and its "negative." As Marx has stated, the separation between labor and property in the product of labor is posited in the initial act of exchange with capital. The product is in reality not the immediate product that appeared as the result of the simple production process, i.e., it is not a mere sum of the costs of production. Rather, here capital appears as a commodity, and this commodity itself possesses the property of surplus value as expressed in its "higher price." The immediacy of the commodity contains within itself, or is the supersession of, both contradiction and mediation.

The property of surplus value—the "higher price"—is here briefly explained in terms of the relation between the objectified labor time (money) that is employed by the capitalist and the living labor that is purchased. The price of the commodity first of all reflects the price of labor, or the amount of objectified labor that is needed to reproduce living labor (necessary labor time). In addition, it reflects a certain amount of objectified labor time that exceeds the latter.[37] Thus, the property of surplus value is a function of a relation between necessary labor time and surplus labor time. The worker has been forced to work for a period of time that is longer than that which is needed to keep him alive.

The deep, underlying logical structure of this exposition is indebted to Hegel's analysis of the property of "the thing." Just as the thing first appears as a mere sum of indifferent determinations, so too does "the product" initially appear (e.g., to the classical political economists) as a mere sum of the costs of production. Diversity is the illusory being of the thing-in-itself. The latter is an essential identity. Likewise, "the product" is not a mere sum, since it is first of all a new use value. In addition, because it is the result of a production process that is for capital, it "comes into existence" as an exchange value; and not just as an exchange value, but increased exchange value, or at a "higher price." The problem of course is, whence the "higher price?"

The thing-in-itself is the superseded mediation of a negative self-relation. It emerges into existence not as an immediate something, but as a result of ground-determination. It relates to itself as to an "other." This self-relation constitutes the determinateness that is property. Likewise, the commodity contains within itself the mediating process of production. The form and content of the process are superseded, and hence preserved in the form and matter of the commodity. The latter is not only superseded mediation, but also presupposes the opposition and contradiction between capital and its negation. The "higher price," or the property of surplus value, is thus a function of the fact that the commodity embodies within itself contradiction and mediation. It in a very real sense relates to itself as to an "other." It is a use value, but at the very same time, it embodies the contradiction between capital and labor. Consequently, it possesses the *property* of surplus value.

Hegel characterizes property as the middle term between the extremes that constitute the thing-in-itself (SL 490, STWII 137-38). Because the self-related negativity of the thing-in-itself possesses a determinateness that is its property, the property must first be conceived of as the middle term between the thing-in-itself and its "other." Looked at more closely, the middle term becomes the self-subsistent thing itself (SL 491, STWII 138). It turns out that property in fact constitutes the subsistence of the thing.

Likewise, Marx describes the property of surplus value—bourgeois wealth—as exchange value that mediates between the extremes of exchange value and use value. He states that:

> This intermediary situation always appears as the economic relation in its completeness, because it comprises the opposed poles, and ultimately always appears as a one-sidedly higher power vis-à-vis the extremes themselves; because the movement, or the relation, which originally appears as mediatary between the extremes necessarily develops dialectically to where it appears as mediation with itself, as the subject for whom the extremes are merely its moments, whose autonomous presupposition it supersedes in order to posit itself, through their supersession, as that which alone is autonomous. . . . Where it is posited as middle term, exchange value is always the total economic expression, itself one-sided against the extremes.[38]

Exchange value as surplus value—a property of the commodity in its "higher price"—is that which brings about the mediation between capital as money and labor as use value (N 332, MEW 250). Furthermore, capital now appears as an entire process of self-multiplication. The opposition between capital (money) and living-labor is superseded in the production process and its result, the product. The "higher price" of the commodity thus represents the "autonomy" of capital, because it contains the property of surplus value.

At this point in his exposition, if Marx had continued to follow the logical progression of categories found in the SL, he would have moved from a consideration of the property of surplus value to a consideration of the many matters and forms that are superseded in the product by the activity of living labor. As we shall see in the following chapter, however, Marx moved at this point from a consideration of the higher price of the commodity to "the essential relation" between the "whole" of capital and its "fractional parts."

According to the logical schema developed by Hegel in the SL, Marx should have done otherwise than he did. Hegel moves from a consideration of the nature of "the thing" (*Die Sache*) and its properties, to a consideration of the many matters and forms that are superseded in the activity that is "the thing." Although Marx does not immediately follow this logical progression and incorporate these categories in the exposition that follows his consideration of the higher price of the commodity, he does so some pages further in the manuscript, specifically on pages 360 and following in the Nicolaus translation. Here, the subject is what it had been some forty pages earlier, the nature of the higher price of the commodity; or, what the capitalist receives for free as a result of a production process that is for capital.

In addition to receiving a certain amount of labor time for free, capital also receives something else for free in the simple production process. It receives the preservation and maintenance of raw material and instrument of production. These are preserved, and achieve a higher use value. That is, apart from contact with living-labor they exist in a mere "one-sided objective form" (*einseitiger gegenständlicher Form*) (N 360, MEW 277). They are mere "things" (*bloßes Ding*) that are subject to "dissolution" (*Auflösung*) by chemical processes.

Because they are material things subject to dissolution, their form as objectified labor time may vanish. The latter is an "external form" (*äußerliche Form*) that has been impressed upon "material substance" (*das Stoffliche*), or "matter" (*Substanz*). There is therefore an indifference between the matter and the form (N 360, MEW 277). Because the matter of raw material and instrument of production are subject to "dissolution," so too is their form.

When raw material and instrument are brought into contact with labor's "form-giving activity," their matter is reanimated. It ceases to exist in a "dead state," as an "external indifferent form on the matter." Living labor preserves the material in a definite form, by determining the matter to the purpose of labor. The cotton becomes yarn, the yarn fabric, and the fabric becomes printed, which is a garment. Thus the matter of cotton is preserved in this process, rather than succumbing to its dissolution. The matter "becomes extinct in one form of use value in order to make way for a higher one, until the object is in being as an object of direct consumption" (*in der einen Form des Gebrauchwerts geht er unter, um einer höhren Platz zu machen, bis der Gegenstand als Gegenstand der unmittelbaren Konsumption da ist*) (N 361, MEW 278).

The commodity, then, contains within it the various matters of the use values that have been superseded in order to be posited in its higher use value.[39] But because the production process is for capital, it is not merely the use value of raw material and instruments of production that are preserved (N 363, MEW 280). Each is a specific quantity of exchange value, or objectified labor. Living-labor also acts to preserve the quantity of labor time that is objectified in them. The capitalist obtains this preservation free of charge.

The commodity then not only possesses the property of surplus value as expressed in its higher price, but also contains within itself the many matters and forms of the use values that have been superseded. Because the latter are at the same time exchange values, the commodity likewise preserves within itself—in its price—their exchange values, as a consequence of living-labor's "form-giving activity."

The logical structure of Marx's exposition of the commodity as the supersession of the many matters that are preserved in it, parallels Hegel's exposition of the many matters that are superseded in "the thing." The development of the properties of the thing leads Hegel to an exposition of the various self-subsistent matters out of which the thing is composed (SL 492-94, STWII 139-42). Because the self-subsistent matters as such are not limited to "this" thing, "they pass out of and beyond" (*Sie gehen über dieses Ding hinaus*) it. "The thing" may therefore be conceived of as a mere collection of such matters (SL 494, STWII 141).

We have seen that Marx contends that the commodity contains within itself the many matters of the use values that have been superseded in this their higher use value. The many matters or use values each contain a form that is external to their "natural material." Because each is liable to "dissolution" as matter, the whole thing is liable to dissolution, i.e., the form and matter. Likewise, Hegel maintains that because "the thing" consists of a mere collection of matters, it is liable to "dissolution" (*Auflösung*) (SL 494-95, STWII 142-42). The thing in this sense is reducible to the matters out of which it is composed. In its determinateness it is therefore the "dissolution of itself."

The various matters nevertheless do combine to form the thing. The thing is in itself the interrelation of these matters (SL 495, STWII 143). The subsistence of each is a function of the relation of one to another in the one thing. Each is therefore superseded in its determinateness in relation to the others. Likewise, Marx concludes that the matters of the many use values that served in the production process are preserved, since they are superseded in their relation to one another in the one commodity, for example, the garment.

Furthermore, Hegel demonstrates that it is only as a result of the fact that the thing-in-itself is a negative self-relation, that it is prevented from dissolving into the various self-subsistent matters. The logical structure of Marx's exposition likewise leads him to conclude that it is only insofar as the commodity is a product of living-labor that has been appropriated by capital, that it is able to preserve within itself the many matters of prior use values and their exchange values.

---

[1] In the dialectical exposition of an organic whole, the examination of a particular moment of that whole is recognized as prescinding from the totality. One's examination of this particular "moment" must, therefore, be seen as a foreshadowing, or an adumbration, of this totality, for as the whole is immanent in all its "parts." In some instances, the whole is so apparent in the "part," that one's examination of the part cannot help but incorporate the multiple levels from which one is abstracting.

So for example, in the following section, Marx's stated purpose is the exposition of the "pure form" of the economic relation that transpires in the exchange between equals. He is solely interested in examining the three formally distinct moments in the exchange of equivalents: The subjects of the relation, the exchangers; the objects of their exchange, the equivalents; and, the act of exchange itself, that is, the mediation through which the subjects are posited as exchangers, and their objects as equivalents.

Yet Marx recognizes that the exchange between equals is both a natural and a social relation. On the hand, it presupposes that the subjects are of a specific biological and psychological make-up. On the other, the exchange presupposes that the subjects appear within a particular institutional framework, which provides the conditions of the possibility for such an exchange. Marx recognizes, and states as much, that a comprehensive exposition of this seemingly simple act would require not only an examination of the physical, chemical, emotional, and psychological foundations of the subjects' motives; but, likewise, a complete exposition of the social and legal institutions that the act presupposes.

In this case, therefore, not only is Marx prescinding from the economic whole that is capitalist production, but likewise from the psychological, social, and legal "wholes" as well. We have, in effect, an abstraction from a totality of totalities. (I am indebted to Professor Burkhard Tuschling of the Institut fur Philosophie, Philipps-Universität, Marburg, Germany, for this insight.)

Yet, Marx states: ". . . the content, outside this form (i.e., the pure form of the economic relation of the exchange of equivalents) here still falls entirely outside economics, or is posited as a natural [or social, as the case may be — MM] content distinct from the economic, a content about which it may be said that it is still entirely separated from the economic relation because it still directly coincides with it . . ." (N 241). The psychological, social or legal "totalities" are, therefore, in this respect, irrelevant to the exposition. Because Marx is at present engaged in the dialectical exposition of a particular moment of the totality of capital, he not only abstracts from it, but also from a myriad of totalities.

Since my primary concern is to explicate the deep, logical structure of Marx's dialectical exposition of capital in general, I cannot hope to capture the richness of the text, and its implications, in my exposition. This portion of the text simply cannot be reduced to an economic exposition. Indeed, not only is Hegel's SL at work in these pages, but his Philosophy of Right also plays an important role. (Again, I am indebted to Professor Tuschling for this insight.)

[2] "The alteration is only a change of a state, and the subject of the transition is posited as remaining the same in the process" (*Die Veränderung ist nur Änderung eines Zustands, und das Übergehende ist als darin dasselbe bleibend gesetzt*) (SL 373, STW 444).

[3] "Equality and freedom are thus not only respected in exchange based on exchange value but, also the exchange of exchange values is the productive, real basis of all equality and freedom" (*Gleichheit und Freiheit sind also nicht nur respektiert im Austausch, der auf Tauschwerten beruht, sondern der Austausch von Tauschwerten is de producktive, reale Basis aller Gleichheit und Freiheit*) (N 245, MEW 170).

[4] "Each appears toward the other as an owner of money, and, as regards the process of exchange, as money itself. Thus indifference and equal worthiness are expressly contained in the form of a thing" (*Jeder erscheint als Besitzer des Geldes dem andren gegenüber, selbst als Geld, soweit der Prozeß des Austauschs betrachtet wird. Darum ist de Gleichgültigkeit und Gleichgeltendheit in der Form des Sache ausdrücklich vorhanden*) (N 246, MEW 171-72).

[5] "It is thus, on one side, the regression of exchange value into labour, on the other side, that of money into exchange value, which is now posited, however, in a more profound character. With circulation, the determined price is presupposed, and circulation as money posits it only formally. The determinateness of exchange value itself, or the measure of price, must now itself appear as an act of circulation. Posited in this way, exchange value is capital and circulation is posited at the same time as an act of production" (*Es ist also einerseits das Rückgehn des Tauschwerts in die Arbeit, andrerseits des Gelds in den Tauschwert; der aber jetzt in einer vertieften Bestimmung gestezt ist. Bei der Zirkulation ist der bestimmte Preis vorausgesetzt, und sie als Geld setzt ihn nur formell. Die Bestimmtheit des Tauschwerts selbst, oder das Maß des Preises, muß jetzt selbst als Akt der Zirkulation erscheinen. So gesetzt ist der Tauschwert das Kapital, und die Zirkulation zugleich als Akt der Produktion gesetzt*) (N 235, MEW 161).

[6] "This unity thus posited as the totality of the process of determining, in which it is itself determined as indifference, is a contradiction in every respect. . . . " (*Diese Einheit, so gesetzt als die Totalität des Bestimmens, wie sie selbst darin als Indifferenz bestimmt ist, ist der allseitige Widerspruch. . . .*) (SL 379, STW 451).

[7] "As thus the contradiction of itself and its determinedness, of its implicit determination and its posited determinatedness, it is the negative totality whose determinatenesses have sublated themselves in themselves and in so doing have sublated this fundamental one-sidedness of theirs, their merely implicit being" (*So der Widerspruch ihrer selbst und ihres Bestimmtseins, ihrer an sich seienden Bestimmung und ihrer gesetzten Bestimmtheit, ist sie die negative Totalität, deren Bestimmtheiten sich an ihnen selbst und damit diese ihre Grundeinseitigkeit, ihr Ansichsein, aufgehoben haben*) (SL 384, STW 456).

[8] "Money has negated itself as something which merely dissolves in circulation, but it has also equally negated itself as something which takes up an independent attitude toward circulation. This negation, as a single whole, in its positive aspects, contains the first elements of capital" (*Geld hat sich negiert, als bloß in der Zirkulation aufgehend; es hat sich aber ebenso negiert, als selbständig ihr gegenübertretend. Diese Negation zusammengefaßt, in ihren positiven Bestimmungen, enthält die ersten Elemente des Kapitals*) (N 253, MEW 178).

[9] *Er kann sich nicht an sich selbst von neuem entzünden. Die Zirkulation trägt daher nicht in sich selbst das Prinzip der Selbsterneuerung. Die Momente derselben sind ihr vorausgesetzt, nicht von ihr selbst gesetzt. Waren müssen stets von neuem und von außen hier in sie geworf en werden wie Brenmaterial ins Feuer. Sonst erlischt sie in Indifferenz* (N 255, MEW 179-80).

[10] *In sich selbst betrachtet, ist sie die Vermittlung vorausgesetzter Extreme. Aber sie setzt diese Extreme nicht. Muß also doch nicht nur in jedem ihrer Momente, sondern als Ganzes der Vermittlung, als totaler Prozeß selbst vermittelt sein. Ihr unmittelbares Sein ist daher reiner Schein. Sie ist das Phänomen eines hinter ihr vorgehenden Prozesses* (N255, MEW 180).

[11] Illusory being is therefore the illusory being of essence. Thus illusory being therefore is said to presuppose a process of mediation. This process is a process of mediation of presupposed extremes, which it as immediate being—as pure illusion—does not posit. "Illusion is thus a determination of Essence itself, but one that is only a moment of itself, and Essence is Illusion itself in-itself" (*Der Schein ist also das Wesen selbst, aber das Wesen in einer Bestimmtheit, aber so, daß sie nur sein Moment ist, und das Wesen ist das Scheinen seiner in sich selbst*) (SL 398, STWII 23); cf. Harris, *An Interpretation*, p. 156.

[12] What had been perceived as simple circulation now is perceived as commodity capital (C-M-M-C) and commercial capital (M-C-C-M). Thus, simple circulation can no longer be perceived as what it was, rather its "immediate being is therefore pure illusion." In short, "it is the mediation of presupposed extremes," but "it does not posit these extremes."

[13] *Daß der aus der Zirkulation herstammende und sie daher voraussetzende Tauschwert sich in ihr und durch sie erhalt; sich nicht verliert, indem er in sie eingeht; sie nicht als die Bewegung seines Verschwindens, sondern vielmehr als die Bewegung seines wirklichen Sichsetzens als Tauschwert, die Realisierung seiner als Tauschwerts ist* (MEW 184).

[14] *Das Kapital als der Zirkulation vorausgesetzte oder die Zirkulation voraussetzende und sich in ihr erhaltende Tauschwert ist nicht nur in jedem Moment idealiter jedes der beiden in der einfachen Zirkulation enthaltnen Momente, sondern es nimmt abwechselend die Form des einen und des andren an, aber nicht mehr so, daß es wie in der einfachen Zirkulation nur aus dem einen in das andre übergeht, sondern in jeder der Bestimmungen zugleich Beziehung auf die entgegengesetzte ist, d.h., sie ideell in sich enthält* (MEW 186).

[15] "But this immediacy, instead of being able to form the starting point is, on the contrary, immediacy only as the return or as reflection itself. Reflection therefore is the movement that starts or returns only insofar as the negative has already returned into itself" (*Statt von dieser Unmittelbarkeit anfangen zu können, ist diese vielmehr erst als die Rückkehr oder als die Reflexion selbst. Die Reflexion ist also die Bewegung, die, indem sie die Rückkehr ist, erst darin das ist, das anfängt oder das zurückkehrt*) (SL 401, STWII 26).

[16] Exchange value as capital: ". . . preserves its identity with itself in each of the different substances. It therefore always remains money and always commodity. It is in every movement both of the moments which disappear into one another in circulation. But it is this only because it itself is a constantly self-renewing circular course of exchanges" (*in jeder der verschiednen Substanzen seine Identität mit sich selbst erhalt. Er bleibt also immer Geld und immer Ware. Er ist in jedem Moment beides der in der Zirkulation das eine in das andre verschwindenden Momente. Er ist dies aber nur, indem er selbst ein stets sich erneuernder Kreislauf von Austauschen ist*) (N 260-61, MEW 185).

[17] "For Proudhon in his polemic against Bastiat, Gratuite du Credit, everything comes down to his own wish to reduce the exchange between capital and labour to the simple exchange of commodities as exchange values, to the moments of simple circulation, i.e., he abstracts from just the specific difference on which everything depends" (*Proudon in der Streitschrifft gegen Bastiat: "Gratuite du Credit" lauft alles darauf hinaus, daß er den*

Austausch zwischen Kapital und Arbeit auf den einfachen Austausch von Waren als Tauschwerten, auf die Momente der einfachen Zirkulation reduzieren will, d.h., eben von dem spezifischen Unterschied, auf den alles ankommt, abstrahiert) (N 265, MEW 189).

[18] "If, then, the specification of capital is abstracted away, and only the content is emphasized, as which it is a necessary moment of all labour, then of course nothing is easier than to demonstrate that capital is a necessary condition for all human production" (*Wird so von der bestimmten Form des Kapitals abstrahiert und nur der Inhalt betont, als welcher es ein notwendiges Moment aller Arbeit ist, so ist naturlich nichts leichter zu beweisen, als daß Kapital eine notwendige Bedingung aller menschlichen Produktion ist*) (N 258, MEW 182).

[19] "In the first place, then, each is, only insofar as the other is; it is what it is, through the other, through its own non-being; it is only a positedness; secondly it is, insofar as the other is not; it is what it is, through the nonbeing of the other; it is reflection-into-self" (*Jedes ist so überhaupt erstens, insofern das Andere ist; es ist durch das Andere, durch sein eigenes Nichtsein das, was es ist; es ist nur Gesetztsein. Zweitens: es ist, insofern das Andere nicht ist; es ist durch das Nichtsein des Anderen das, was es ist; es ist Reflexion-in-sich*) (SL 425, STWII 57).

[20] Marx states that the relation between capital and labor may appear as peculiar, insofar as, while labor obtains an exchange value in the exchange between the two, capital obtains a use value. Nevertheless, the capitalist obtains wealth and the worker a use-value that is immediately consumed. Despite the seemingly peculiar result, Marx states: "This appears as a dialectic which produces precisely the opposite of what was to be expected" (*Es erscheint dies als eine Dialektik, die grade in das Umgekehrte von dem umschlägt, was erwartet werden sollte*) (N 295, MEW 217).

[21] "Labour posited as not-capital as such is: (1) not-objectified labour, conceived negatively (itself still objective: the not-objective itself in objective form). As such it is not-raw material, not-instrument of labour, not-raw product: labour separated from all means and objects of labour, from its entire objectivity. This living labour, existing as an abstraction from these moments of its actual reality (also, not-value); this complete denudation, purely subjective existence of labour, stripped of all objectivity. Labour as absolute poverty: poverty not as shortage, but as total exclusion of objective wealth . . . (2) Not-objectified labour, not-value, conceived positively, or as a negativity in relation to itself, is the not-objectified, hence not-objective, i.e., subjective existence of labour itself. Labour is not as an object, but as activity; not as itself value, but as the living source of value. Namely, it is general wealth (in contrast to capital in which it exists objectively, as reality) as the general possibility of the same, which proves itself in action. Thus, it is not at all contradictory, or rather the in-every-way mutually contradictory statements that labour is absolute poverty as object, on one side, and is, on the other side, the general possibility of wealth as subject and as activity, are reciprocally determined and follow from the essence of labour, such as it is presupposed by capital as its contradiction and as its contradictory being, as such as it, in turn, presupposes capital" (*Die Arbeit als das Nicht-Kapital als solches gesetzt, ist: 1. Nicht-vergegenständlichte Arbeit, negative gefaßt [selbst noch gegenständlich; das Nichtgegenständliche selbst in objektiver Form]. Als solche ist sie Nicht-Rohstoff, Nicht-Arbeitsgegenständen, von ihrer ganzen Objektivität getrennt Arbeit. Die lebendige als Abstraktion von diesen Momenten ihrer realen Wirklichkeit existierende Arbeit [ebenso Nicht-Wert]; diese völlige Entblößung, aller Objektivität bare, rein subjektive existenz der Arbeit. Die Arbeit als die absolute Armut: die Armut, nicht als Mangel, sondern als völlige Ausschliessen des gegenständlichen Reichtums. Oder auch als der existierende Nicht-Wert und daher rein gegenständliche Gebrauchswert, ohne Vermittlung existierend, kann diese Gegenständlichkeit nur eine nicht von der Person*

getrennt: nur eine mit ihrer unmittelbaren Leiblichkeit zusammenfallende sein. Indem die Gegenständlichkeit rein unmittelbar ist, ist sie ebenso unmittelbar Nicht-Gegenständlichkeit. In andren Worten keine außer dem unmittelbaren Dasein des Individuums selbst fallende Gegenständlichkeit. 2. Nicht-vergegenständlichte Arbeit, Nicht-Wert, positiv gefaßt, oder sich auf sich beziehende Negativität, ist sie die nicht-vergegenständlichte, also ungegenständlicht, i.e., subjektive Existenz der Arbeit selbst. Die Arbeit nicht als Gegenstand, sondern als Tätigkeit; nicht als selbst Wert, sondern als die lebendige Quelle des Werts. Der allgemeine Reichtum, gegenüber dem Kapital, worin er gegenständlich, als Wirklichkeit existiert, als allgemeine Möglichkeit desselben, die sich in der Action als solche bewahrt. Es widerspricht sich also in keiner Weise oder vielmehr der in jeder Weise sich widersprechende Satz, daß die Arbeit einerseits die absolute Armut als Gegenstand, andrerseits die allgemeine Möglichkeit des Reichtums als Subjekt und als Tätigkeit ist, bedingen sich wechselseitig und folgen aus dem Wesen der Arbeit, wie sie als Gegensatz, als gegensätzliches Dasein des Kapitals vom Kapital vorausgesetzt ist und andrerseits ihrerseits das Kapital voraussetzt) (N 295-96, MEW 217-18).

Conversely, Marx contends we may conceive of capital in its contradictory being in relation to labour. First, positively, i.e., "as a negativity of itself," it is the "not-objectified source of value." It is value itself, i.e., not non-value or the living source of value; but rather general wealth as a process within which are posited moments of itself. It is therefore not-objectified insofar as it is itself all of its self-posited moments. Thus conceived negatively, it is not non-objectified labour; or, it is raw-material, instrument of labour, raw product, labour itself, et al.

[22] "Essence as ground excludes itself from itself, it posits itself; its positedness—which is what is excluded—is only as positedness; as identity of the negative with itself. This self-subsistence is the negative posited as negative; it is self-contradictory and therefore remains immediately the essence as in its ground" (*Das Wesen schliesst als Grund sich von sich selbst aus, es setzt sich; sein Gesetzsein—welches das Ausgeschlossene ist—ist nur als Gesetzsein, als Identität des Negativen mit sich selbst. Dies Selbständige ist das Negative, gesetzt als Negatives; em sich selbst Widersprechendes, das daher unmittelbar im Wesen als seinem Grunde bleibt*) (SL 435, STWII 69).

[23] "Ground, on the other hand, is real mediation because it contains reflection as sublated reflection; it is essence that through its non-being, returns into and posits itself" (*Der Grund dagegen ist die reale Vermittlung, weil er die Reflexion als aufgehobene Reflexion enthalt; er is das durch sein Nicht-sein in sich zurückkehrende und sich setzende Wesen*) (SL 445, STWII 82).

[24] "Through the exchange with the worker, capital has appropriated labour itself; labour has become one of its moments, which now acts as a fructifying vitality upon its merely existent and hence dead objectivity" (*Durch den Austauch mit dem Arbeiter hat sich das Kapital die Arbeit selbst angeeignet; sie ist eins seiner Momente geworden, die nun als befruchtende Lebendigkeit auf seine nur daseiende und daher tote Gegenständlichkeit wirkt*) (N 298, MEW 219).

[25] "The relation of capital, in its content, to labour, of objectified labour to living labour—in this relation, where capital appears as passive towards labour, it is its passive being, as a particular matter, which enters into relation with the forming activity of labour—can, in general, be nothing more than the relation of labour to its objectivity, its material . . ." (*Die Beziehung des Kapitals seinem Inhalt nach auf die Arbeit, der vergegenständlichten Arbeit auf die lebendige Arbeit—in dieser Beziehung, wo das Kapital passiv gegen die Arbeit erscheint, ist es sein passives Dasein, als besondre Substanz, das in bezug auf die Arbeit als formende Tätigkeit trit— kann überhaupt nur die Beziehung der Arbeit auf ihre Gegenständlichkeit, ihren Stoff sein*) (N 298, MEW 220).

[26] *Das Verzehren ist nicht einfaches Verzehren des Stofflichen, sondern Verzehren des Verzehrens selbst; im Aufheben des stofflichen aufheben dieses Aufhebens und daher Setzen desselben. Die formgebende Tätigkeit verzehrt den Gegenstand und verzehrt sich selbst, aber sie verzehrt nur die gegebne Form des Gegenstands, um ihn in neuer gegenständlicher form zu setzen, und sie verzehrt sich selbst nur in ihrer subjektiven Form als Tätigkeit. Sie verzehrt das Gegenständliche des Gegenstandes—die Gleichgültigkeit gegen die form—und das subjekitive der Tätigkeit; formt den einen, materialisiert die andre* (N 301, MEW 222).

[27] "Thus, if at the end of the process of production, which was begun with the presuppositions of capital, capital appears to have vanished as a formal relation, then this can have taken place only because the invisible threads which draw it through the process have yet to be observed" (*Wenn daher am Ende des produktionsprozesses, der unter der Voraussetzung des Kapitals begonnen war, das kapital am Ende, als formbeziehung, verschwundern erscheint, kann dies nur der Fall sein, weil die unsichtbaren Fäden, die es durch denselben durchzieht übersehn worden sind*) (N 304, MEW 225).

[28] "The different modes in which the values existed were a mere semblance; value itself formed the constantly self-identical essence within their disappearance. Regarded as value, the product has in this respect not become product, but rather remained identical, unchanged value, which merely exists in a different mode, which is, however, irrelevant to it and which can be exchanged for money" (*Die verschiednen Existenzweisen der werte waren reiner Schein, der Wert selbst bildete in ihrem Verschwinden das sich gleichbleibende Wesen. Das Produkt, als Wert betrachtet, ist dieser Seite nach nicht Produkt, sondern vielmehr identisch geblieben, unveränderter Wert, der nur in einer andren Existenzweise ist, die ihm aber auch gleichgültig ist und gegen Geld ausgetauscht werden kann*) (N312-13, MEW 233).

[29] "That means, in other words, nothing more than that the production process in its material aspect has been irrelevant to value; that value therefore has remained identical with itself and has merely taken on another mode of existence" (*D.h. in andren Worten nichts, als daß der Produktionsprozess nach seiner stofflichen Seite gleichgültig fur den Wert war; daß er daher identisch mit sich geblieben ist und nur eine andre stoffliche Existenzweise angenommen hat, in andrer Substanz und Form materialisiert ist*) (N 313, MEW 233).

[30] *Kapital ist unmittelbare Einheit von Produkt und Geld. . . . So ist es wieder selbst ein Unmittelbares, und seine Entwicklung besteht darin, als diese Einheit—die als bestimmtes und daher einfaches Verhältnis gesetzt ist—sich selbst zu setzen und aufzuheben. Die Einheit erscheint zunächst im Kapital als etwas Einfaches* (N 332, MEW 251).

[31] "Now because existence is essentially mediation-with-self, the determinations of the mediation are present in it, but in such a manner that they are also reflected into themselves and their subsistence is essential and immediate. As the immediacy that posits itself through sublation, existence is negative unity and a being-within-self; it therefore determines itself immediately as an existent and as thing" (*Weil nun die Existenz wesentilich die mit sich identische Vermittlung ist, so hat sie die Bestimmungen der Vermittlung an ihr, aber so, daß sie zugleich in sich reflektierte sind und das wesentliche und unmittelbare Bestehen haben. Als die durch Aufheben sich setzende Unmittelbarkeit ist die Existenz negative Einheit und Insichsein; sie bestimmt sich daher unmittelbar als ein Existierendes und als Ding*) (SL 483-84, STWII 128-29).

[32] What Hegel terms the thing-in-itself contains a side that is said to be ". . . the unmoved, indeterminate unity precisely because it has the determination of being sublated mediation and therefore of being only the substrate of the determinate being" (. . . *die unbewegte, unbestimmte Einheit, weil es eben die Bestimmung hat, die aufgehobene Vermittlung zu sein, und daher nur die Grundlage desselben*) (SL 485, STWII 130).

As such it ought not contain a manifoldness, and it obtains this only when brought into relation with external reflection, i.e., only in relation to another. From a perspective that is external to the thing-in-itself, it appears to be a mere sum of indifferent determinations.

[33] "This reproduction of the 100 thallers is a simple retention of self-equivalence, except that it is mediated through the material production process" (*Diese Reproduktion der 100 Taler ist einfaches Sichselbstgleichbleiben, bloß daß es durch den materiellen Produktionsprozeß vermittelt ist*) (N 313, MEW 233-34).

[34] "The only process, as regards value, is that it sometimes appears as a whole, unity; then as a division of this unity into certain amounts; finally, as sum" (*Der einzige Prozeß in bezug auf den Wert, daß er einmal als ein Ganzes, Einheit; dann als Teilung dieser Einheit in bestimmte Anzahl; endlich als Summe erscheint*) (N 314, MEW 235).

[35] "In short, if this not-realization, i.e. the non-multiplication of the value of capital, is presupposed, then what is presupposed is that capital is not a real element of production, that it is not a specific relation of production; then a condition is presupposed in which the production costs do not have the form of capital and where capital is not posited as the condition of production" (*Kurz, dies Nichtverwerten, d.h. das Nichtvervielfältigen des Werts des Kapitals vorausgesetzt, ist vorausgesetzt, dass es kein wirkliches Glied der Production, kein besonders Produktionsverhältnis; ist ein Zustand vorausgesetzt, worin die Produktionskosten nicht die Form des Kapitals haben und das Kapital nicht als Bedingung der Produktion gesetzt ist*) (N 317, MEW 237-38).

[36] "The surplus value which capital has at the end of the production process—a surplus value which, as a higher price of the product, is realized only in circulation, but like all prices, is realized in it by already being ideally presupposed to it, determined before they enter into it—signifies, that the labour time objectified in the product—or amount of labour (expressed passively, the magnitude of labour appears as an amount of space; but expressed in motion, it is measurable only in time)—is greater than that which was present in the original components of capital. This in turn is possible only if the labour objectified in the price of labour is smaller than the living labour time purchased with it" (*Der Mehrwert, den das Kapital am Ende des Produktionsprozesses hat—ein Mehrwert, der als höherer Preis des Produkts erst in der Zirkulation realisiert wird, aber wie alle Preise in ihr realisiert werden, dadurch, daß sie schon ideell ihr vorausgesetzt sind, bestimmt sind, ehe sie in sie eingehn—heißt, dem aligemeinen Begriff des Tauschwerts gemäß ausgedrückt, daß die im Produkt vergegenständlichte Arbeitzeit—oder Quantum Arbeit [ruhend ausgedrückt, erscheint die Größe der Arbeit als Raumquantum, aber bewegt ausgedrückt, ist sie nur durch die Zeit meßbar]—größer ist als die in den ursprünglichen Bestandteilen des Kapitals vorhande*) (N 321, MEW 240).

[37] "Surplus value in general is value in excess of the equivalent. The equivalent, by definition, is only the identity of value with itself. Hence surplus value can never sprout out of the equivalent: nor can it do so originally out of circulation; it has to arise from the production process of capital itself. The matter can also be expressed in this way: if the worker needs only half a working day in order to live a whole day, then, in order to keep him alive as a worker, he needs to work only half a day. The second half of the labour day is forced labour; surplus labour. What appears as surplus value on capital's side appears identically on the worker's side as surplus labour in excess of his requirements for keeping himself alive" (*Mehrwert ist überhaupt Wert uber das Äquivalent hinaus. Äquivalent seiner Bestimmung nach ist nur die Identität des Werts mit sich. Aus dem Äquivalent heraus kann daher nie der Mehrvert entspriessen; also auch nicht ursprünglich aus der Zirkulation; er muß aus dem Produktionsprozeß des Kapitals selbst entspringen. Die Sache kann auch so ausgedrückt werden: Wenn der Arbeiter nur einen halben Arbeitstag braucht, um einen ganzen zu leben, so braucht er, um seine Existenz als Arbeiter zu fristen, nur einen halben*

Tag zu arbeiten. Die zweite Hälfte des Arbeitstags ist Zwangsarbeit; surplus Arbeit. Was auf seiten des Kapitals als Mehrwert erscheint, erscheint exakt auf seite des Arbeiters als Mehrarbeit über sein Bedürfnis als Arbeiter hinaus, also über sein unmittelbares Bedürfnis zur Erhaltung seiner Lebendigkeit hinaus) (N 324, MEW 243-44).

[38] *Diese Mitte erscheint immer als das vollendete ökonomische Verhältnis, weil es die Gegensätze zusammenfaßt, und erscheint schließlich immer als eine einseitig höhere Potenz gegenüber den Extremen selbst; weil die Bewegung oder das Verhältnis, das als vermittelnd zwischen den Extremen urspünglich erscheint, dialektisch dazu notwendig fortrührt, daß es als Vermittlung mit sich selbst erscheint, als das Subjekt, dessen Momente nur die Extreme sind, deren selbsändige Voraussetzung es aufhebt, um sich durch ihre Aufhebung selbst als das allein Selbständige zu setzen* (N 332, MEW 250).

[39] "Material as well as form, matter like form, are preserved by further labour—preserved as use value, until they obtain the form of use value as such, whose use is consumption. It is therefore already a part of the simple production process that the earlier stage of production is preserved by the later, and that positing the higher use value preserves the old, or, the old use value is transformed to the extent that it is raised to a higher use value" (*Das Material sowohl wie die Form, der Stoff wie die Form wird erhalten durch die fernere Arbeit—als Gebrauchwerte erhalten, bis sie die Gestalt des Gebrauchswerts als solches erhalten, dessen Gebrauch die Konsumption ist. Es liegt also im einfachen Produktionsprozeß, daß die frühere Stufe der Produktion erhalten wird durch die spätere und daß durch das Setzen des höheren Gebrauchswerts der alte erhalten oder nur soweit verändert wird, als er erhöht wird als Gebrauchswert*) (N 361, MEW 278-79).

CHAPTER 4

CAPITAL AS IT PROCEEDS FROM ITSELF

The development of the "becoming of capital" had disclosed the point at which capital "comes into existence" as "the product." As such, it contains in itself the contradiction and mediation that had gone before. Contradiction and mediation are now expressed in the higher price of the commodity, which represents the property of surplus value. We saw in the last chapter that Marx's exposition of the nature of surplus value had benefited from Hegel's exposition of *die Sache Selbst*. In a section that follows, Marx is concerned to show that the essence of surplus value is a function of a relation between the "whole" and the "parts" of capital. Once he has determined the ground of the production process, he must then analyze the composition of the product.

1. THE PARTS OF CAPITAL AND THE FORCE OF THEIR EXPRESSION

In producing a commodity, labor acts to preserve both the use values and the exchange values that comprise the simple production process. The capitalist obtains two things free of charge. He obtains the surplus labor that increases the value of his capital; and, in addition, he gets the use value and exchange value of previously objectified labor.

Labor is the real foundation of the product of capital. Labor is fixed in the commodity. Its form-giving activity is the "temporality" of the commodity.[1] The commodity therefore has another content as ground of its existence besides the form and matter that distinguish one thing from another. Living labor's form-giving activity has served as the substrate of the commodity's existence. Because labor is a moment of the self-preservation and multiplication of capital, it is exchange value that in truth is the "temporality" of the commodity. Labor acts to preserve the use value of the material conditions of production, and thereby preserves capital.[2]

A distinction is made within the commodity between its form and matter—its material existence—and the "eternal existence" of value. The latter is surplus value that is a consequence of the distinction between necessary and surplus labor time. Marx states:

> If the capitalist employs labor only in order to create surplus value—to create value in addition to that already present—then it can be seen as soon as he

> orders work to stop that his already present capital as well becomes devalued; that living labor hence not only adds new value, but, the very act of adding a new value to the old one, maintains, eternalizes it.[3]

The product possesses within itself "eternal value" as a consequence of the worker's activity, which is itself a moment of capital. Capital appropriates labor's activity, and thereby eternalizes itself in the form of the product. It is thus the "law of capital" (*Gesetz des Kapital*) to perpetuate itself in the form of surplus value; and it does this by creating more and more surplus labor. Marx presents us with a brief excursus on the "law of capital," and the way in which it works to structure a world according to its needs (N 325, MEW 253).

The "law of capital" is realized only gradually and as a consequence of acting on and shaping successive generations of laborers. The population of society must increasingly reflect capital's "ceaseless striving" (*rastlose Streben*) toward the general form of wealth. The many use values that issue from the production process will increasingly be a result of surplus labor. This "ceaseless striving" continues until capital has created and molded a world according to its own needs.

The logical form of this exposition clearly reflects indebtedness to Hegel's exposition of the way in which essence emerges into the immediacy of being. Hegel demonstrates that since "the thing" is a result of the "self-propelling content" of essence, it is a determinate being that nevertheless is an essential immediacy. A distinction is therefore to be noted between its appearance as a mere determinate being and an "enduring element," or an "eternal element." He states: "According to the first side it is a determinate being, but one which is contingent, unessential and, in keeping with its immediacy, is subject to transition, coming-to-be and ceasing-to-be" (*Nach der ersten Seite ist er als ein Dasein, aber als ein zufälliges, unwesentliches, das nach seiner Unmittelbarkeit dem Übergehen, Entstehen und Vergehen unterworfen ist*) (SL 501, STWII 151). In its material existence, "the thing" is subject to transitoriness. Yet insofar as it is not merely determinate being, but rather essential immediacy, it possesses an "enduring element" within itself; it possesses an essential content. Hegel states: "According to the other side, it is the simple content determination exempt from this flux, the enduring element of it" (*Nach der andern Seite ist er die einfache, jenem Wechsel entnommene Inhaltsbestimmung, das Bleibende desselben*) (SL 501, STWII 151).

Hegel shows that a distinction between mere immediacy and an "enduring element" necessarily results in a distinction between mere appearance and the "law of appearance"—an "inwardly diverse content," and a "determinate, essential content" (SL 502, STWII 151-52). The determination of the "law of appearance" shows that the existent possesses within itself the matter and form that characterize "thinghood"; while, at the same time, it possesses a content that constitutes the "substrate of appearance," the permanence of law.

The law realizes itself only gradually by a process of immediate identity with appearance, and then the supersession of appearance. This successive supersession of appearance creates a "world-in-and-for-itself." Appearance begins to lose its "essenceless manifoldness" (SL 508-9).

The law is completely realized when it obtains immediate existence in and though its own negative self-relation. It has become the "totality of the content of the world of Appearance and the ground of all its manifoldness" (SL 510). The gradual realization of the law results in a world that is a function of "negative self-relation."

This realization is precisely what Marx contends is the ultimate goal of the "law of capital," that is, that it structure a world based solely on the contradiction between capital and labor. Though he will elaborate on this later, here he contends that its "historic destiny" is fulfilled when surplus labor is the sole ground of all productive activity (N 325, MEW 253).

The "law of capital," then, begins with the distinction in the commodity between its material existence and "eternal value," that is, with surplus value. In its mania for limitless wealth, capital incessantly drives labor on in the production of general wealth. In short, it creates and molds a world for itself, for the realization of surplus labor time, surplus value. The "law of capital" is thus realized only as an "essential relation for the development of the social productive forces" (N 325, MEW 253).

In the next 150 pages, Marx expounds on the nature of capital as an "essential relation" for the development of productive forces. He defines this "essential relation" as a relation within the product of capital. Here Marx distinguishes the product as "the whole of the working day." "The whole of capital" is equivalent to the product of the whole of the working day. We saw in the last section that surplus value is a function of a relation between necessary and surplus labor time. Here Marx demonstrates that the "essential relation" is a relation within "the whole of capital"—the whole of the working day—and the "fractional parts" of that day that are devoted to either necessary or surplus labor.

Surplus value (relative) is always equal to the relation between the whole working day and that part of the working day that is required by the worker to enable him to survive.[4] Any decrease in necessary labor time, or any increase in productivity, necessarily results in an increase in surplus labor, hence surplus value.[5]

In summarizing this essential relation between the whole and parts of capital, Marx reiterates that an increase in the productive force of living labor necessarily results in an increase in the whole of capital. This increase is not a function of an increase in the quantity of the product, but results from a decrease in necessary labor while maintaining a full working day (N 339, MEW 257). The "whole of capital," and in particular its surplus value, is a function of the relation between the "fractional parts" of necessary and surplus labor time that comprise the whole of the working day.[6]

The more developed capital becomes the more surplus labor it creates. The more surplus labor it creates, the more it must develop the productive forces in order to realize more surplus value, but at a smaller proportion. Marx states that capital's internally posited limitation always remains the relation between the entire working day and the fractional part that expresses necessary labor. He states:

> It can only move within these boundaries. The smaller already the fractional part falling to necessary labor, the greater the surplus labor, the less can any increase in productive force perceptibly diminish necessary labor, since the denominator has grown enormously. The self-realization of capital becomes more difficult to the extent that it has already been realized.[7]

Though capital may always try to decrease necessary labor time, it can never make it equal zero. Surplus value can never be equal to the whole of the working day. A certain part of the working day must always be exchanged for necessary labor.

To this point, Marx has developed only the essential relation between "the two parts of capital," that is, between the two parts of the living work day, the one that represents wages and the other that represents capital (N 354, MEW 272). The two other "parts" of capital are the raw material of labor and the instrument of production. What effect, then, does a growth in both raw material and the instrument of production have on the relation between necessary and surplus labor time, both absolute and relative? The relation between the "invariable parts" and the "variable parts" of the whole of capital determines the extent to which capital is productive of surplus value.

An increase in relative surplus value would entail a concomitant increase in both raw material and the instrument of production (N 380, MEW 294). This part of capital has grown, while the exchange with living labor has diminished (N 384-85, MEW 298-99). The surplus value may rise, but because there is absolutely less living labor in relation to capital, the rate of profit declines. In short, the "invariable part" of capital grows in relation to the "variable part"; consequently, for capital to maintain its growth rate, more living labor must be employed.[8] An increase in simultaneous working days entails an increase in living labor, hence capital must solicit the increase of the working population. Yet, while capital tends to increase the laboring population, it equally tends to reduce its necessary part, that is, to constantly increase a reserve labor pool (N 400, MEW 314).

These various tendencies of capital are said by Marx to be the "natural forces" (*Naturkrafte*) of capital as social labor (N 400, MEW 314). The "natural forces" of capital are (1) to constantly reduce necessary labor time; (2) to constantly create surplus labor time so as to create more and more surplus value; (3) to increase the laboring population, and at the same time, (4) to decrease the part that serves as living labor. Although Marx terms these various tendencies the "natural forces" of capital, he also maintains that they are internally posited limitations to its creation (N 404, MEW 318). While necessary labor is the source of its flourishing, it eventually impedes its growth. The increase of surplus labor time as a "natural force," is an "internal boundary" (*Schränke*) or an internally posited limitation on its growth (N 404, MEW 318). In fact, all the "natural forces" that are posited by capital turn out to be so many "internal boundaries," limitations that are created by its own development, by relations among its own "parts" (N 404, MEW 318).

We see here in the terminology employed and in the very structure and organization of the material, the influences of Hegel's exposition of the "essential relation" between "whole" and "parts." The relation between the world-as-both-in-and-for-itself and Appearance is further determined as an "essential relation" between "whole" and "parts." The whole is said to appear as an existent, which contains within itself "parts" that unite to constitute it (SL 514, STWII 167). These parts may likewise be taken as that which serves as the ground or substrate of the existence of the whole. In which case, one abstracts away from the whole as self-subsistent existent, and focuses on the interrelation among the parts (SL 514-15, STWII 167-68).

On further determination, however, we see that the whole indeed consists of parts, such that it is nothing without them (SL 516, STWII 168-69). Likewise, the parts are self-subsistent only as parts of a whole. Thus, the "essential relation" of whole and parts shows itself as a single identity of which both are moments. The unity of whole and parts has progressed from an abstract one to a fluid whole. The "essential relation" so determines itself that it becomes a "variable whole" consisting of interrelating "parts" whose relationship is in turn determined by the "whole." In this case the determination of the essential relation is no longer a relation of whole and parts. Rather, the mediating relation between whole and parts gives way to a relation of "force" and its expression (SL 517, STWII 170-71).

The "whole," now termed the "force" of essence, reacts on its parts, and structures their interrelation according to its own tendencies. The "parts" become, in turn, the condition for the expression of this "force." Because they contain within themselves the force that structures their interrelations, they are themselves so many forces, against which the force of essence is active (SL 519-20, STWII 174-75). In short, the "parts" have become so many solicited forces, or internally posited limitations, through which the force of essence is expressed (SL 522-23, STWII 177-78).[9] These limitations are, of course, of its own making.

Marx sees this movement as the outcome of the "natural force" of capital, that is, that it should generate within itself an internal limitation or an "internal boundary" to its own expansion, as a function of its own interrelated parts. He adds that while capital posits these "internal boundaries," it nevertheless tries to supersede and "leap-over" them: they are constantly posited as limitations, yet just as much superseded. He states: "Capital, as the positing of surplus labor, is equally and in the same moment the positing and not-positing of necessary labor; it exists only insofar as necessary labor both exists and does not exist."[10] As a consequence, it is "equally a tendency of capital to make human labor (relatively) superfluous, so as to drive it, as human labor, towards infinity" (*Es ist ebensosehr Tendenz des Kapitals, menschliche Arbeit überflüssig zu machen [relativ] als menschliche Arbeit ins Maßlose zu treiben*) (N 399, MEW 313). Capital drives labor toward infinity as a consequence of the "internal boundaries" that are created by its "natural force" (N 404, MEW 318).

Hegel had also demonstrated that the "force" of essence posits its own internal limitations and, at the same time, supersedes them, only to posit them anew. The one force solicits and posits the other as opposed to itself, and then supersedes this its own moment, in the overcoming of its own "internal boundaries." The expression of force entails an "infinite impulse" that drives itself onward by constantly positing and superseding its own self-created barriers.

2. CONSUMPTION CAPACITY AND THE RELATION BETWEEN INNER AND OUTER

The production process has resulted in a product, which, as a commodity, possesses within itself the relation between necessary and surplus labor time. Its price manifests the impulse within capital to constantly reduce necessary labor in order to realize surplus value, both absolute and relative. It therefore embodies the opposition and contradiction between capital and wage-labor.

In the last section, we saw that the exposition of the relation between the "whole" and the "parts" of capital led Marx to a treatment of its own self-created internal limitations. Capital was seen to have posited these barriers, only to supersede them and posit them anew. In this way, it drives human labor toward "infinity."

Following this treatment of capital's own internally posited limitations, Marx considers the relation between capital's production process and simple circulation. Because we are dealing with capital in its process of "self-formation," circulation is not yet a determinant of capital. It is therefore referred to as an "external condition" or "outer barrier" to capital's process of "actualization."

The production process has resulted in the production of the product, which possesses a price that reflects both the contradiction between capital and living labor, and the "natural forces" of capital. The product must now realize its price in a process of circulation and be exchanged for money. In short, though it may be expressed in terms of money (it has a price), it nevertheless is this value only "in-itself" (N 402, MEW 316).[11]

Marx maintains that the products realization in circulation presupposes two conditions: (1) that there is a need for it as a use value; (2) that there is enough money in circulation to accommodate the newly created surplus value (N 405, MEW 318-19). As for the first, the number of commodities that are produced is determined by the natural composition of the product. The number of specific use values must be limited, because there is just so much need for them.[12] As to the second, not only must there exist a need for the product, but there must also exist the money to realize its price.[13] The existence of surplus money in turn presupposes that surplus money had been realized as a consequence of the production of surplus value.

Whereas the former limitations had been internal to, or posited within, the production process itself, the limitations of consumption capacity and available equivalents appear as limitations that lie outside it (N 404, MEW 318).[14] The two external conditions are overcome as limitations only by a constant expansion of the sphere of circulation, which is accompanied by the creation of production facilities within this sphere.[15]

Until capital has reduced its outer barriers in simple circulation, it consists of three processes. Because the commodity is money only "in-itself," the unity of production and "actualization" or circulation, is not "immediate," but only a process. Each of the three processes exists "indifferently" or "independently" alongside one another. In which case, the production process, the realization of surplus value, and the realization of the price of the commodity in exchange form a mere "external unity."[16] Because we are still examining the "becoming of capital," capital is not yet a determinant of circulation. The "transition from one into the other" of the three processes is as yet merely accidental.[17]

Though they form an "external," or immediate unity, they at the same time, form an "inner unity." But their "inner unity" does not yet form a "totality" (*Totalität*) (N 403, 414-5, MEW 317, 327-28). It is nevertheless the case that regarded as a "whole" or as a "totality," "this inner unity must necessarily maintain itself to the extent that the whole of production rests on capital, and it must therefore realize all the necessary moments of its self-formation, and must contain the determinants necessary to make these moments actual" (*muß diese sich bewähren, soweit das Ganze der Produktion auf dem Kapital beruht, also es die notwendigen Momente seiner Selbstgestaltung alle realisieren muß und die Bedingungen fur die Verwirklichung derselben enthalten*) (N 403, MEW 317).

Marx is indebted for the logical structure of this formulation to Hegel's exposition of the relation between "inner" and "outer." Hegel describes the result of the "inner" tendencies of the force of essence, as an emergent relation between essence and determinate being. In the infinite movement of force, force posits that which is external to itself. A distinction emerges between the reflection-into-self that is force and an external immediacy. This distinction between the "inner" of essence and the "outer" of determinate being is a function of a "becoming-other as a transition of itself into externality" (*Anderswerden als Übersetzen ihrer selbst in die Äußerlichkeit*) (SL 524, STWII 179). The "inner" of essence is thus determined over and against the "outer" that is the form of being. The unity that exists between the two is at first an immediate unity (SL 525-26, STWII 180-81).

The result of the inner movement or force of essence is *die Sache Selbst*. The latter is at first "in-itself" the mediated unity of the "inner" and the "outer." That is, it ought to be, or it is ideally, realized as an identity or the "totality" that consists of the mediation between its moments of inner and outer (SL 527, STWII 183-84). As yet, however, the inner and outer are merely "indifferent" (*gleichgültige*) or "external form" (*äußere Form*) determinations that exist alongside one another. They therefore form an "external unity," because their "transition from one into the other" (*übergehen beider ineinander*) is merely "immediate" (*unmittelbar*) (SL 528, STWII 185).

In addition to the limitations internal to the force of essence in its expression, other limitations to its realization as a totality are external to it per se. To realize a totality of related moments, a process of mediation is required to bring about a real unity of the inner and outer. Though they form an "external," or an immediate unity, they nevertheless form an "inner unity," because "the nature of the relation has shown that these determinations constitute one identity and one alone" (*die Natur des Verhältnisses hat gezeigt, daß diese Bestimmungen schlechtin nur eine Identität ausmachen*) (SL 525, STWII 181). They do not, however, as yet form a "totality."

Marx contends that the "inner unity" of production and simple circulation must maintain itself, because both are determined as "moments" of capital. Their "external" or "immediate" unity must develop to the point at which the two form "moments" of a single identity or "totality" that is capital. Though the product is at first merely "in-itself" the unity of the two, it is presupposed that capital in its self-formation will reduce its "external conditions"—simple circulation—to a moment of its own production. Insofar as it does this, capital is said to have "realized" or "actualized" all the necessary moments of its "actualization" (N 414-15, 447, MEW 327-28, 361). The "indifferent" relation between production and circulation is superseded, so that both now develop as moments of a single identity or "totality." It nevertheless remains the case, that both the inner and outer barriers to the production process are constantly superseded only to be posited anew.[18]

This exposition closely follows Hegel's treatment of the development of the relation between "inner" and "outer." The latter form merely an "external" or "immediate" unity in the beginning of the self-formation of essence. In this case, essence has not yet "externalized and brought forth itself out of inwardness by its actuality" (*sich aus der Innerlichkeit durch seine Tätigkeit noch nicht entaussert und hervorgebracht*) (SL 526, STWII 183). The two form-determinations nevertheless constitute a single identity. They are two form-determinations of a "third" that links them together to form a unity (SL 526, STWII 182). They then develop to the point where they are two "moments" of this single identity. The two are superseded as "indifferent" in the self-formation of essence, and thereby constitute a mediated identity (SL 527-28, STWII 184-85). Once essence has reduced its "external conditions"—i.e., appearance—to a moment of its own process of self-development, essence is said to have "realized" or "actualized" all the moments that are necessary for its "actualization" (SL 528, STWII 185).

3. CAPITAL AS IT PROCEEDS FROM ITSELF: THE ATTRIBUTES OF MONEY AS REALIZED CAPITAL

We have seen that the content of the production process and circulation—its "external condition"—are a single content. In the process or "transition of one into the other," their indifference toward one another is superseded in their identity. Capital is now seen as the identity of the superseded moments of production and circulation. Because capital has reduced the two to moments of itself, capital is "actualized."

So far, Marx has traced only the "becoming of capital" as a realized "totality." He has shown how capital arises from it presuppositions and reduces the latter to moments of itself. Now, however, Marx must show how capital transforms these presuppositions, so that it will no longer appear as arising from them, but as that which posits its own presuppositions as a self-causing agent.

The deep, logical structure of such an exposition will entail such categories as "actuality," "possibility," and "necessity." We will see in it, as in the preceding exposition, that Marx is indebted to Hegel for his presentation of capital as a self-causing agent. Hegel provides the framework or categorical schema that enabled Marx to show how capital transforms the presuppositions of its becoming, into "moments" of itself.

The exposition of the self-formation or "becoming of capital" has proceeded to the point where capital is now "actualized" as a "totality." Marx had specified that the production process must proceed to its end, to the emergence of the commodity. The commodity was at first capital as "in-itself." This characterization of the commodity as capital "in-itself" had been a function of the fact that the commodity had not yet realized its price in the exchange for money. Marx had described this state of affairs as entailing an indifferent, external relation between the production process and simple circulation. Despite the fact that the two moments exist external to one another, they nevertheless constitute the inner unity of capital as a totality of production and realization. This inner unity is at first merely implicit, or it is posited as a possibility.[19]

With the completion of this third process taken as given, once the commodity has been exchanged for money, capital is realized as a totality. Capital is thus no longer merely "in-itself," but, through the process of its realization in circulation, it has become both in and for itself as money (N 405, MEW 319). It is defined as a totality of moments wherein "there appears nothing higher in-itself, nothing legitimate for itself, outside this circle of social production and exchange" (*nichts als An-sich-Höheres, Fur-sich-selbst-Berechtigtes, außer diesem Zirkel der gesellschaftlichen Production und Austauschs erscheint*) (N 409, MEW 323). Thus, while production and realization may be indifferent, independent, indeed contradictory moments, capital is "by its concept" (*seinem Begriff nach*) the unity of the two (N 415, MEW 328). Both are posited in the essence of capital.[20]

We have seen then that the product has emerged from the production process with all the determinations that are presupposed to it, and has entered into the circulation process. The commodity realizes its price in the exchange for money, and subsequently drops out of the process in consumption. The process of realization of capital has come to an end with the realization of the price of the commodity in money. Capital has begun from itself in money and now returns to itself again in the form of money. The entire process entailed a beginning from itself, and an arrival at itself (N 447-8, MEW 360-61). Marx states:

> Capital is thus now posited as money again, and money therefore posited in the new aspect of realized capital, not merely as realized price of the commodity. Or, the commodity realized in the price is now realized capital.[21]

All capital's prior determinations are said to have vanished in its realized form as money. Capital no longer appears in the form of a "relation between two opposed determinations—objectified and living labor—or necessary and surplus labor" (*als Beziehung zweier qualitativ ungleicher — vergenständlichter und lebendiger Arbeit — oder der notwendigen Arbeit und der geschaffnen Surplusarbeit*) (N 448, MEW 361).

This "mode of presentation" of the realization of capital as a "totality," reflects Marx's employment of Hegel's exposition of the emergence of "the absolute." The self-development or "becoming of essence" has proceeded to the point where essence is "actual" as a "totality" (SL 528, STWII 185). Essence is now an "Absolute *Sache*," as a unity of being and essence. *Die Sache Selbst* had initially been merely "in-itself" a totality of opposed moments. Because the inner and outer remained a mere implicit, immediate unity, the absolute *Sache* could not be realized as both in and for itself a totality. But the absolute *Sache* becomes a totality once both the inner and outer are realized as a unity of opposed moments within itself. It is the "absolute unity" of being and essence (SL 530-31, STWII 187-88).

Because the absolute is a unity of form and content, it is an absolute identity. All that formerly appeared in the development of essence now appear as so many moments in its becoming "actual," its becoming "the absolute" (SL 531, STWII 188). The latter is the ground or foundation of all prior developments. It must be conceived therefore as having begun from itself, only to arrive at itself as this "totality." The absolute posits all that was before it as its own presuppositions, for the purpose of "arriving at itself."[22]

In the Absolute, all traces of its becoming have vanished. This absolute identity is therefore determinate. That is, because the absolute is a result—albeit a result of its own prepositing—it nevertheless is initially posited as "the negative of reflection and the process of determining as such" (*das Negative der Reflexion und des Bestimmens überhaupt*) (SL 533, STWII 190). In short, the absolute in its arrival at itself stands initially over and against the opposition and manifoldness that has led to it. It is therefore external to the process. Because its existence is a function of becoming, it is something imperfect. It is not "the absolute absolute," but the absolute in a "determinateness." It is a "form determination," or "the absolute in a determinateness," or "an attribute of the absolute absolute" (SL 533-34, STWII 191-92).

Although the attribute is a form determination of the absolute, a mere relative absolute, it nevertheless is at the same time the form of the absolute. It therefore contains within itself the entire content of the absolute. Furthermore, the attribute as a totality is posited as the absolute's "true and sole subsistence," even though this determination of the absolute is likewise posited as its "unessential subsistence" (SL 533-34, STWII 191-92).

Marx's development of capital in its realized form as money reflects the logical structure of this exposition. All its prior determinations have vanished in it as money, and capital now acquires all the attributes that are a function of its being money.[23] Capital thus returns to itself in the form of money, and, as such, relates to itself as its own measure.[24]

A second attribute of capital in its realized form as money, is money in its role as a medium of circulation (N 448, MEW 361). Marx had defined money in its second form as a medium of circulation as the negation of itself as a measure. It appeared only to vanish again in the exchange for commodities, which were in turn consumed. Here, rather than money merely exchanging itself for a commodity and thereby vanishing in circulation, capital as money will be exchanged for those particular value-elements that enable it to begin its course as capital anew.[25]

Thus, in its initial form as realized capital, capital acquires all those properties that are a function of its being money, with this difference. Its existence as money, as a measure and a medium of circulation, is a transformation that is merely "formal" (N 448-49, MEW 361-62). As a measure, it is surplus labor that is objectified in a specific commodity. As a medium of circulation, its disappearance into the "becoming of capital" is merely formal, because it again stands at the beginning of the production process.

The structure of the presentation of realized capital as money as a measure and a medium of circulation, and the charaterization of the latter as transformations that are merely "formal," recalls Hegel's development of the attributes of the absolute. For Hegel, the absolute as a "determinateness," or an attribute, signifies that the absolute is in a mere "form determination." Thus, while it is the case that the attribute contains within itself all prior determinations as superseded, the determination in which it is posited is also an unessential subsistence. The transformation of the absolute into an attribute is therefore a transformation that is merely "formal," because the attribute will again be submerged into the becoming of essence.

The attribute is initially the absolute as in a simple identity with itself. It is then taken as a negation, or, "its form determination, by virtue of which it is attribute, is therefore posited, immediately as mere illusory being—the negation as negative" (*seine Formbestimmung, wodurch es Attribut ist, ist daher auch gesetzt, unmittelbar als bloßer Schein—das Negative als Negative*) (SL 534, STWII 192). Just as the attribute had resulted immediately from the exposition of the absolute so too does the exposition immediately submerge the attribute and its distinguishing act in the becoming of essence, into the simple absolute. It is merely a "way or manner" of existence of the absolute. In short, what had been taken as determinations or differentiations of the absolute are in fact mere "formal distinctions," mere formal-reflections-into-self of the absolute itself.

When the attribute as a negation is taken as a negative, and not simply as a mere formal distinction, it is termed a "mode" of the absolute. A "mode" is described as a reflection of the absolute that is wholly external to it. It is not merely formally distinct, but is the self-externalization of the absolute. In the mode, the absolute is rendered a plurality.

The third form of realized capital as money is likewise contrasted to, and presupposes, the prior two forms. The realization of capital in the attributes of money as a measure and as a medium of exchange is a mere formal transformation. The transformation of realized capital into the third form of money is not a mere formal change, but entails the formation of a difference within capital itself.

Recall that money in its third form is the negation of circulation as a negation; it is an independent value in a negative relation with respect to circulation. Here where capital appears as money in its third form, capital itself becomes a commodity, but one that enters into circulation in the form of self-sufficient value (N 449, MEW 362). In other words, capital as money in its third form becomes another capital.[26] In its third form, capital has posited itself as external to itself, but not as another which is other than itself, but rather, as another form of itself, as a particular manifestation of itself.

Marx completes his exposition of the formal determinations of realized capital with a summary of what has thus far transpired. When money first stood at the beginning of the production process, the "presuppositions" of capital "appeared to come in from the outside" (*erschienen die Vorausetzungen selbst äußerlich*) as external presuppositions for the arising of capital (N 450, MEW 363). This "second" return of money to the beginning of the realization process of capital, affords a chance to clarify certain issues that had remained unclear upon the "first" entrance of money into the realization process, i.e., "as money in transition from its role as value to its role as capital" (*dem Geld, daß aus seiner Bestimmung als Wert in die des Kapitals übergeht*) (N 450, MEW 363). Marx suggests that these difficulties are themselves solved in and through the process of production and realization. He states:

> In the first encounter, the presuppositions themselves appeared to come in from the outside, out of circulation; as external presuppositions for the arising of capital; hence not emergent from its inner essence, and not explained by it. These external presuppositions will now appear as moments of the motion of capital itself, so that it has itself—regardless how they may arise historically—preposited them as its own moments.[27]

This summary again parallels the way Hegel ends his exposition of essence as "actuality." In a summary analysis, Hegel contends that when essence had first been realized as the absolute, it appeared as the result of a process. With this exposition of the absolute from a simple identity through attribute as negation to mode, the absolute has completed its "reflective movement," and become identical-to-itself in a return-to-self. Where the absolute first appeared as though it were determined by that which is external to it, now all the determinations that arise do so within the absolute itself, in addition to having their beginning in it (SL 535-36, STWII 194). Though it had presupposed moments that were external to itself, all the moments that appear in it now are determinations of its own reflective movement. It now posits all the determinations in its movement as an identity-with-itself.

4. SURPLUS LABOR AS THE REAL NECESSITY FOR NEW SURPLUS LABOR

Money as realized or actualized capital represents a completed circuit of production and circulation, in which the entire process is now circumscribed by capital itself. As opposed to the transition from money to capital, capital in this instance has begun from itself only to arrive at itself in its money form. We stand now again at the beginning of the entire process of realization. Marx is very careful at this particular point in the exposition to define what this "new aspect" of money as realized capital is, or represents. He is careful to specify the exact nature of the foundation of realized capital in its money form.

Surplus value had appeared within the production process as surplus labor, which is itself living labor (N 450-51, MEW 364). Living labor had worked on the objective conditions of production in its production of surplus value. At the end of the production process, surplus labor appears in an "objectified form" (*vergegenständlicht*) as surplus product; or, what is the same, surplus product is a specific sum of objectified living labor: the sum of surplus labor (N 451, MEW 364).

The surplus product becomes surplus capital with the exchange for money. The completed development is the surplus product "in its totality" (*in seiner Totalität*) (N 451, MEW 364). Because surplus capital is the result of both the production and realization process, and it is itself nothing other than objectified surplus labor, all the conditions that served to create this new value appear as so many embodiments of surplus labor. The objective conditions of surplus labor "therefore now appear, are therefore now posited, as the product, result, objective form, external existence of surplus labor itself" (*erscheinen daher jetzt, sind daher jetzt gesetzt als Produkt, Resultat, objective Form, äußerliche Existenz der Surplusarbeit selbst*) (N 452, MEW 365).

Surplus capital, or money in its "new aspect" as realized capital, represents a state of affairs wherein labor has reproduced its own conditions for capital. Living labor is now the "value-creating possibility" (*wertschaffende Möglichkeit*) (N 453, MEW 366). The realization of capital "lies as a possibility within the womb of living labor" (*in ihm als Möglichkeit liegende Verwertung*). Capital has gained complete mastery over "the value-creating possibility" in its realized form as money.

Money in its form as realized capital, therefore, contains all the determinations that had been a result of the prior self-formation of capital. It is objectified living labor, and therefore contains within itself the "not-being" (*Nichtsein*), or "the other-being" (*Anderssein*), or the "being of another opposite itself" (*Sein des andren gegen sie selbst*) of capital (N 454, MEW 367). In its new aspect as realized capital "as money, its potential to be transformed into capital is already posited in it."[28]

The above formulation clearly benefited from Hegel's exposition of "Actuality." In his initial treatment of the absolute *Sache*, Hegel had developed an "exposition" of the absolute. This exposition entailed presenting the latter as an implicit unity of the inner and outer. All prior determinations were seen to have vanished in this "absolute identity." The exposition of the absolute had merely been the development of the form of the absolute. This "self-manifestation" of the absolute entailed an implicit unity of existence and essence. "Actuality" as absolute form is the "immediate form-unity of inner and outer" (SL 542, STWII 202). It is an immediacy as determined over and against a fully explicit or developed actuality. Or, it is actuality as against possibility (SL 542, STWII 202).

Hegel begins his treatment of the complete development of the absolute—the absolute in its totality—with an exposition of the formal nature of actuality, the absolute form. It is initially characterized as an "immediate, unreflected actuality," and as such it is analogous to any being or existent in general. Yet it is not merely an immediate existent, because it is the "form-unity of being within self or inwardness and outwardness" (SL 542, STWII 202). Because it is not merely external, but contains within itself all the determinations that characterize the "inner," it contains an "in-itself" or possibility. What is actual is just as much possible as it is actual.

What appears as an "immediate, unreflected actuality" is the result of a long process, and in fact it is the unity of being and essence. When looked at closely therefore this immediate existence contains within itself the movement that characterizes all prior determinations. What is called the "inner" or moment of essentiality within this immediate being is possibility. The latter is the "negative of actuality" (SL 543, STWII 203). Thus, this immediacy is really an actuality that contains within itself possibility. Possibility exists within actuality. It is the "not being in itself" *(nicht an sich zu sein)* of actuality; or, it is merely an "other-being" (*Anderssein*), or the being of another opposite itself (SL 543-44, STWII 203-4).

The logical form of this exposition is also present in Marx's description of money at this point. Money as realized capital contains within it all that has thus far transpired. It contains within it the "negative" of capital. The negative of capital is the source of the possibility that now resides within money. Marx describes in detail the process through which money realizes the possibility that is posited within it. Because it is the mere possibility of surplus capital—it is surplus labor in objective form—it must of necessity divide into a double form in order to realize itself as capital. If it is to serve as the possibility for an increase in surplus capital, it must split itself into the "actual conditions of value-creation" (*realen Bedingungen der Wertschopfung*) (N 455, MEW 368).

Thus, labor's own product splits into two component parts: (1) the objective conditions for the realization of new labor; and (2) a labor fund for maintaining "the possibility of this living labor, i.e., of living labor capacity as alive" (*der Möglichkeit dieser lebendigen Arbeit, d.h. des lebendigen Arbeitsvermogens als eines lebendigen*) (N 455, MEW 368). In addition to having reproduced the objective conditions of production, labor has at the same time created a fund for its own maintenance.

When the newly created surplus capital is divided into the objective conditions of production and the labor fund, it becomes the "real possibility" (*reale Möglichkeit*) of new surplus labor, and hence of surplus capital (N 455, MEW 368). Surplus capital can become the "real possibility" of new surplus labor only when it is converted into a labor fund. The realization of the possibility that is posited within money results in the "actual conditions of value-creation," which in turn is the "real possibility" of new surplus capital. In fact, the production by labor of this surplus is likewise said to be the creation of the "real necessity" (*reale Notwendigkeit*) of new surplus labor (N 455, MEW 368).

The logical form of this presentation of the creation of the actual conditions for the real necessity of capitalist production reflects Hegel's exposition of the emergence of "real necessity" (*reale Notwendigkeit*) (SL 549, STWII 211). The possibility that exists within actuality is the "negative being" of actuality, the "being of another opposite itself." It therefore lacks something, and points to this other. Because the "in-itself" or possibility is a moment within the absolute form—a moment within actuality—it supersedes itself. Possibility as superseded thereby becomes actuality (SL 544, 205).

But this actuality is not the primary or immediate unreflected actuality that we started with. "Reflected actuality" is a unity of itself and possibility. The truth of the immediate existence of actuality is that its very existence is a function of its "negative being," or of possibility. Conversely, possibility exists in relation to what is actual. It therefore has determined itself to be an immediate existence.

This unity of possibility and actuality is "contingent actuality." It is contingent precisely because it has possibility immediately within it. Since it is a mere possibility, it could be otherwise. Similarly, the possibility that exists within contingent actuality is a mere immediate possible. It is "equally an in-itself that lacks actuality," and for that reason it is only an immediate existence that lacks its own full development.

The movement of each moment into the other leads to its "necessity." Contingent actuality becomes what is necessary precisely because this actuality is at the same time immediately determined as a possible. Formal necessity is in turn "real actuality" *(reale Wirklichkeit)*, or the "thing of many properties" (*das Ding von vielen Eigenschaften*), or "the existent world" (*die existierende Welt*) (SL 546, STWII 208).

Real actuality also contains possibility immediately within it. It too contains the moment of the in-itself. For Hegel, "This possibility as the in-itself of real actuality is itself real possibility, and first of all, the in-itself as pregnant with content" (*Diese Möglichkeit als das Ansichsein der realen Wirklichkeit ist selbst reale Möglichkeit, zunächst das inhaltsvolle Ansichsein*) (SL 547, STWII 208). Real possibility is further distinguished from formal possibility, since it contains the determination of actuality within itself.[29]

It is the case then that "the existent world," or the "existing multiplicity of circumstances," is a function of both "real actuality" and "real possibility." It is not yet actuality as a totality both in and for itself. It is as yet "real possibility."

The supersession of real possibility "produces the same moments that are already in being" (*bringt also dieselben schon vorhandenen Momente hervor*) (SL 548, STWII 210). But instead of this production as having been a function of moments that are contingent or external to one another, "each grows out of the other; consequently, in this negation it also is not a transition, but a going-together-with-itself" (*jedes aus dem anderen werdend; sie ist daher in dieser Negation auch nicht ein Übergehen, sondern ein Zusammengehen mit sich selbst*) (SL 548, STWII 210). This "going-together-with-itself" is in fact a reproduction and growth of the very same "circle of conditions" (*Kreis der Bedingungen*) from which the negation had emerged. Here each of the moments that make up the circle of conditions become what they already are. What is different from what had originally transpired—in the initial production of the circle of conditions—is that reproduction entails not a "coming-to-be-from-another," but rather a self-propelling "coming-to-be."

The supersession of the duality of actuality and possibility that real possibility is, entails that the very same conditions that served as foundation for its negation and recreation should again reappear. Such necessity Hegel terms "real necessity." So much so is the necessity of this reproduction of the circle of conditions a function of real possibility that: "Real possibility and necessity are therefore only seemingly different; this is an identity which does not have to become but is already presupposed and lies at their base" (*Reale Möglichkeit und die Notwendigkeit sind daher nur scheinbar unterschieden; diese ist eine Identität, die nicht erst wird, sondern schon vorausgesetzt ist und zugrunde liegt*) (SL 549, STWII 211).

Marx's exposition of the "real necessity" of capitalist production follows closely Hegel's exposition of the emergence of "real necessity." Money contains in itself the possibility of surplus capital. This possibility is itself a function of the "possibility that lies in the womb of living labor" (N 453, MEW 366). Money splits into the duality of the "actual conditions of the creation of surplus capital," that is, the objective conditions and a labor fund (N 455, MEW 368). The objective conditions and a labor fund are, in turn, the basis of the "real possibility" of the reproduction of the very same conditions; and, in fact, they lead to the "real necessity" of the production and reproduction of those same conditions (N 455, MEW 368).

That Marx is indeed following the logical progression of Hegel's exposition is also seen in his consideration of surplus capital from what he terms "the standpoint of capital." Once he has developed the "real necessity" of the creation and recreation of surplus capital, he then discusses the contingencies that are still contained in what he calls capital I.

Marx's point here is that the money that had been used to initiate the original production process that led to surplus capital, must be seen to have been introduced by the capitalist (N 456, MEW 369). The formation of surplus capital I presupposes prior existing values that had been introduced by the capitalist—had been an act of the capitalist's. Surplus capital I, therefore, contains as its content values that are not, strictly speaking, values that are solely the result of surplus labor. Marx is careful to add, however, that these preexisting values are only formally different from surplus capital, since living labor must replace these values as well.

The formation of surplus capital II presupposes only that the capitalist has already appropriated alien labor without exchange (N 457, MEW 370). This precondition not only maintains capital, but also serves as the basis for its growth. With the emergence of surplus capital II, nothing is present in either the production or realization process that is not grounded in surplus labor. Nothing enters the process out of circulation that did not originate within the "possibilities that lie within labor's own womb." Nothing appears that is not a function of capital's own "immanent essence," within the necessity that is the expansion and intensification of capital.[30] Capital therefore "no longer proceeds from presuppositions in order to become, but rather it is itself presupposed and proceeds from itself to create the conditions of its maintenance and growth" (*nicht mehr von Voraussetzungen aus, um zu werden, sondern ist selbst vorausgesetzt und, von sich ausgehend, schafft die Voraussetzungen seiner Erhaltung und Wachstums selbst*) (N 460, MEW 372).

Hegel concludes his treatment of "Actuality" with the development of "absolute necessity." The production and reproduction of the "circle of conditions" that had resulted from "real necessity," nevertheless contains moments within itself that had entered the process from outside. "Real necessity" is as yet a mere relative necessity, precisely because "it has a presupposition from which it begins, it has its starting point in the contingent" (*Sie hat nämlich eine Voraussetzung, von der sie anfängt, sie hat an dem Zufälligen ihren Ausgangspunkt*) (SL 549, STWII 211). While the truth of contingent actuality had been formal necessity, which thereby entailed a "circle of conditions," it nevertheless is an immediate, unreflected actuality. Real necessity—the initial reproduction—began therefore "from the unity of possible and the actual which is not yet reflected into self—this presupposing and the self-returning movement are still separate" (*von jener noch nicht in sich reflektierten Einheit des Möglichen und Wirklichen an—dieses Voraussetzen und die in sich zurückkehrende Bewegung ist noch getrennt*) (SL 550, STWII 212). Though it may in fact result in a self-propelling movement, it origins are in an "other."

The return or reproductive movement that is entailed in the negation of real possibility, and hence the emergence of real necessity, results in what Hegel terms "absolute necessity" (*Absolute Notwendigkeit*) (SL 550, STWII 213). It is an actuality that can no longer be otherwise, since it is the necessity of the reproductive movement. It is the constant movement of reproduction. Hegel describes it as follows: "Thus form in its realization has penetrated all its differences and made itself transparent and is, as absolute necessity, only this simple self-identity of being in its negation, or in essence" (*So hat die Form in ihrer Realisierung alle ihre Unterschiede durchdrungen und sich durchsichtig gemacht und ist als absolute Notwendigkeit nur diese einfache Identität des Seins in seiner Negation oder in dem Wesen mit sich selbst*) (SL 551-52, STWII 214).

That which is absolutely necessary contains within itself no presuppositions which it itself does not posit. It no longer proceeds from presuppositions in order to become, but rather it is itself presupposed, and proceeds from itself to produce and reproduce the conditions of its maintenance and growth. It is "the beginning from itself which first is the positing of this self from which the beginning is made" (*das Anfangen von sich selbst ist erst das Setzen dieses Selbsts, von dem das Anfangen ist*) (SL 556, STWII 220).

Thus, the deep, logical structure of Marx's exposition of surplus capital II follows Hegel's treatment of "absolute necessity." With the creation of surplus capital II, capital "proceeds from itself" in producing and reproducing the conditions for its own existence. Marx lauds the scientific method he employs, while condemning the classical political economists, since their method prevents them from seeing capital as a historical mode of production (N 460-61, MEW 372-73).

5. CAPITAL AND WAGE-LABOR: THE ABSOLUTE RELATION

At this point in the exposition, Marx takes a closer look at the outcome of the creation and recreation of surplus capital II. At the end of the production of surplus capital II, all the conditions and presuppositions of the becoming of capital vanish. Capital now posits the conditions for its own realization, in accordance with its "immanent essence." As such it posits the raw material, the instrument of production, the labor fund and the conditions for its circulation. The sum total of its conditions are said to be the property of capital.

The initial production process that resulted in the creation of surplus capital I began with a simple exchange between objectified labor and living labor. This "simple exchange" was based entirely on the "laws of exchange of equivalents as measured by the quantity of labor or labor time contained in them" (N 457, MEW 370). This simple exchange of equivalents in turn presupposed the legal institutions that provided the framework to insure everyone's right to property over his own products and their free disposition (N 457-8, MEW 370).

Marx discerns, however, that as a consequence of the creation of surplus capital II, the right of property undergoes a "dialectical conversion" (*dialektischer Umschlag*) (N 458, MEW 370). In short, it "becomes the right to an alien product, or the right of property over alien labor, the right to appropriate alien labor without equivalent" *(das Recht auf fremdes Produkt oder in das Eigentumsrecht auf fremde Arbeit, das Recht, sich fremde Arbeit ohne Äquivalent anzueignen . . . zu verhalten*) (N 458, MEW 370). Money as surplus capital is exchanged for living labor, the living possibility of value-creation—a mere use value. Labor in turn creates a surplus product for capital. Consequently, the product of labor's efforts becomes the property of capital, and capital has acquired the right of property over the product without an exchange of equivalents.[31]

With the creation of surplus capital II, the "dialectical conversion" is complete. Living labor's own product now confronts it as the objective conditions for the production of capital. As Marx states:

> The objective conditions of living labor appear as separated, independent values opposite living labor capacity as subjective being, which therefore appears to them only as a value of another kind (not as value, but different from them, as use value).[32]

Capital relates to living labor as to the possibility of its own existence, while labor, in turn, relates to the objective conditions of production as alien. Indeed, labor relates to its own laboring capacity as alien.

The "simple exchange" that takes place after the creation of surplus capital II is in fact the "mere illusion" (*bloßer Schein*) of an exchange of equivalents. On the surface, objectified labor is exchanged for its equivalent in living labor. However, as Marx has shown, what actually takes place is just the opposite.[33]

Hegel's exposition of "absolute necessity" lays bare, as it were, the logical form of this "dialectical conversion," which is a consequence of surplus capital II. In absolute necessity, the negativity of essence served as the foundation of the possibility or "in-itself" of formal actuality. In the development of formal necessity, real actuality as an immediate "circle of conditions" contained within itself its negation or its "real possibility." The negation of this "in-itself" of real actuality entailed the recreation or reproduction of the very same "circle of conditions" that had served as its foundation. This "going-together-with-itself" is, at the same time, the "real necessity" of the continued return-to-self of the circle of conditions.

"Real necessity" was seen to have had its conditions and its ground in that which is external to itself. From a formal standpoint it is necessary, yet its content has been limited. Form is now said to have "penetrated all its differences," with the positing of the "circle of conditions," or *die Sache* as absolute. In its return-to-self, which is at the same time a repelling of itself from itself, "absolute necessity" has only itself as a ground and condition. "Absolute necessity" is the "reflection or form of the absolute." It is the unity of being and essence.

In its determination as essence, absolute necessity entails the "absolute conversion of its actuality into its possibility and of its possibility into actuality" (*das absolute Umkehren ihrer Wirklichkeit in ihre Möglichkeit und ihrer Möglichkeit in Wirklichkeit*) (SL 552, STWII 215). Yet, at the same time, however, in its determination of being, absolute necessity entails that its differences have the appearance of "a simply affirmative multiplicity, a differentiated actuality which had the shape of others, self-subsistent relatively to one another" (*seinde Mannigfaltigkeit, als unterschiedene Wirklichkeit, welche die Gestalt von selbstandigen Anderen gegeneinander hat*) (SL 552, STWII 215).

Thus, with the emergence and development of "absolute necessity," the "absolute conversion" of actuality into possibility and vice versa is complete. On the other hand, however, its determinations have the appearance of being. That is, they appear as separated, independent sides, as what Hegel terms, "free actualities" (*freie Wirklichkeiten*). Essence is therefore concealed in the separated, independent sides. Any contact between the sides appears as a mere "empty externality" (*leere Äußerlichkeit*). Despite the fact that contact between the sides appears as an "empty externality," what actually takes place between them is just the opposite. This "contact" between them is an "illusory show" (*Scheinen*) for what is actually transpiring beneath the surface. For the truth is that they stand in a relation of "absolute negativity" toward one another.

The "absolute conversion" of possibility into actuality and vice versa, remains concealed in its appearance in the form of being, beneath or behind the separated, independent sides of the identity. Marx sees that this separation is precisely what transpires at this point, despite the "dialectical conversion." Even though the actual ground of production is living labor, the objective conditions of living labor nevertheless "appear as separated, independent values opposite living labor." Capital and labor appear therefore as though they were independent "free actualities."

Hegel demonstrates that the "contact" between such "free actualities" appears as a mere "empty externality." Such "contact" conceals essence. As a "mere semblance," it conceals the fact that the two sides are mediated by the deepest of antitheses. The truth of the matter is, they stand in a relation of "absolute negativity" toward one another.

Marx's exposition reflects the same logical progression, when he maintains that the real relation between capital and labor is concealed by "simple exchange." This "simple exchange" is a "mere semblance"—the illusion—of an exchange of equivalents. It appears as though wage-labor is merely exchanging the price of its commodity for money. The actual state of affairs, however, entails a "dialectical conversion," and a relation of "negation" between capital and its "other-being," wage-labor. Thus, while capital and wage-labor appear as wholly separated—with wealth or property on the one side, and alien labor on the other—the most important outcome is the production and reproduction of the relation of capital and labor. This "social relation" or "production relation," as Marx calls it, appears as an even more important consequence of the process than its material results (N 458, MEW 370). He states:

> And even more particularly, within this process the worker produces himself as labor capacity, as well as the capital confronting him, while at the same time the capitalist produces himself as capital as well as the living labor capacity confronting him. Each reproduces itself, by reproducing its other, its negation. The capitalist produces labor as alien; labor produces the product as alien. The capitalist produces the worker, and the worker the capitalist, etc.[34]

Hegel maintains that the sides actually stand in a relation of "absolute negativity" (*absolute Negativität*) toward one another (SL 553, STWII 216). The determinateness or apparent separation of the one over and against the other is the determinateness of essence. The two sides stand therefore in an "absolute relation," wherein the one, in and through its own negation, constitutes the other and vice versa. The negation of possibility entails the production and reproduction of actuality; and, likewise, the negation of actuality entails the production and reproduction of possibility. Hegel states: "This identity of being with itself in its negation is now substance. It is this unity as in its negation, or as in contingency, as such it is substance as relation to itself" (*Diese Identität des Seins in seiner Negation mit sich selbst, so ist sie nun Substanz. Sie ist diese Einheit als in ihrer Negation oder als in der Zufälligkeit; so ist sie die Substanz als Verhältnis zu sich selbst*) (SL 553, STWII 217).

6. THE POWER OF THE CAPITALIST

In the emergence of surplus capital II, capital has rid itself of all the contingencies and externalities that served as the basis of its becoming. Capital "no longer proceeds from presupposition in order to become, but rather it is itself presupposed, and proceeds from itself to create the conditions of its maintenance and growth."

Because capital posits the conditions of its own realization, it is now an identity of a production process and a process of realization (N 458-9, MEW 370-71). It is now a "totality." It is thus the unity of its different moments of production and reproduction. As this unity in its different moments, capital is the "power" (*Macht*) that drives the production process toward its realization (N 453, MEW 366). Specifically, it is the "power" that is independent of living labor, and which rules over it. It does so through labor's own action. Capital is "objectified labor as mastery, command over living labor" (*vergegenständlichte Arbeit als Herrschaft, Kommando über lebendige*) (N 453, MEW 367).

Marx further describes capital as "substance" (*Substanz*) in comparison to living labor, which is the "insubstantial" (*substanzloses*) (N 454, MEW 366). Living labor appears as a "mere accessory" (*Akzessorium*) to the "substance" (*Substanz*) that is capital (N 462, MEW 373). Labor endows capital with a power of its own, while at the same time, it acts to reduce itself to mere subsistence, an "accessory." While creating capital, it destroys itself. In this manner, capital posits or causes itself to exist through its negation of labor, while at the same time, causes labor to wear itself out as a mere use value, a means. Marx also states that capital is an "acting cause," to labor as a "produced effect."[35] When labor sells itself as a commodity, "he sells himself not as a cause but as effect" (*verkauft er sich nicht als cause, sondern als effect*) (N 571, MEW 473). Capital is an active power or cause in relation to living labor, which in turn is produced effect. Only insofar as capital causes living labor to exist as its produced effect, can capital produce and reproduce itself (N 457, MEW 369).

This is a crucial point in the development of Marx's exposition. Capital is now its own self-causing unity. The exposition from this point on will focus on the manner in which capital alters its own presuppositions in ways that are suitable to its own ends.

We have seen Marx's debt to Hegel throughout his treatment of the "becoming of capital." Hegel had developed the logical schema that Marx used to organize his economic data into a dialectical exposition of the "organic development" of capital. Hegel had also demonstrated that once an organic unity has become, it must be conceived of as a unity of distinct moments. In Hegel's exposition, so to conceive organic unity means that the "absolute relation" that results from "absolute necessity" is the mediated unity of being and essence. This unity is what has traditionally been referred to as "substance" (SL 555, STWII 219). "Substance" no longer proceeds from presuppositions, but it is itself presupposed, and proceeds from itself to create the conditions of its own self-movement. In short, it is self-causing. As a self-causing unity, substance must first of all be seen as "power" (*Macht*). Because it "proceeds from itself" in its self-movement, it is the power that unites its own moments, its own "accidents."

On the one hand, therefore, it is a simple unity, a totality. On the other hand, however, substance is a "flux of accidents" (*Wechsel der Akzidenzen*) (SL 556, STWII 220). It is a differentiation of itself into moments that comprise its unity. As such, it is the "power" that posits determinations within itself, and distinguishes them from itself. Insofar as substance as power posits its accidents in its reflection-into-self, it is the "cause" (*Ursache*) of the accidents it "effects" (*Wirkung*). Actual substance is defined as power that in its return-to-self posits or causes a determinateness, which in turn is taken as an effect. The effect is necessary in relation to the cause, for it is only insofar as the effect is necessary that the cause may be seen as self-moving.

This logical progression from substance as power to substance as cause in relation to effect, is reflected in Marx's exposition of capital as a self-causing unity of different moments. Capital is the "power" that drives the production process toward realization (N 453, MEW 366). It is "substance" in relation to living labor, its "accessory." It is an "active cause," and labor is its "produced effect"; and it is only insofar as capital causes living labor to exist as its produced effect, that it can reproduce itself.

At this particular juncture, Marx introduces the "for-itself" existence of capital, the capitalist. In the causal relation between capital and living labor, Marx states, "the objective conditions of labor attain a subjective existence vis-à-vis living labor capacity—capital turns into capitalist . . ." (*Die objectiven Bedingungen der Arbeit erhalten subjective Existenz gegenüber dem lebendigen Arbeitsvermögen—aus dem Kapital wird der Kapitalist*) (N 462, MEW 374). Marx elsewhere is careful to specify the terms under which one may identify the two. Thus while capital is essentially capitalist, it is, at the same time, "an element of his existence distinct from him, or production in general, capital" (*unterschiednes Element seines Bestehns oder die Production überhaupt Kapital*) (N 513, MEW 420).

Nevertheless, in becoming a reality that posits its own conditions for its own realization, in accord with its "immanent essence," capital attains a "for-itself" existence in the form of the capitalist (N 461-2, MEW 374-5).[36]

The capitalist "represents value for-itself, money in its third moment, wealth, by means of simple appropriation of alien labor" (*repräsentiert der Kapitalist für sich seienden Wert, Geld im dritten Moment, Reichtum, durch einfache Anegnung fremder Arbeit*) (N 456, MEW 369).

This appropriation of the product of living labor without exchange, places the capitalist in a position in which he is able to cause the process to begin again and again (N 457, MEW 370). In this way, surplus capital allows the capitalist to continually posit living labor as a cause of the maintenance and growth of surplus capital. Marx states:

> The objective conditions of living labour are presupposed as having an existence independently of it, as the objectivity of a subject distinct from living labour capacity and standing independently over against it; the reproduction and realization, i.e., the expansion of these objective conditions is therefore at the same time their own reproduction and new production as the wealth of an alien subject indifferently and independently standing over against labour capacity.[37]

The capitalist as active power causes the existence of wage-labor, which now exists as capital's produced effect. Wage-labor in turn becomes a cause of the maintenance and growth of surplus capital. Capital thus posits or conditions the process of its realization.

The above characterization of capital and its relation to living-labor reflects an indebtedness for logical form to Hegel and his exposition of substance as cause. We have seen that the relation between an effect and its cause is for Hegel a necessary one. The cause produces an effect, and is thereby self-moving. Hegel continues when he suggests that a cause is always a particular cause, with a particular effect. The cause initially stands to the effect as a contingent causality (SL 560, STWII 225). As such, the cause contains a content that is indifferent to the form-determinations of the causal relation. Both the cause and the effect are immediate actualities, or finite substances.

The cause of an act is therefore the inner disposition of an active subject (SL 561, MEW 226). Any other determinations that this finite substance may possess are irrelevant with respect to the form-determinations of the causal relation. The cause of the motion of the paint and the form of the painting, is the active subject or the painter. The activity—painting—exists as a particular disposition within the active subject. Whatever else the painter may be is of little consequence to the act of painting. While the other determinations of this finite substance are irrelevant to its being an active cause, it nevertheless serves as the "substrate" of the disposition.

The substrates of the causal relation, however, are not simply immediate actualities. They themselves are substances. The form-determinations of the relation are not merely external, but are posited within the respective substances. The substance that is cause first obtains its power in an external manner. The power in turn is posited in the substance. The substance then relates negatively to itself, and thereby causes an effect. At first, the effect is also an external determination of another substance. The latter receives a "determination alien to its original self-identity" (*eine seiner ursprünglichen Identität mit sich . . . fremde Bestimmung*) (SL 564, STWII 231). When it then assumes this "alien determination" within itself, the substance relates negatively to itself, and thereby becomes itself a cause with an effect.

In this manner, causality conditions its own activity. It posits or presupposes itself by first creating the conditions for the emergence of an "active subject" with the power, in turn, to cause an "alien determination" in another substance. This presupposing act of causality entails that one substance—the "active subject"—be the "active substance," while the other a "passive substance." Here an active substance, as cause, relates negatively to itself, and thereby mediates itself with itself through the effect as its negation (SL 566, STWII 233). The effect, in turn, as passive substance, no longer relates to causality externally. Rather, because it has been preposited or conditioned in and through the relation, when it is acted upon by the active substance, it supersedes this conditionedness, and thereby becomes so determined.

Because the passive substance receives these determinations through the activity of what is essentially external to itself, it "suffers violence" (*leidet sie Gewalt*) (SL 567, STWII 235). Hegel goes on to say that insofar as it suffers violence, the passive substance is an entirely "alien being."[38] Furthermore, it is the case that, because the passive substance assumes the conditions that are requisite for the "violence" of an active substance, its own activity makes it a passive substance. When it receives the act of "violence," therefore, it only displays what it is in-itself. In this way, it comes to be its own effect, that is, it displays itself as the cause of its own predicament (SL 568, STWII 236). It will, however, be exposed as active, or rather reactive, upon further development.

Labor relates to capital as the produced effect to the active cause. From another perspective, the capitalist causes the existence of living labor, so that capital may begin the process again and again. Thus, the wage-laborer is determined by the activity of the capitalist in and through "simple exchange." It is clear that for Marx, this "exchange" is actually an act of violence, that is, this exchange is not an exchange at all. Rather, it is the exploitation of wage-labor by capital (N 462, MEW 374). Wage-labor is therefore an "alien being." It assimilates this act of violence and, in turn, becomes the cause of the reproduction and expansion of capital. In this way, labor's own activity becomes the cause of its own predicament (N 462, MEW 374).

In the final analysis, Marx maintains that the most important outcome of capital as having become a unity of production and realization—a self-causing unity—is that the process entails the reproduction of the relation between capitalist and worker (N 458, 370). In this reciprocal causal relation, the capitalist acts to ensure that the worker produces and reproduces himself as penurious living labor, while working, at the same time, to maintain himself as independent value for-itself.

Likewise, for Hegel, the passive substance receives the activity of the active subject as a positedness in-itself, supersedes its conditions and becomes itself a cause. Its own act is a reaction against the first active cause. In and through the first cause, the passive substance acquires a negative self-relation and, in turn, posits the first cause as its own effect. Its action, or rather reaction, serves to bring about again the causal agency in the first cause.[39]

So for Marx. The capitalist acts to ensure that the worker produces and reproduces himself as living labor. Living labor in turn acts on the objective conditons of production, and thus perpetuates the existence of the capitalist. As he states: "Each reproduces itself, by reproducing its other, its negation" (*Jedes reproduziert sich selbst, indem es sein andres, seine Negation reproduziert*) (N 458, MEW 371).

---

[1] "Labour is the living, form-giving fire; it is the transitoriness of things, their temporality, as their formation by living time" (*Die Arbeit ist das lebendige, gestaltende Feuer; die Vergänglichkeit der Dinge, ihre Zeitlichkeit, als ihre Formung durch die lebendige Zeit*) (N 361, MEW 278).

[2] "But, as ongoing labour, it is itself already incorporated in capital, and a moment of the same. This force of labour therefore appears as the self-preserving force of capital. The worker has merely added new labour; as for previous labour—owing to the existence of capital—this has an eternal existence as value, quite independent of its material existence. This is how the matter appears to capital and to the worker" (*Als solche gegenwärtige Arbeit aber ist sie selbst schon dem Kapital einverleibt, ein Moment desselben. Diese erhaltende Kraft der Arbeit erscheint also als Selbsterhaltungskraft des Kapitals. Der Arbeiter hat nur neue Arbeit hinzugefugt; die vergangne—indem das kapital existiert—hat eine ewige Existenz als Wert, durchaus unabhangig von seinem stofflichen Dasein. So erscheint die Sache dem Kapital und dem Arbeiter*) (N 364, MEW 281).

[3] *Wenn der Kapitalist bloß arbeiten läßt, um Mehrwert zu schaffen—um noch nicht vorhandnen Wert zu schaffen—so zeigt sich, dass, sobald er aufhört, arbeiten zu lassen, auch sein schon vorhandnes Kapital entwertet wird; daß also die lebendige Arbeit nicht nur neuen Wert zufügt, sondern durch den* very act of adding a new value to the old one, maintains, eternalizes it) (N 365, MEW 282).

[4] "By appropriating the entire day's work and then consuming it in the production process with the materials of which his capital consists, but by giving in exchange only the labour objectified in the worker—i.e., half a day's work—the capitalist creates the surplus value of his capital; in this case, half a day of objectified labour" (N 334).

[5] "At no time has he [Ricardo] shown that there is an essential relation between the whole of the labour objectified in capital and the living work day (whether the latter is represented as one working day of 50 times 12 hours, or as 12 hrs. of labour by 50 workers, is the same thing as far as the relation goes), and that this essential relation is just the relation between the equivalent of the objectified labour with which the worker is paid, and the living working day; where the whole is the day itself, and the essential relation is the variable relation (the day itself is a constant) between the fractional part of the necessary hours of labour and the hours of surplus labour" (*Er hat nirgends entwickelt, daß ein immanentes Verhältnis stattfindet zwischen dam Ganzen der im Kapital vergegenständlichten Arbeit und dem lebendigen Arbeitstag [ob dieser als ein Arbeitstag von 50 + 12 Stunden oder als zwölfstündliche Arbeit von 50 Arbeiten vorgestellt wird, ist für das Verhältnis dasselbe] und daß dieses immanente Verhältnis eben das Verhältnis des Bruchteils des lebendigen Arbeitstags, oder des Äquivalents für die vergegenstänlichte Arbeit, womit der Arbeiter bezahlt wird, zu dem lebendigen Arbeitstag ist; wo das Ganze der Tag selbst und das immnanente Verhaltnis das variable Verhältnis [der Tag selbst is konstante Größe] zwischen dem Bruchteil der notwendigen Arbeitsstunden und der Surplusarbeitsstunden*) (N 352, MEW 270).

[6] "Thus the absolute sum by which capital increases its value through a given increase of the productive force depends on the given fractional part of the working day which represents necessary labour, and which therefore expresses the original relation of necessary labour to the living work day" (N 340).

[7] *Innerhalb dieser Grenzen kann es sich allein bewegen. Je kleiner schon der Bruchteil, der auf die notwendige Arbeit fällt, je größer die Surplusarbeit, desto weniger kann irgendeine Vermehrung der Produktivkraft die notwendige Arbeit sensibly vermindern; da der Nenner enorm gewachsen ist* (N 340, MEW 259).

[8] We may see, then, that capital attempts to overcome the restriction of relative surplus value by increasing absolute surplus labour time, i.e., the multiplication of simultaneous working days. It nevertheless at the same time seeks to reduce living labour to a minimum, because its existence depends upon the reduction of necessary labour time in favor of surplus labour time. Marx states: "Capital must therefore constantly posit necessary labour in order to posit surplus labour; it has to multiply it (namely the simultaneous working days) in order to multiply the surplus; but at the same time it must sublate them as necessary, in order to posit them as surplus labour" (*Das Kapital muß daher beständig notwendige Arbeit setzen, um Surplusarbeit zu setzen; es muß sie vermehren [nämlich die gleichzeitigen Arbeitstage], um das Surplus vermehren zu können; aber es muß sie ebensosehr aufheben als notwendige, um sie als Surplusarbeit zu setzen*) (N 399, MEW 313).

[9] Miller translates *Anstoss* as "impulse." I feel that this term is somewhat awkward, in that though it does adequatedly convey the sense of that which is "internally posited," it does not convey the sense of a limitation. The "whole," or the "force" of essence, structures its "parts." As so structured, the "parts" react back upon the original force; they, in turn, themselves become "countervailing forces," and as such are superseded limitations.

[10] *Das Kapital als Setzen der Surplusarbeit ist ebensosehr und in demselben Moment Setzen und Nichtsetzen der notwendigen Arbeit; es ist nur, insofern sie ist und zugleich nicht ist* (N 399, MEW 314).

[11] "There now appears, as the result of this unity of the process of production and the process of realization, the product of the process, i.e., capital itself, emerging as product from the process whose presupposition it was—as a product which is a value, or value itself appears as the product of the process, and specifically a higher value, because it contains more objectified labour than the value which formed the point of departure. This value as such is

money. However, this is the case only in itself; it is not posited as such; that which is posited at the outset, which is on hand, is a commodity with a certain (ideal) price, i.e., which exists only ideally (*ideell*) as a certain sum of money, and which first has to realize itself as such in the exchange process, hence has to re-enter the process of simple circulation in order to be posited as money" (*Als Resultat dieser Einheit von Produktions— und Verwertungsprozeß erscheint nun das Produkt des Prozesses, d.h. das Kapital selbst, wie es als Produkt aus dem Prozesse hervorgeht, dessen Voraussetzung es war—als Produkt, das Wert ist, oder der Wert selbst erscheint als Produkt dieses Prozesses, und zwar ein höherer Wert, weil mehr vergegenständlichte Arbeit enthaltend als der, von dem ursprünglich ausgegangen worden. Dieser Wert als solcher ist Geld. Indes ist dies nur an sich der Fall; es is nicht als solches gesetzt; was zunächst gesetzt ist, vorhanden ist, ist eine Ware von einem bestimmten [ideelen] Preise, d.h., die nur ideell als eine bestimmte Geldsumme existiert und die sich erst im Austausch als solche realisieren soll, also erst wieder in den Prozeß der einfachen Zirkulation eingehen muß, um als Geld gesetzt zu werden*) (N 402, MEW 315-16).

[12] "Hence, as use value, the product contains a barrier—precisely the barrier consisting of the need for it—which, however, is measured not by the need of the producers but by the total need of all those engaged in exchange" (*Als Gebrauchswert hat daher das Produkt in sich selbst eine Schranke—eben die Schranke des Bedüfnisses danach—die aber nicht am Bedürfnis des Produzenten, sondern dem Gesamtbedürfnis der Austauschenden nun gemessen wird*) (N 405, MEW 319).

[13] "As a new value and as value as such, however, it seems to encounter a barrier in the magnitude of available equivalents, primarily money, not as medium of circulation but as money. The surplus value (distinct, obviously from the original value) requires a surplus equivalent. This now appears as a second barrier" (*Als Neuwert und Wert überhaupt aber scheint es Schranke zu haben an der Große vorhandner Äquivalent, zunächst Geld, nicht als Zirkulationsmittel, sondern als Geld. Der Surpluswert [versteht sich vom ursprünglichen von selbst] erheischt ein Surplusäquivalent. Dies erscheint jetzt als zweite Schranke* (N 405, MEW 319).

[14] "Inside the production process, realization appeared totally identical with the production of surplus labour (the objectification of surplus time), and hence appeared to have no bounds other than those partly presupposed and partly posited within this process itself, but which are always posited within it as barriers to be forcibly overcome. There now appear barriers to it which lie outside it" (*Innerhalb des Produktionsprozesses erschien die Verwertung gänzlich identisch mit der Produktion von Surplusarbeit [der Vergagenständlichung von Surpluszeit] und daher ohne weitre Grenzen als die, die innerhalb dieses Prozessess selbst teils vorausgesetzt, teils gesetzt werden; die aber immer so als zu überwältigende Schranken in ihm gesetzt sind. Jetzt erscheinen Schranken desselben, die ausserhalb desselben liegen*) (N 404, MEW 318).

[15] "The creation by capital of absolute surplus value—more objectified labour—is conditional upon an expansion, specifically a constant expansion, of the sphere of circulation. The surplus value created at one point requires the creation of surplus value at another point, for which it may be exchanged; if only, initially, the production of more gold and silver, more money, so that, if surplus value cannot directly become capital again, it may exist in the form of money as the possibility of new capital. A precondition of production based on capital is therefore the production of a constantly widening sphere of circulation, whether the sphere itself is directly expanded or whether more points within it are created as points of production. While circulation appeared at first as a constant magnitude, it here appears as a moving magnitude, being expanded by production itself. Accordingly, it already appears as a moment of production itself" (N 407).

[16] "The three processes of which capital forms the unity are external; they are separate in time and space. As such, the transition from one into the other, i.e., their unity as regards the individual capitalist, is accidental. Despite their inner unity, they exist independently alongside one another, each as the presupposition of the other" (*Die 3 Prozesse, deren Einheit das Kapital bildet, sind äußerliche, Zeit und Raum nach außereinander liegend. Als solcher ist der Übergang aus dem einen in den andern, d.h., ihre Einheit in bezug auf die einzelnen Kapitalisten betrachtet, zufällig. Sie existieren unabhängig nebeneinander, trotz ihrer innern Einheit und jeder als Voraussetzung des andern*) (N 403, MEW 317).

[17] "So far in the realization process, we have only the indifference of the individual moments toward one another; that they determine each other internally and search for each other externally. . . . The inner necessity of moments which belong together, and their indifferent, independent existence towards one another, are already the foundation of contradiction" (*Bisher haben wir bei dem Verwertungsprozeß bloß die Gleichgültigkeit der einzelnen Momente gegeneinander; daß sie sich innerlich bedingen und äußerlich suchen; aber finden können oder nicht, decken können oder nicht, entsprechen können oder nicht. Die inner Nötwendigkeit des Zusammengehörigen und seine gleichgültige selbständige Existenz gegeneinander schon Grundlage von Widersprüchen*) (N 415, MEW 327-28).

[18] "But from the fact that capital posits every such limit as a barrier and hence gets ideally beyond it, it does not by any means follow that it has really overcome it, and, since every such barrier contradicts its character, its production moves in contradictions which are constantly overcome but just as constantly posited. Furthermore. The universality towards which it irresistibly strives encounters barriers in its own nature, which will, at a certain stage of its development, allow it to be recognized as being itself the greatest barrier to this tendency, and hence will drive towards its own sublation" (*Daraus aber, daß das Kapital jede solche Grenze als Schranke setzt und daher ideell darüber und da jede solche Schranke seiner Bestimmung widerspricht, bewegt sich seine Produktion in Widersprüchen, die beständig überwunden, aber ebenso beständig gesetzt werden. Noch mehr. Die Universalität, nach der es unaufhaltsam hintreibt, findet Schranken an seiner eignen Natur, die auf einer gewissen Stufe seiner Entwicklung es selbst als die größte Schranke dieser Tendenz werden erkennen lassen und daher zu seiner Aufhebung durch es selbst hintreiben*) (N 410, MEW 323-24).

[19] "At the point where we stand now, where capital is being examined only in general, the real difficulties of this third process are present only as possibilities, and are therefore superseded again as possibilities. Therefore, the product now posited as having been transformed back into money" (*Die wirklichen Schwierigkeiten dieses dritten Prozesses sind auf dem Punkt, wo wir jetzt stehn, wo das Kapital nur im allgemeinen betrachtet wird—nur als Möglichkeiten vorhanden und daher ebenso als Möglichkeiten aufgehoben. Produkt also jetzt gesetzt als wieder in Geld verwandelt*) (N 447, MEW 361).

[20] "Exchange does not change the inner characteristics of realization; but it projects them to the outside; gives them a reciprocally independent form, and thereby lets their unity exist merely as an inner necessity, which must therefore come forcibly to the surface in crises. Both are therefore posited in the essence of capital: the devaluation of capital in the production process, as well as the supersession of devaluation and the creation of the conditions for the realization of capital" (*Der Austausch ändert nicht die innren Bedingungen der Verwertung; aber er wirft sie nach außen; gibt ihnen selbständige Form gegeneinander und laßt so die innere Einheit nur als innre Nötwendigkeit existerert, die sich daher außerlich gewaltsam in den Krisen äußert. Beides ist daher im Wesen des Kapitals gesetzt: sowohl die Entwertung des Kapitals durch den Produktionssprozeß als die Aufhebung derselben und das Herstellen der Bedingungen fur die Verwertung des Kapitals*) (N 447, MEW 360).

[21] *Das Kapital ist jetzt also wieder als Geld gesetzt und das Geld daher in der neuen Bestimmung von realisierten Kapital, nicht bloß als realisierter Preis der Ware. Oder die im Preis realisierte Ware ist jetzt realisiertes Kapital* (N 447, MEW 361).

[22] "But the exposition of the absolute is, in fact, its own act, which begins from itself and arrives at itself" (*In der Tat aber ist das Auslegen des Absoluten sein eigenes Tun, und das bei sich anfängt, wie es bei sich ankommt*) (SL 532, STWII 190)

[23] "When capital is posited as money, it is therefore posited in the first aspect, as measure of value" (*Indem das Kapital als Geld gesetzt ist, ist es so in der ersten Bestimmung des Geldes gesetzt, als Maß des Werts*) (N 448, MEW 361).

Furthermore, Marx states: "In accord with the initial nature of money, the only apparent feature by which capital—when transformed into money—may be measured is the new value which it has created; i.e., the first aspect of money as the general measure of surplus value—of the realization of capital" (*Zunächst, der Natur des Geldes nach erscheint am Kapital—indem es in Geld verwandelt ist—nur gemessen der Neuwert, den es geschaffen; d.h., es wiederholt sich die erste Bestimmung des Geldes als des allgemeinen Maßes der Waren; jetzt als Maß des Mehrwerts—der Verwertung des Kapitals*) (N 448, MEW 361).

[24] "... the measure of its realization is posited in its own form—as a proportion of the capital returned (returned to its money form) from the production process and from exchange, relative to the original capital" (... *ist das Maß seiner Verwertung in seiner eignen Form gesetzt—als Proportion des aus dem Produktionsprozeß und dem Austausch retournierten Kapitals [zu seiner Geldform retournierten] zum ursprünglichen Kapital*) (N 448, MEW 361).

[25] "The second form of money was that of the medium of circulation, and in this regard the money form of capital appeared as a mere vanishing moment for the purpose of exchanging it again, but not, as in the case of money as a medium of circulation in general, an exchange in return for commodities—use values—for final consumption, but rather an exchange in return for those particular use values in which it is able to begin its course as capital anew" (N 448).

[26] "This third form presupposes capital in the earlier forms and at the same time forms the transition from capital to the particular capitals, the real capitals, since now, in this last form, capital already in its very concept divides into two capitals with an independent existence. Along with duality, plurality in general is given. Such is the march of this development" (*Diese dritte Form unterstellt das Kapital in den früheren und bildet zugleich den Übergang aus dem Kapital in die besondren Kapitalien, die realen Kapitalien; da jetzt, in dieser letzten Form, das Kapital seinem Begriff nach sich schon in zwei Kapitalien von selbständigem Bestehn scheidet. Mit der Zweiheit ist dann die Mehrheit überhaupt gegeben.* Such is the march of this development) (N 449, MEW 362).

[27] *Beim ersten Vorkommen erschienen die Voraussetzungen selbst äußerlich, aus der Zirkulation herkommend; als äussere Voraussetzungen fur die Entstehung des Kapitals; daher nicht aus seinem inneren Wesen hervorgehend und nicht aus demselben erklärt. Diese äußerlichen Voraussetzungen werden jetzt als Moments der Bewegung des Kapitals selbst erscheinen, so dass es selbst sie—wie sie immer historisch entstehen mögen—als seine eignen Momente vorausgesetzt hat* (N 450, MEW 363-64).

[28] "In surplus capital, all moments are products of alien labour—alien surplus labour transformed into capital ... finally the amount of material and instrument required so that new surplus labour can realize itself in them, or a new surplus value can be created" (*In dem Surpluskapital sind alle Momente Produkt der fremden Arbeit—in Kapital verwandelte fremde Surplusarbeit . . . endlich das notige Quantum von Material und*

Instrument, damit sich neue Surplusarbeit in ihm verwirklichen oder neuer Mehrwert geschaffen werden kann) (N 453, MEW 366).

[29] "The real possibility of something is therefore the existing multiplicity of circumstances which are connected to it" (*Die reale Möglichkeit einer Sache ist daher die daseiende Mannigfaltigkeit von Umstanden, die sich auf sie beziehen*) (SL 547, STWII 209).

[30] "Once production founded on capital is presupposed—money has become transformed into capital actually only at the end of the first production process, which resulted in its reproduction and in the new production of surplus capital I; surplus capital I, however, is itself posited, realized as surplus capital, only when it has produced surplus capital II, i.e., as soon as these presuppositions of money, while it is in the process of passing over into capital, which still lie outside the movement of real capital have vanished, and when capital has therefore itself posited, and posited in accordance with its immanent essence, the conditions which form its point of departure in production—then the condition that the capitalist, in order to posit himself as capital, must bring values into circulation which he created with his own labour—or by some other means, excepting only already available, previous wage-labour—belongs among the antediluvian conditions of capital, belongs to its historic presuppositions, which precisely as such historic presuppositions, are past and gone, and hence belong to the history of formation, but in no way to its contemporary history, i.e., not to the real system of the mode of production ruled by it" (N 459, MEW 371-72.)

Furthermore, he states: "The conditions and presuppositions of the becoming, of the arising, of capital presuppose precisely that it is not yet in being but merely in becoming; they therefore disappear as real capital arises, capital which itself, on the basis of its own reality, posits the conditions for its realization" (N 459, MEW 371).

[31] "The right of property is converted, to become, on the one side, the right to appropriated alien labour, and the other, the duty of respecting the product of one's own labour itself, as values belonging to others" (*Das Eigentumsrecht schlägt um in das Recht auf der einen Seite, sich fremde Arbeit anzueignen, und die Pflicht auf der andren, das Produkt der eignen Arbeit und die eigne Arbeit selbst als andern gehörige Werte zu respektieren*) (N 458, MEW 371).

[32] *Die objektiven Bedingungen der lebendigen Arbeit erscheinen als getrennte, verselbständigte Werte gegen das lebendige Arbeitsvermögen als subjektives Dasein, das ihnen gegenüber daher auch nur als Wert von einer andren Art (nicht als Wert, sondern als Gebrauchswert von ihnen verschieden) erscheint* (N 461, MEW 374).

[33] "The relation of exchange has thus dropped away entirely, or is a mere semblance. Furthermore, the right of property originally appeared to be based on one's own labour. Property now appears as the right to alien labour, and as the impossibility of labour appropriating its own product. The complete separation between property, and, even more so, wealth, and labour, now appears as a consequence of the law which began with their identity" (*Das Verhältnis des Austauschs ist also gänzlich weggefallen oder ist bloßer Schein. Ferner erschien ursprünglich das Eigentumsrecht gegründet auf die eigne Arbeit. Eigentum erscheint jetzt als Recht auf fremde Arbeit und als Unmöglichkeit der Arbeit, sich ihr eignes Produkt anzueignen. Die völlige Trennung zwischen Eigentum und noch mehr Reichtum und Arbeit erscheint jetzt als Konsequenz des Gesetzes, das von ihrer Identität ausging*) (N 458, MEW 371).

[34] *Und zwar produziert innerhalb dieses Prozesses der Arbeiter sich selbst als Arbeitsvermögen und das ihm gegenüberstehende Kapital, wie andrerseits der Kapitalist sich produziert als Kapital und das ihm gegenüberstehende lebendige Arbeitsvermögen. Jedes reproduziert sich selbst, indem es sein andres, seine Negation reproduziert. Der Kapitalist produziert die Arbeit als fremdes; die Arbeit produziert das Produkt als*

fremdes. Das Kapitalist produziert den Arbeiter und der Arbeiter den Kapitalisten etc. (N 458, MEW 371).

[35] "Value of labour presupposes in principle that living labour is not equal to its product, or, what is the same, that it is sold not as an acting cause, but as itself a produced effect" (*Wert der Arbeit unterstellt überhaupt, daß die lebendige Arbeit nicht gleich ihrem Produkt, oder was dasselbe ist, daß sie verkauft wird nicht als wirkende Ursache, sondern selbst produzierter Effekt*) (N 575, MEW 478).

[36] "Now, if we initially examine the relation such as it has become, value having become capital, and living labour confronting it as mere use value, so that living labour appears as a mere means to realize objectified, dead labour, to penetrate it with an animating soul while losing its own soul to it—and having produced, as the end-product, alien wealth on one side and, on the other, the penury which is living labour capacity's sole possession—then the matter is simply this, that the process itself, in and by itself, posits the real objective conditions of living labour . . . and posits them as alien, independent existences—or as the mode of existence of an alien person, as self-sufficient values for-themselves, and hence as values which form wealth alien to an isolated and subjective labour capacity, wealth of and for the capitalist" (*Betrachten wir nun zunächst das gewordne Verhältnis, das Gewordensein des Werts zu Kapital und die lebendige Arbeit als ihm bloss gegenüberstehnden Gebrauchswert, so daß die lebendige Arbeit als bloßes Mittel erscheint, um die vergegenständlichte, tote Arbeit zu verwerten, mit belebender Seele zu durchdringen und ihre eigne Seele an sie zu verlieren—und als Resultat einerseits den geschaffnen Reichturn als fremd, als eigen aber nur die Bedürftigkeit des lebendigen Arbeitsvermögens produziert zu habe—so erscheint die Sache einfach die, daß um und durch den Prozeß selbst gesetzt sind die sachlichen Bedingungen der lebendige Arbeit . . . gesetzt sind als fremde, selbständige Existenze—oder als Existenzweise einer fremden Person, als an sich gegenüber dem lebendigen Arbeitsvermögen, das ebenfalls von ihnen isoliert, subjektiv dasteht, an sich festhaltende, für sich seiende Werte und daher Werte, die dem Arbeitsvermögen fremden Reichtum, den Reichtum des Kapitailisten bilden*) (N 461, MEW 373-74).

[37] *Die objektiven Bedingungen des lebendigen Arbeitsvermögens sind vorausgesetzt als ihm gegenüber selbständige Existenz, als die Objektivität eines vom dem lebendigen Arbeitsvermögen unterschiednen und ihm selbständig gegenüberstehenden Subjekts; die Reproduktion und Verwertung, d.h., die Erweiterung dieser objektiven Bedingungen, ist daher zugleich die Reproduktion und Neuproduktion ihrer als des Reichtums eines fremden Subjekts, dem Arbeitsvermögen gleichgültig und selbständig gegenüberstehend* (N 462, MEW 374).

[38] "Violence is the manifestation of power, or power as external. But power is external only insofar as causal substance in its action, that is, in the positing of itself, is at the same time presupposing, that is, it posits itself as sublated. Conversely, the act of violence is equally an act of power. It is only on an other presupposed by itself on which the violent cause acts, its effect thereon is a negative relation to itself, or the manifestation of itself. The passive is the self-subsistent that is only something posited, something that is broken within itself; an actuality which is condition, and condition, too, which is now in its truth, that is, an actuality that is only a possibility, or, conversely, an in-itself that is only the determinateness of the in-itself, is only passive. Therefore not only is it possible to do violence to that which suffers it, but also violence must be done to it; that which acts violently on the other can do so only because it is the power over it, the power in which it manifests both itself and the other" (SL 567, STWII 235).

[39] "That first cause, which first acts and receives its effect back into itself as reaction, then reappears as cause, whereby the action, which is infinite causality runs on into the spuriously infinite progress, is bent round and becomes an action that returns into itself, an infinite reciprocal action" (SL 569, STWII 237).

CHAPTER 5

THE *BEGRIFF* OF CAPITAL

In chapters three and four, we examined Marx's exposition of the essence of capitalist production. His presentation entailed a movement from the abstract to progressively more concrete determinations, which, in turn, involved a series of correlated moments. Each individual series, or stage, in the development of the exposition contained two phases in the development of a single, more concrete whole. We saw, for example, that the identity of the initial return movement of the production process of capital depends on the contradiction between capital and its "non being," or living labor; that capitalist production is the ground of the product; that the product contains surplus value as its property; that surplus value can be analyzed as a relation between the whole of the working day and its fractional parts, necessary and surplus labor time; and, finally, that the relationship and tension between the parts within the whole is the natural force of capital that constantly reduces necessary labor time. All of these twofold relations are superseded when capital is described as a unity of production and its process of actualization. This characteristic is further developed in Marx's presentation of capital as a self-causing unity.

Thus, we have reached the point at which capital can be presented as a "totality" of inseparable moments. This whole has been present since the beginning as the organizing principle of the entire exposition. Capital as a unity of production and circulation is that "organic unity" which is the groundof the entire development. In its "immediate being ," capital is commodity and monetary circulation. But monetary circulation presupposes the system of capitalist production. Thus, capital as a whole consists of both production and circulation.

Throughout this exposition, Hegel's SL has played an explicit role. Marx viewed Hegel's presentation of the logic of essence as an adequate conceptual schema in which to lay bare the nature of capitalist production. As a consequence, Marx was able to perceive aspects of capital never before seen in the economic data.

For Hegel, the logic of essence entails a progressive movement from the abstract to the concrete. This movement entails a series of dyadic relations between specific categories. Within each stage of the series, the two correlated categories are shown to be aspects of a single, more concrete whole. The entire series is superseded, when the exposition of essence becomes actuality. Actuality is further developed as a self-causing unity of inseparable moments, which has, in fact, been present from the outset of the exposition. Through the categories employed in being, we saw the immediate forms of existence of this organic whole, but the foundation of the relations between the categories remained implicit. In essence, the nature of this underlying reality is developed. The foundation of the relation between categories is therefore posited or set out. In the final stages of the development of essence, we see that the underlying reality of the entire development is itself a unity of being and essence.

This unity of being and essence, or the concept, is fully explicated within the remaining chapters of the SL. The concept has been immanent within the entire development as the foundation of the many categories of the two preceding parts and the organizing principle of the whole. But now in this third part, its development becomes the focus of the exposition. The precise nature of the development of the concept differs essentially from the exposition of being and essence. In being, the categories had merely passed over into each other. Because the whole was merely implicit, the transition of one category into the next had characterized their precise ordering. In essence, being is set out as what it essentially is, and each category is reflected in the next.

The nature of the development of the categories in the concept is not a transition or a reflection. The development of the categories is a function of making explicit what is implicit, an explication of what had been merely immanent. Whereas in being and essence the principle of the whole is merely immanent, in the concept the whole itself is developed. Each category, therefore, represents the whole of the organic unity, viewed from a certain perspective. Each is therefore both the whole of the system and a specific moment of it.

The general motif continues to be a movement from the abstract to the concrete. Thus, while it is the case that each category is the whole of the system from a certain point of view, the relation between categories continues necessarily as one from the abstract to the concrete. The precise positioning of each category is therefore a function of its relation to the others as determined by the whole of the concrete, organic unity.

To give an example of this rather complex relation of categories, we may use Hegel's presentation of the relation among universality, particularity, and individuality. Hegel states that universality is the whole of the concept itself as well as one moment within it. The concept is thus defined as universal, because it is the organizing principle of the whole. But universality is also merely one of its constitutive moments. Universality is the most abstract moment that characterizes the whole, and it differentiates itself into particular moments. The particular moments are the universal in a more concrete determination. Each particular moment is the universal, and therefore the whole, but each is also a particular aspect or moment of the whole. Each moment thus manifests the whole as self-differentiating. Since each particular moment contains within itself the universal, it is likewise a self-identity, or an individual. Individuality is both a concretization of the universal and a specific characteristic of the organic system.

In what follows we shall see that Marx remains logically consistent and continues to employ the SL in his exposition of the nature of capital in general. Once capital is exposed as a self-causing unity, however, the logic of the development differs essentially from the exposition of monetary circulation and the essence of capitalist production. The relation between economic categories will not be a function of transition or reflection. Rather, the relation between economic categories in the exposition of capital as a self-causing unity will simply explicate what before was implicit.

When capital is described as a self-causing unity the whole of capital has emerged, and the organic development of capital is complete. The exposition will no longer center on the "becoming" of capital, but on capital as it "proceeds from itself." Each economic category will manifest the whole of capital from a certain perspective. Each economic category is the whole of the system, and a particular moment of it. As with Hegel's SL, the overall progression of the categories continues to be a movement from the abstract to the concrete, although each economic category is the whole of capital from a particular point of view. The ordering of the categories is therefore a function of their relation to each other, as determined by the concrete, organic system of capital.

Thus, we shall see that capital is a universal. It is the organizing principle of the whole as a concrete, organic unity. As Marx specified in the "Introduction," capital determines the relative importance of its own moments. Universality will also be a particular moment of capital as organic unity. Capital as "circulating capital" differentiates itself into particular moments. It must proceed to this "particularization" of itself. Each particular moment is a specific characteristic of circulating capital; each is a concrete determination of it. The particular moments are the whole of capital, when viewed from a certain perspective. Each is the totality, and, at the same time, a particular moment of the totality. Because each particular moment contains within itself the determination of capital, it is an individual stage in the entire process. It exists in space and time as an individual moment of circulating capital.

The third part of the *Grundrisse* is divided into two specific stages in the development of the exposition of the *begriff* of capital. The first stage is an exposition of capital as a unity of "form-determinations." It is a logical exposition of the movement of circulating capital per se. This part of the exposition presents the moments that capital preposits and passes through for its maintenance and growth. The second stage describes the process of the "objectification" of the productive forces of capital. It presupposes the logical exposition of the nature of circulating capital and shows how capital attains to its "material presence" in this self-movement.

In presenting capital as a self-causing unity, the exposition of capital's "becoming" is complete. All the conditions for its realization are now posited by it. Marx states:

> These presuppositions, which originally appeared as conditions of its becoming—and hence could not spring from its action as capital—now appear as results of its own realization, reality, as posited by it—not as conditions of its arising, but as results of its presence.[1]

Thus, whereas what had come before in the exposition of capital had concerned the process of its "becoming," the exposition now focuses on capital as it has become.

The exposition of the "form-determinations" of capital—capital as it "proceeds from itself"—entails three phases. In the first phase, Marx considers the moments contained in the concept of "circulating capital." He presents capital as a differentiated whole, comprised of its own particular moments. Capital is the organizing principle. It therefore determines the nature of each moment and their relation to each other.

The exposition of capital as an organic system, as a "totality," cannot be presented all at once, as it were. Rather, in the second phase each moment of the entire process is carefully examined in its own right and in relation to the other moments. In this exposition of the "divisions," "partitions," or "differences" within capital, Marx reintroduces the elements that had been presented as conditions of capital's "becoming." Only this time, these elements are examined from the perspective of capital as it has become. Once Marx has explicated the nature of the individual moments of the process, in the third and final phase he demonstrates that circulating capital is essentially a "series of mediations." Each moment is described as "the possibility of going over into its other, next phase, and is thus the possibility of the whole process."

In his organization of the text, Marx is indebted to the first section of the third part of the SL, entitled "The Subjective Concept." In this section, Hegel presents the concept of the concept and shows it to be a differentiated whole that is comprised of its own particular moments. The concept is an organic system that determines the nature of each of its moments as well as their relation to each other. Each is therefore shown to be a phase within the entire development of the system.

In the second chapter of the first part, entitled "The Judgement," Hegel details the various moments that are entailed in the self-differentiating whole. In the "partition" of, or the "divisions" within, the concept, categories that had been incorporated in the analysis of the concept's "becoming" reappear at a higher level. They have been preserved, yet transformed, as moments in the development of the concept. What had been indifferent, self-subsistent moments of the concept are now seen as different moments in a "series of mediations." The judgement gives way to the syllogism.

Hegel contends that the syllogism is the concept set out as a unity of its different moments. Because the syllogism is the completed concept, the concept is rational. Hegel states: "Everything is a syllogism, a universal that through particularity is united with individuality (SL 669)." The importance of this statement for Hegel cannot be overemphasized. Everything that is complete in its nature is a totality and, therefore, a unity of determinate concepts; that is, a totality is rational, and as such forms a syllogism of its determinate concepts. Conversely, when reason grasps its object, it "rises above the finite, conditioned, sensuous," and grasps its object as a unity of determinate extremes. Thus, reason is able to grasp and penetrate the very nature of the unconditioned, or the "thing-in-itself," precisely because, as the "thing-in-itself" is a unity of determinate concepts, so too does reason grasp its object. In effect, the object forms a series of syllogisms within itself, and reason grasps it as such. Reason is therefore able to come to know the object as it exists in itself.

Anyone who follows Hegel cannot ignore this basic tenet. Everything that is real, everything that is completely actual, everything that has attained to its concept, is rational. It is therefore a series of syllogisms. In addition, one who wishes to comprehend a systematic, organic unity along the lines laid down by Hegel must recognize this fact, and seek to grasp the subject matter as rational.

This most important element in Hegel's scientific method was by no means lost to Marx. Marx conceived of capital as a systematic, organic unity; he saw it as rational. He therefore sought to articulate its inner structure as such, that is, as rational. Each individual phase or moment in the "metamorphosis" of capital, serves as the "middle term," or mediates between other phases or moments, and is itself mediated by these other phases when they serve as "middle terms" in the self-movement of capital. The dialectical exposition of capital articulates capital as a "series of mediations" or syllogisms, which combine to form the whole.

1. CAPITAL AS A UNITY OF FORM-DETERMINATIONS: THE CONCEPT OF CAPITAL IN GENERAL

With the production of surplus capital II, capital stands in a position to posit its own conditions for its realization. Marx states: ". . . as soon as capital has become capital as such, it creates its own presuppositions, i.e., the possession of the real conditions of the creation of new values without exchange—by means of its own production process" (. . . *so bald das Kapital als solches geworden ist, schafft es seine eignen Voraussetzungen, nämlich den Besitz der realen Bedingungen für Schopfung von Neuwerten ohne Austausch—durch seinen eignen Produktionsprozeß*) (N 460, MEW 372).

These conditions entail that the power of an active subject, the capitalist, posits the negation of itself in the form of living labor. Living labor, as a condition of the activity of the capitalist, assumes the determinations posited within it by capital's act of violence, and becomes the "alien being" of "alien labor." In this alienated state, it becomes a cause of, or produces surplus capital. As a result, the process may be started again and again. In short, capital has become the cause of itself.

All the conditions necessary for its maintenance and growth have now been posited by capital (N 463-64, MEW 376-77). The true nature of capital thus emerges only at the end of the second cycle, with the realization of surplus capital II (N 514, MEW 421). Capital is now a "simple unity," which differentiates itself from itself in order to posit itself anew. Marx states: "The circulation of capital constantly ignites itself anew, divides into its different moments, and is a *perpetuum mobile*" (*Die Zirkulation des Kapitals entzündet sich an sich selbst stets von neuem, dirimiert sich in ihre verschiednen Momente und ist ein perpetuum mobile*) (N 516, MEW 423).

Money as money began at an "infinite number of points and returned to an infinite number of points" (*unendlich vielen Punkten aus und kehrte an unendlich vielen Punkten zurück*) (N 516, MEW 423). Money realized in simple circulation "vanishes in its other," in its exchange for the commodity. As the "vanishing of the one into the other," simple circulation was "beyond production" (N 514, MEW 421). Likewise, production appeared as "over and against" circulation. Circulation was an external limitation to the "actualization" of the product insofar as it had not yet been the circulation of capital. At the end of the second cycle, however, capital is a "simple unity" of production and circulation. Marx states:

> Production originally appeared to lie beyond circulation, and circulation beyond production. The circulation of capital—circulation posited as the circulation of capital—embraces both moments. Production appears in it as the conclusion and the point of departure of circulation, and visa versa. The

> independence of circulation is here reduced to a mere semblance, as is the otherworldliness of production.[2]

Capital is a simple identity, which posits or divides into these different moments of itself. Capital "embraces" (*in sich fasst*) its moments within its "simple unity." Marx states: "It (capital) becomes qualitatively altered in circulation and the totality of the moments of its circulation are themselves the moments of its production—its reproduction as well as its new production" (*Es ändert sich qualitativ in dem Umlauf, und die Totalität der Momente seines Umlaufs sind selbst die Momente seiner Produktion—seiner Reproduktion sowohl wie seiner Neuproduktion*) (N 516 MEW 423). Simple circulation is no longer "over and against" capital, and production is no longer external to circulation. Rather, we have the circulation of capital, which is a totality of moments that entail the mediation of capital with itself through its negation, or living labor.

Hegel's exposition of essence provided Marx with the conceptual tools that enabled him to present the presuppositions of a capitalist system of production. Capital is now conceived of as a self-causing system. Hegel also provided Marx with the conceptual tools for his exposition of capital as a self-causing system. This initial formulation of the general concept of capital is clearly indebted to Hegel's consideration of the concept of the concept. The causal relation between active and passive substance attains to what Hegel calls "the concept itself": substance as "absolute power" differentiated into a relation, which entails two simple moments (SL 578, STWII 246). The one—the active substance—had posited or caused its effect in a passive substance as its negation. The passive substance is the condition of the movement of substance. The active substance becomes itself only in relation to what is powerless. Its movement consists in positing its other, and thereby relating itself to itself through this other. The relation itself is determined as a self-related negativity.

The passive substance assumes the determinations posited in it by the cause. It becomes a cause or acquires the power to act, then reacts on passive substance, and begins the process anew. The whole process is "bent round and becomes an action that returns into itself, an infinite reciprocal action" (*umgebogen und zu einem in sich zurückkehrenden, einem unendlichen Wechselwirken wird)* (SL 569, STWII 237). This infinite return-into-itself is the supersession of substance and the emergence of the concept.

Hegel characterized being as a mere "passing over into another." With the transition into essence, being was illusory being. With the development of essence, essence was "over and against" being (SL 596, STWII 269). Essence was the negation of mere being, because it entailed the positing of negation, or mediation. The concept is the unity of being and essence, or being-in-and-for-itself. It is being that entails "the infinite mediation and negativity of being within itself" *(die unendlich Vermittlung und Negativität desselben in sich selbst)* (SL 596, STWII 269). Hegel initially describes the concept as a "simple identity," a unity that contains self-differentiations within itself (SL 577, STWII 245). This unity "embraces" (*in sich fasst*) its differences within its "simple identity" (SL 600, STWII 274).

In the concept of the concept, Hegel provides an outline of being-in-and-for-itself. Being-in-and-for-itself is immediately a positedness that contains self-differentiations or determinatenesses within itself. Yet it is nevertheless absolutely self-related in its differentiations as immediately a "simple identity" (*einfache Identität*) (SL 582, STWII 251-52).[3] Hegel demonstrates that the infinite self-return of the concept entails differentiations within a simple unity (SL 596, STWII 269). Insofar as this "simple unity" contains or "embraces" its own differentiations, it is "filled with content" (*inhaltsvolle*) (SL 601, STWII 274). The differentiations are qualitatively distinct moments of itself. This simple unity is the universal to its moments, which are its particularity.

Marx contends that with the emergence of capital as a "simple unity," the simple circulation of commodity and money gives way to the "content-filled" (*inhaltsvolle*) circulation of capital (N 517, 521, MEW 424, 428). Circulating capital is "pregnant with content" (N 517, 521, MEW 424, 428). It is now a totality that contains within itself qualitatively distinct moments or "particularizations" of itself (N 517, 520, MEW 424, 427). Circulating capital is a process of mediation, whose moments are nothing other than capital in a determinate form (N 514, MEW 421).

In considering the circulation of capital, and its qualitatively different moments, Marx maintains that the "great differentiation within it" is between the production process and circulation, "both as moments of its circulation."[4] These two great moments are themselves considered totalities.[5] Capital is a totality of moments, each of which is a totality. In our investigation into the nature of the "simple unity" of circulating capital, Marx tells us that "we can take circulation or production as the point of departure" (*Wir können dabei ausgehn von der Zirkulation oder von der Production*) (N 520, MEW 427). When we begin with production, or when we take production as the totality, circulation must be taken as one of its moments. Likewise, production will appear as a moment of circulation, when circulation is regarded as the totality of the production process.

Marx also claims that capital must proceed to these specifications. Production and circulation are two particular moments in the process of circulation; each appears in a "duality" (*Zweiheit*) (N 520, MEW 427). On one hand, each is a particular moment of circulating capital; on the other, each must be considered in relation to the other because each is a particular moment of capital.[6]

This mode of presentation clearly echoes Hegel's description of universality in its particularity. The pure concept is described as an utterly simple determination (SL 601, STWII 274). It is, however, a determination that contains qualitatively distinct moments as its content: the concept is "pregnant with content." These moments are posited in the infinite self-return of the concept. The pure relation of the concept to itself is the universality of the concept, as an infinite positing of itself through negation (SL 601, STWII 274). It is therefore a simple relation to itself within itself, and it contains absolute mediation, though it is not mediated (SL 601, STWII 274).

The concept is, then, a universal as a simple unity, or a content consisting of qualitatively distinct moments.[7] The determinateness or the content of the universal is particularity. The latter is the necessary determination of the universal in its infinite self-movement. Because particularity is a necessary determination of the universal, it too is a totality. That is, since particularity contains universality within itself, it must be seen as a totality (SL 605-6, STWII 280-81). Thus, the universal is a totality of moments, and each moment is, in turn, a totality.

As the universal thus particularizes itself, particularity appears in a "dual form." As the determination of the universal, or its difference, the particular contains a necessary relation to the universal in its "reflection-into-self." Insofar as it is this difference, it contains a "reference outward, the reflection-into-other" (*nach außen, die Reflexion-in-sich*) (SL 604, STWII 278). Its reference outward entails that particularity is distinguished from an other, while its reference into self entails that the particular is in-itself the universal. Each particular is therefore coordinated with the other, since each is a moment of the universal. Insofar as particularity is determined by universality, it assumes universality's characteristics. It is therefore a simple determination, which is also a self-related determinateness. At the same time, because particularity is thus self-related or a determinate determinateness, it is also individuality (SL 612, STWII 288).

Individuality is said to be differentiation as such, in which the universal becomes "external to itself" (*außer sich)* and thereby enters into actuality. In individuality, the different moments of universality become fixed (SL 621, STWII 299). Further, the individual is described as a "qualitative one or a this" (*qualitative Eins oder Dieses*) (SL 621, STWII 300). As such it is to be distinguished from an other, which is equally qualitatively determined. Yet, insofar as they are determined by the universal, their exclusive relation, each to the other, is nevertheless an essential one.

Once Marx had discussed the "great differentiation" within capital, and shown how each "particularization" must be conceived of in a "duality," he considers the spatial and temporal moments of each process (N 518-533, MEW 424-38). Though circulating capital is a unity of qualitatively distinct moments, each moment is fixed in space and time (N 521, MEW 428). Marx examines the spatial and temporal aspects of each moment as determinants of the circulation of capital.

The temporal moment, or the length of time capital remains within the production process, is a function of technological conditions. The time that capital spends in the production phase is dependent on the development of the productive forces. Other factors will enter later, but the time capital spends in the production process depends on the labor time necessary for making the product. The spatial moment is a function of the time from the completed transformation of capital into the product, until it becomes transformed into money (N 518, MEW 426). Marx suggests that the frequency with which capital can repeat the production process, or the process of "self-realization," in a given amount of time, is a function of the speed with which this space of time may be run through (N 518, MEW 426).

Because the qualitative moments of production and circulation are separated in space and time, Marx considers them "individual, mutually indifferent processes" (*besondre, gegeneinander gleichgültige Prozesse*) (N 535, MEW 441). Nevertheless, their relation to each other is a function of their relation to circulating capital.

2. THE DIVISIONS IN CIRCULATING CAPITAL

Capital is a self-differentiating system. It must proceed to qualitatively distinct "particularizations" of itself in its self-realization. These "individual, mutually indifferent processes" are also inseparable from one another, because they are coordinated in their relation to circulating capital. The process of capital's self-differentiation must, however, be examined in detail. Recall that the many phases through which capital passes in its "becoming" have not been annihilated, but are in fact superseded in its unity. They must therefore be reexamined, not as they had been, but as they are now, as moments of circulating capital.

Marx's concern at this point is not directly with the production process. He made clear its role in the actualization process of circulating capital in the previous exposition. Rather, he is concerned to determine whether any moments other than living labor capacity are productive of capital. He therefore focuses on the transformation of the product into a commodity, the transformation of the commodity into capital as money, and finally the transformation of capital as money into the conditions of production.

At this point, Marx characterizes this "process of transformation" (*Verwandlungsprozeß*) as a "qualitative process of value" (*qualitativer Prozeß des Werts*). He states:

> Circulation as we regard it here is a process of transformation, a qualitative process of value, as it appears in the different form of money, production (actualization process), product, retransformation into money and surplus value . . . in this transition from one form to another" (*Die Zirkulation, wie wir sie betrachten, ist Verwandlungsprozeß, qualitativer Prozeß des Werts, wie er in der verschiednen Form von Geld, Produktionsprozeß, Produkt, Rückverwandlungsprozesses in Geld und Surpluskapital erscheint . . . in diesem Übergehn aus einer Bestimmung in die andre neue Bestimmungen sich erzeugen*) (N 524, MEW 430).

Moreover, each of these determinate, qualitatively different forms are a "division" (*Teilung*), a "partition," or a "difference" (*Unterschied*) within capital, the subject of the whole movement (N 521, 535-36, 539, 620, 661). Rather than stages through which capital must pass in its becoming, these forms are now "moments of its metamorphosis" or development (N 536). They are separated in space and time, and appear as "individual, mutually indifferent processes" (N 535). Insofar as the individual moments stand, at least initially, over against each other, Marx maintains that value must undergo a "series of mediations," in order to again arrive at the beginning of the production process as its condition (N 332, 535-36, 626, 637, 647, 667).

Marx's exposition of this "simple unity" begins at the beginning with the "immediate product," but with this difference. Each of the many phases through which capital has passed, are now taken as determinate, qualitatively distinct forms of capital itself. They are not examined as stages through which capital must pass in its becoming, but as phases in its metamorphosis.

This procedure reflects precisely Hegel's exposition of the development of the concept as a self-differentiating system. In "The Concept of the Concept," the concept is a simple unity that posits within itself qualitatively distinct moments. These moments were developed as individual, mutually indifferent moments that are nevertheless inseparable from each other. Yet this development is merely the presentation of the concept of the concept. It is by no means the fully articulated and organized system. Its differentiations must now be spelled out in articulated detail.

The emergence of this "simple unity" does not annihilate the many phases of being and essence. Rather, they are each superseded in its unity. Hegel tells us that we must now retrace the many phases through which the concept had passed in its "becoming," only this time, we do so from the perspective of the realized concept. In it, all the many categories that comprise the sections of being and essence reappear, but at a higher level of exposition. They are now considered determinate, qualitatively different forms of the concept itself (SL 624, STWII 302-3). They are therefore "divisions" (*Teilung*), "partitions," or "differences" (*Unterschied*) within the concept, as the subject of the entire development (SL 627-30, STWII 306-10).

In the exposition of individuality, the concept appear as "external to itself" (SL 627-30, STWII 306-10). Its various moments have become fixed, and it has become actual. As these moments now stand indifferently over and against each other, the concept has posited within itself a "division" between them. "The judgement" is the "determinate being or otherness of the concept which had not yet restored itself to the unity whereby it is as concept" (*das Dasein oder das Anderssein des Begriff, welcher sich noch nicht zu der Einheit*) (SL 627 STWII 306). Thus, while it is the case that the concept is a system of interrelated moments, it is first only a relation of self-subsistent moments that are indifferent to one another. Hegel must demonstrate how the integration of these moments will produce the unity that is the system. This demonstration examines the transformation of the concept in its "immediate being" or original partition to its self-mediated universality. Hegel therefore begins his exposition of the concept at the beginning, that is, with an "immediate being," which is at first merely over and against an abstract or undetermined universal.

Marx likewise begins his reexamination of the concept of capital at a higher level with an "immediate being." In the exposition of circulating capital, capital initially appears as "individual, mutually indifferent processes." Marx must therefore show how these indifferent moments are related as "moments of the metamorphosis" of capital. Marx begins his exposition of the development with the "immediate product" (*unmittelbar Produkt*), which is a qualitatively determined use-value (N533-4, MEW 440). It is not immediately capital, or, it is capital in an as yet unrealized form. In fact, capital in its money form stands indifferently over and against this particular, qualitatively determined use-value (N 534, MEW 440). Money merely picks out one characteristic of the product, namely, that the product is a particular embodiment of labor time. Insofar at it is a use-value with many different qualities—it is a material being subject to the laws of decomposition, etc.—it may never actually be exchanged for money (N 534-35, MEW 440-41).

The logical form of this exposition is indebted to Hegel's analysis of the qualitative judgment of existence. The "immediate being" initially stands opposed to an abstract universal. It is a mere qualitatively determined, immediate being (SL 631, STWII 311). Likewise, the universal is at first merely an abstract determination of the subject. It is one aspect or characteristic that inheres in the subject to the exclusion of others. The subject is the "something of many qualities," or, the "thing of manifold properties" (SL 634-35, STWII 315-16). The predicate is merely one of its properties. The subject and predicate are not therefore immediately related.

The final result of the first form of the judgment, however, is that both the individual and the universal are no longer taken in an abstract or immediate sense. In the judgment of existence, the content of the judgment had been the immediate, or abstract, indeterminateness of both subject and predicate. In the judgment of reflection, also termed the judgment of quantity, subject and predicate are related in an essential determination (SL 643-44, STWII 326-27). The individual now contains in-itself the essential determination expressed by the universal, under which it is subsumed (SL 644-45, STWII 327-28). In the quantitative judgment of reflection, many individuals will be united in an essential determinateness.

Marx's examination of the second moment of the metamorphosis of capital reflects this logical progression of quality to quantity. The second moment or phase in the exposition recalls the development of the transformation of the product into a commodity. The product is quantitatively determined as a commodity. Insofar as it is also a particular embodiment of labor time, it may be equated with other particular embodiments of labor time. Marx states that the product is not really complete until it is on the market, until its price is posited (N 533-34, MEW 440). When it is on the market, or when it is transformed into a commodity, it is now quantitatively determined. It thus possesses a property that makes it equal to all other commodities (N 534, 631). Insofar as its price has been posited, the commodity may be said to equal a specific amount of money. Each commodity is related to the other through money. It is as yet, however, merely in-itself capital as money. It must be realized as such.

In so ordering his presentation, Marx remains logically consistent to Hegel's treatment of the judgment. We see in the universal judgment, that the particular individual has become an individual that directly attains universality (SL 647-50, STWII 331). In this form of the judgment, a property that belongs to all individuals unites them. The subject of the universal judgment expresses the individual as a genus (SL 648, STWII 332). Thus the subject has been raised to universality, and is as a result equated with the predicate. Likewise, the predicate is completely determined within itself, such that it now contains this individuality. Nevertheless, the subject merely contains that predicate in-itself in a still undetermined manner. The predicate expresses its "inner nature" (*innere Natur*) (SL 650, STWII 334).

In the judgment of necessity, the subject and predicate are in substantial identity. As Hegel states, in this form of the judgment, the copula that joins the subject and predicate has the meaning of necessity. The subject is completely determined by the universal, and conversely, the universal is in an essential relation with itself as this individual (SL 651-52, STWII 335-36). In this sense, then, the individual is not only a concrete individual, but also "the being of another" (SL 652). Each concrete individual is equated with, or related to, the other through this third, or the universal.

In a logical progression of economic categories, Marx's exposition of the commodity at this juncture recalls the exposition of the relation between the commodity and money. As money was separated from the commodity, and now represents exchange value, so the commodity must now be related to money. This relation is expressed as the price of the commodity (N 533-34, MEW 440). When the commodity attains a price—is on the market—it is now actually identified with a certain sum of money. Moreover, through price in its relation to money, the commodity is equated with, or related to, all other commodities.

Marx reiterates, however, a limiting condition of money circulation, and of production based on capital. While it is the case that the price of the commodity has been posited, and therefore, the product has been transformed into a commodity, it may nevertheless fail to be realized in a money form (N 535, MEW 441). It is in some sense a "matter of chance" or problematic whether the commodity will actually be exchanged for money. That it ought to be is one thing. Something may occur, however, that makes it impossible to exchange one commodity for another through the medium of money, for example, a monetary crisis, poor quality of the material, or a lack of demand may result in a "pure loss." Nevertheless, the development of the "metamorphosis" of capital presupposes that this phase is superseded, and it is assumed that the commodity is indeed salable, and hence exchanged for money (N 535-6, MEW 441-42).

In Hegel's "Judgement of the Concept," the relation between the subject (the concrete individual in general) and the predicate is a relation between the individual and its constitution. The individual ought to be what the predicate expresses. Yet because it is a particular or an immediate individual, it is not itself a universal. Though it is of a certain constitution, it equally falls short of what it is supposed to be. In the "Assertoric Judgement," it is at least problematic whether the subject will meet the criteria given in its essential nature. Finally, in the "Apodectic Judgement," Hegel shows that the subject realizes its essential nature, only when it is a unity of its immediate determinations and universality.

The most important result of this development is that, while the individual attains to universality, universality is also particularized in the form of the immediate individual. Thus, the universal now permeates both the subject and predicate. The two possess the same content, but more important, they are determined by the same form relation. This relation is itself the extremes of subject and predicate. Subject and predicate have therefore become form determinations of the universal. The universal is thus expressed by the "filled copula" of the judgment. It is the "copula filled with content," because it is now the concept itself which emerges from the "original partition" of judgment (SL 663, STWII 351).

Marx's consideration of the relation between commodity and money, once the former has been realized in the latter, reflects the logical form of this development. The relation between the two is no longer a mere "vanishing of the one into the other" (N 535-36, MEW 441-2). In simple circulation, money was transformed into the commodity, and consumption completed the process. The presuppositions of money circulation had been outside it, and it constantly required the introduction of commodities from the outside to begin the process of C-M-M-C anew. Marx states:

> Money became transformed into commodity through circulation, and in the exchange of M-C, consumption completed the process; or, the commodity was exchanged for money—and in the exchange C-M, M was either a vanishing moment itself to be exchanged for C again, in which case the process ended with consumption again, or the money withdrew from circulation and transformed itself into dead treasure, merely symbolic wealth. At no point did the process ignite from within, but rather the presuppositions of money circulation lay outside it, and it constantly required a new push from the outside. Insofar as both moments were exchanged, their change of form within circulation was merely formal. But insofar as content entered in, it dropped out of the economic process; content did not form a part of it. The commodity did not sustain itself as money, nor money as commodity; each was either one or the other.[8]

Now, however, the commodity and money are united, insofar as both are moments of circulating capital. Value is the content, which is at one time commodity, then money and vice versa; or, value is the form of the relation between the moments. In short, commodity and money are the form determinations of circulating capital. Marx states:

> Capital is now posited, however, as not merely sustaining itself formally, but as realizing itself as value, as value relating to itself as value in every one of the moments of its metamorphosis, in which it appears at one time as money, at another time as commodity, then again as exchange value, then again as use value. The passage from one moment to the other appears as a particular process, but each of these processes is the transition to the other. Capital is thus posited as value-in-process which is capital in every moment. It is thus

> posited as circulating capital; in every moment capital, and circulating from one form into the next.[9]

The relation between money and commodity, Marx states, is a relation "filled with content."

3. CIRCULATING CAPITAL AS A SERIES OF MEDIATIONS

Once Marx has isolated the different "moments of the metamorphosis," he considers the relation between these different moments from the vantage point of circulating capital. Circulating capital is articulated as a systematic unity of different moments. It is evident from Marx's exposition that he agrees with Hegel that the real—which for him is circulating capital—is rational. Because it is rational, it must be explicated as a system of progressively more determinate mediations.

Marx tells us that within the context set by capital the relation between money and commodity is "filled with content." For Hegel, too, the relation between the subject and predicate is "filled with content," when the immediate individual attains its essential determinations. Universality now permeates both subject and predicate, with the result that the different moments of the concept are related to each other through a series of mediations. It is no longer the case that the indifferent, self-subsistent moments of the concept are separated into the extremes of the judgment. Rather, as Hegel states: "Through this impregnation of the copula the judgement has become the syllogism" (SL 663, STWII 351).

Marx first explains circulating capital as a series of mediations that involve the product, the commodity, and money. Circulating capital is a series within which each moment is both an "extreme" and a "middle term." The moments are now "filled with content" precisely because each mediates the other, in a continual process of the transformation of value from the "immediate product" to the conditions for the renewal of the production process (N 521, 535, MEW 427, 442).[10] The product is brought to the market and thereby becomes a commodity. Insofar as it has attained to this form, it can be exchanged for money. The product, through its transformation into a commodity, is mediated by, or attains to the form of, money (N 536-37, 634-37, MEW 443-44, 534-537). Marx states: "The product relates to the commodity as a use value to exchange value, thus the commodity to money. Here one series attains its peak" (*Das Produkt verhält sich zur Ware wie Gebrauchswert zum Tauschwert; so die Ware zum Geld. Hier erreicht die eine Reihe ihre Höhe*) (N 637, MEW 537). Likewise, it is only insofar as the commodity is a particular use value—fulfills some purpose, is in demand—that it may be transformed into money. The commodity, by being a particular use value, is mediated by, or attains to the form of, money (N 535, 637, MEW 442, 537). Finally, when the product is equated with money in its determination of price, it becomes a commodity. Thus, the product, by having been equated with a certain amount of money, becomes a commodity.

Marx also presents the entire series of mediations as a relation of exchange value to use value. Marx states:

> In the circulation of capital we have a series of exchange operations, acts of exchange, each of which represents a qualitatively different moment towards the other, a moment in the reproduction and growth of capital. A system of exchanges, changes of substance, from the standpoint of value as such. Changes of form, from the standpoint of use value. The product relates to the commodity as use value to exchange value, thus the commodity to money. Here one series attains its peak. Money relates to the commodity into which it is retransformed as exchange value to use value, even more so, money to labor.[11]

In money circulation, a mere formal alteration of exchange value occurs, first as money, then as commodity. Both money and the commodity simply vanish, one into the other (N 535-36, MEW 442-43). Money is exchanged for the commodity, and the commodity falls outside circulation, only to be consumed. Simple circulation "consisted of a great number of simultaneous or successive exchanges. Their unity, regarded as circulation, was actually present only from the observer's standpoint" (*Die einfache Zirkulation bestand aus einer Menge gleichzeitiger oder sukzessiver Austausche. Die Einheit derselben als Zirkulation betrachtet, war eigentlich nur vom Standpunkt des Beobachters aus vorhanden*) (N 637, MEW 537).

This transformation of the product into money, and vice versa, now appears as an essential process of capital. The constant continuity of the process from one moment to the next, from one form of value to the next, is therefore given. As Marx states: "The passage from one moment to the other appears as a particular process, but each of these processes is the transition into the other" (*Das Übergehn aus einem Moment in das andre erscheint als besonder Prozeß, aber jeder dieser Prozesse ist das Übergehn in den andren*) (N 536, MEW 442). Each moment, or each form, is in-itself "the possibility of going over into its other, next phase, and is thus the possibility of the whole process." Marx states:

> Insofar as capital in every moment of the process is itself the possibility of going over into its other, next phase, and is thus the possibility of the whole process, which expresses capital's act of life, to that extent each of the moments appears potentially as capital—hence commodity capital, money capital—along with the value positing itself in the production process as capital.[12]

This passage exemplifies Marx's indebtedness to Hegel's presentation of the concept as a "series of mediations." Marx's exposition of the continuity of the process does not, however, represent a general indebtedness to Hegel's exposition of "The Syllogism," but a particular indebtedness to Hegel's exposition of the syllogism of existence, the formal syllogism.

Hegel maintains that in the syllogism, the concept is restored or posited as the unity of its different moments. He states: "Everything is a syllogism, a universal that through particularity is mediated with individuality . . ." (SL 669, STWII 358). Hegel initially presents the concept as a series of mediations, which become progressively more concrete or determinate as the exposition develops. He presents each of the different moments of the concept as an "extreme" and as a "middle term," such that each mediates the other in the unity of the concept.

Hegel begins his exposition of the concept with an "immediate form" of mediation. Here the determinations of the mediation are simple or abstract determinatenesses. In the syllogism of existence, an immediate individual is united with universality through particularity (SL 667-68, STWII 355-56). Yet, since particularity unites individuality and universality in an immediate manner, this mediation between individuality and universality presupposes another mediation. Another mediation must show that the individual unites particularity and universality within itself to account for the fact that particularity mediates universality. Finally, to demonstrate that individuality and particularity are in fact united, it must be shown that universality mediates between the two. The syllogism of existence is therefore presented as a series of syllogisms, wherein each of the moments is presented as middle term, and therefore each is taken as actually uniting within itself the other moments (SL 678-81, STWII 370-74).

The concrete determinations of the syllogism of existence can exist only insofar as each moment maintains this circle. Hegel thereby demonstrates that each of the three moments of the concept presupposes a relation to the other; each mediates between the other two. No one series can exist without the others. Each of the mediations is a continual process of "going over into the other or into its presuppositions" (SL 680-81, STWII 373-74). Each series is, therefore, only insofar as it contains within itself the possibility of "going over into its presupposition." Each is the "positive reflection of one into the other."

Individuality, particularity, and universality are no longer abstract. Rather, each possesses within itself the full determinations of the other two forms. The individual must now be taken not as an immediate individual, but as a universal. The immediate series of mediations has therefore attained a more concrete, a more determinate form. Each moment is an element in a concrete system of interrelated and interpenetrating moments. In the syllogism of reflection and in the first syllogism of necessity, the categorical syllogism, Hegel proves that the concept is a self-mediating system that contains within itself only moments that are posited by it in its self-movement (SL 686-98, STWII 380-95). Each moment is shown to be a mere phase through which the concept must pass in its development.

The process of mediation that constitutes circulating capital likewise attains a more determinate form with the advance of Marx's exposition. The series of mediations among the product, the commodity and money is a continual process of the constant transition of one moment into the next. Money and commodity circulation is no longer a simple or abstract process. It is one "filled with content." Thus, when viewed from the vantage point of circulating capital, the entire series achieves a more concrete, determinate form. The product is not merely the product, but production in general. The commodity is not merely the commodity, but circulation. Finally, money is now capital as money.

The various phases through which capital passed in its "becoming," began conceptually with the transformation of money into the conditions of production (N 619, MEW 519). Because we are now, however, dealing with capital as it has become, we begin with the creation of surplus value in the immediate production process, that is, with the product and its "higher price." Marx summarizes the entire "series of mediations" as follows:

> (1) Creation of surplus value, or immediate production process. Its result, the product. (2) Bringing the product to market. Transformation of product into commodity. (3) (a) Entry of the commodity into ordinary circulation. circulation of the commodity. Its result: transformation into money. This appears as the first moment of ordinary circulation. (B) Retransformation of money into the conditions of production: money circulation; in ordinary circulation, the circulation of commodities and the circulation of money always appear distributed among two different subjects. Capital circulates first as commodity, then as money, and vice versa. (4) Renewal of the production process, which appears here as reproduction of the original capital, and production process of capital.[13]

The series of mediations formed by monetary circulation now takes place within the context of the production of capital—capital as it has become. Production, circulation, and capital as money serve as "extremes" and as "middle terms" in the series.

The product of production based on capital, or production in general, becomes money or surplus capital in and through circulation (N 542-3, 619, 626, 647, 667-68). Circulation, then, mediates between production and capital in its money form (N 542-3, 619, 626, 647, 667-68). Likewise, circulation becomes the circulation of capital through production. Production based on capital mediates between circulation and capital in its money form.[14] Finally, just as circulation mediates between production and money or surplus capital, so too money mediates between production and circulating capital or the conditions of production. Thus, production through capital in its money form becomes the conditions for the production process that emerge from circulation.[15]

This latter moment, where money is exchanged for commodity, is of an entirely different nature than that which had obtained in simple circulation. Here the retransformation of money into commodity is at the same time the retransformation of capital into the material conditions of production. Marx states:

> To the extent that money figures here as medium of circulation, it does so indeed only as mediation of production, on one side with consumption, in the exchange where capital discharges value in the form of the product, and as mediation, on the other side, between production and production, where capital discharges itself in the form of money and draws the commodity in the form of the condition of production into its circulation.[16]

We can see here that, just as Hegel presents the concept as a series of mediations in a more concrete, determinate form in the advance from the syllogism of reflection to the first syllogism of necessity, the categorical syllogism; so too Marx continues his exposition by presenting circulating capital as a series of mediations in a more concrete, determinate form. Production, circulation, and capital as money serve as "extremes" and as "middle terms" in the continual process of circulating capital. Each is a moment in a concrete system of interrelated and interpenetrating moments. Marx thereby presents circulating capital as a self-mediating system, which contains within itself only moments that are posited by it in its self-development. Each moment is a phase in the metamorphosis of circulating capital.

4. CIRCULATING CAPITAL AS A UNITY OF ITS FORM-DETERMINATIONS

While capital must now be grasped as a self-mediating system, the connection among its various moments is by no means an immediate occurrence. The necessity of the continuity of circulating capital determines production and circulation, but they are as yet "particular, mutually indifferent processes" (N 535, 622). They may share an identical content, but they are nevertheless separated by space and time. Here Marx articulates the precise relation of circulation to production as a relation of condition to conditioned. Circulation appears as a determinant of production. Capital is therefore said to be "conditioned qualitatively," since it cannot renew the production phase without passing through the phases of circulation.[17] Thus, though circulation and production are "particular, mutually indifferent processes," they are nevertheless related, since circulation is the condition for the renewal of the production process.[18]

Circulation as a condition is presupposed as having been superseded (N 538-39, 542, 544-46, 619-20). The necessity of the continuity of the passage of circulating capital through its different phases is given. Circulation must therefore always be overcome as a barrier to the production process, and yet it is always posited anew as a condition.[19] It is only insofar as circulation—an "indifferent process"—contains within itself the determination of the universal or capital, that it is transformed into an activity or process that serves as condition to the actual production process (N 535, 622, MEW 449, 536). The production process in turn—an "indifferent process"—is mediated insofar as the circulation process conditions it. Through circulation, value becomes actual; or, the circulation of capital "actualizes value" (N 543). In this manner, though circulation and production share an identical content, they are always related to each other as condition to conditioned. They are always separated in space and time, and thus appear as "particular, mutually indifferent processes."

The logical progression from the exposition of capital as a series of mediations, or a unity in difference, to the exposition of the relation between its moments as a relation of condition to conditioned, follows precisely Hegel's treatment of "The Syllogism of Necessity." In the exposition of the categorical syllogism, Hegel demonstrates that the concept is a universal as a system of interrelated moments. He shows how each moment is a "form-determination" of the universal or the concept itself. Nevertheless, the relation between the moments is a connection that is not an immediate occurrence. Each of the moments is said to possess the universal only in-itself. They therefore must be seen as fixed, indifferent actualities (SL 698, STWII 394-95).

Hegel explains this relation as one that is predicated on the necessity of the concept. The moments share an identical content. They are nevertheless individual, mutually indifferent moments, precisely because they are determined by an immediacy of being (SL 699, STWII 395). Though they share an identical content, they are separated according to the "external diversity of Existence, or mutual indifference of being in the sphere of Appearance" (SL 699, STWII 395). The syllogism of necessity gives way to the hypothetical syllogism.

A relation between "individual, mutually indifferent moments" that share an identical content determined by the necessity of the universal, is a relation of condition to conditioned. The condition is a mediating being that is at once an "indifferent actuality." It is that which allows for the emergence of the conditioned into actuality. Because the condition contains within itself the universal or the concept, it is not an immediate being in the ordinary sense. Rather, it is a "self-superseding being" (*sich aufhebendes Sein*) (SL 700, STWII 397). It thus determines itself as an activity, and serves as the middle term that permits an inner necessity to become a real necessity. The conditioned thereby emerges as a mediated being, and the relation between the two moments, the condition and conditioned, is thus superseded.

With the supersession of the relation between the moments of condition and conditioned, the moments have an identical content, and exhibit an identical form-determination. In "The Disjunctive Syllogism," objective universality determines itself as a totality that is a unity of all form-determinations. It is an "identity that differentiates itself and gathers itself into itself out of the differences" (*unterscheidende und aus diesem Unterschiede sich in sich zusammennehmende*) (SL 701, STWII 398). It is the universal sphere that contains its total "particularizations" (*Besonderung*) (SL 701, STWII 398).

Marx structures his exposition in precisely the same way. He first presents circulating capital as a series of mediations, then the relation of circulation to production as one of condition to conditioned. After Marx proves that this relation must be superseded, he exposes circulating capital as a "unity-in-process"—a totality of the "two great sections of its movement, as a totality of these two processes" (N 546, 620, MEW 453, 520). Marx states:

> The total production process of capital includes both the circulation process proper and the actual production process. These form the two great sections of its movement, which appears as the totality of these two processes. On one side, labour time, on the other, circulation time. And the whole of the movement appears as unity of labour time and circulation time, as unity of production and circulation. This unity itself is motion, process. Capital appears as this unity-in-process of production and circulation, a unity which can be repeated both as the totality of the process of its production, as well as the specific completion of one turnover of the capital, one movement returning into itself.[20]

Circulating capital is the "subject" that predominates over the different phases of its movement. As subject of these metamorphoses, circulating capital proceeds in a spiral, an expanding circle, in a process of actualization (N 620, MEW 520).

Although Marx characterizes circulating capital at this point as a "unity-in-process," he simultaneously claims that circulating capital is posited in each phase as "in an individual determinateness" *(in einer Bestimmtheit)* (N

620, MEW 521). In which case, capital is "restricted to a particular form, which is the negation of itself as the subject of the whole movement" (*als in besondre Gestalt gebannt, die die Negation seiner als des Subjekts der ganzen Bewegung ist*) (N 620, MEW 521). Marx states:

> Therefore, capital in each of its particular phases is the negation of itself as the subject of all the various metamorphoses. Not-circulating capital. Fixed capital, actually fixated capital, fixated in one of the different particular determinatenesses, through which it must move. . . . As the subject moving through all phases, as the moving unity, the unity-in-process of circulation and production, capital is circulating capital; capital as restricted into any of these phases, as posited in its *differentiations*, capital is fixated capital, tied-down capital. As circulating it fixates itself, and as fixated capital it circulates. The differences of circulating capital and fixed capital thus appear initially as form-determinations of capital, depending on whether it appears as the unity of the process or as one of its determinate moments.[21]

The distinction between *circulating* and *fixed* capital is merely a "formal distinction" at this point in the exposition, depending on whether we focus on circulating capital as the unity of the process, or on one of its "specific moments" (N 621-622, MEW 521-522). Marx states:

> Much confusion in political economy has been caused by this, that the aspects of circulating and fixed are initially nothing more than capital itself posited in the two aspects, first as the unity of the process, then as a particular one of its phases, itself in distinction to itself as unity–not as two particular kinds of capital, not capital of two particular kinds, but rather as different *form-determinations* of the same capital.

One and the same capital always appears in both states. Marx emphasizes the importance of grasping these aspects of circulating and fixated capital as *specific form-determinations* of capital generally, since a great many phenomena of the bourgeois economy would otherwise be incomprehensible (N 623, MEW 523).

This development is a critical transition in Marx's exposition. When he moves from a consideration of circulating capital as a "unity-in-process," to circulating capital as simultaneously the negation of itself as the subject of the whole movement, he follows precisely Hegel's exposition of the disjunctive syllogism and the transition to objectivity. Hegel's exposition of the disjunctive syllogism opens up to Marx a vista unavailable to the classical political economists. For example, the classical political economists had failed to fully comprehend the nature of the economic cycle, because either they focused on the aspect of a material product in which it was supposed to be circulating capital or on the fluid nature of the process. They could not hold both thoughts simultaneously in their minds. In short, their method prevented them from grasping circulating and fixated capital as *specific form-determinations* of circulating capital in general. As Marx states: "Capital is not a quantity simply, or an operation simply, but both at the same time" (N 625, MEW 525).

Hegel has demonstrated that the difference between A and B in the hypothetical syllogism becomes an empty name with the supersession of the relation of condition to conditioned. A and B share the same content. They are moments in an underlying network of structural relations that makes necessary their connection in the system. They thus merge into the unity of the whole. The result is an identity that differentiates itself and constitutes itself out of its differences.[22] Hegel explicates this organic unity as the disjunctive syllogism.

In "The Disjunctive Syllogism," determinate moments specify an organizing principle. The whole in turn contains these differentiations as specific form-determinations. Thus, the organizing principle is the subject that specifies itself through alternative form-determinations. The only difference that now exists among form-determinations is one of point of view. One can alternately focus on the unity of the whole, or on its determinate moments. The organizing principle has become an essential moment of its each of its form-determinations. Each moment appears as the totality of what is mediated. Hegel calls this totality "objective universality." Thus, objective universality contains within itself "individual determinatenesses" (*einzelne Bestimmtheit*) (SL 702, STWII 399). Because each differentiation is a specific form-determination, it is the negation of objective universality as the subject of the completed unity (SL 701-2, STWII 398-99). Objective universality has therefore become absolute form and content. It is the unity of its specific form-determinations, and the particularization or differentiation of itself as each of these determinate moments.

In the transition from the disjunctive syllogism to objectivity, Hegel reviews the entire course of the development up to this point (SL 703-4, STWII 400). In the judgment, he had set out in detail the various moments of the self-differentiating whole. Through the development of the "divisions" within the concept, he had shown that the indifferent, self-subsistent moments of the concept are merely different moments in a "series of mediations." In the syllogism, Hegel presented the concept as a unity of its different moments. Each moment is only by means of an other. The supersession of the series of mediations, in turn, produces an immediacy. Objective universality, in its reality, is a being that is identical with the mediation of its moments (SL 704, STWII 401). Hegel calls this being a fact that is in-and-for-itself, or objectivity.

Marx likewise concludes his exposition of circulating capital as unity-in-process with a recapitulation of the entire development up to this point. We can now see that the circulation of capital is a change of forms by means of which value passes through different phases in its metamorphosis. The entire exposition of "capital as it proceeds from itself" had its point of departure in money, and ends in money (N 626, MEW 526). Marx states:

> If we examine the cycle up to this point, we stand at the point of departure again. Capital has become money again. But it is now at the same time posited, it has now become a condition for this money that it becomes capital again, money which preserves and multiples itself through the purchase of labour, by passing through the production process. Its form as money is posited as mere form; one of the many forms through which it moves in its metamorphosis.[23]

Marx tells us that we can view the entire exposition up to this point as of one turnover of capital as such, a single course of circulating capital through its "different moments" (N 626, MEW 526). The process began with money as its point of departure, and ends with money. Money has become a transition point or a point of new departure. Marx also tells us, however, that money is a "vanishing terminal point," and only a seeming point of departure. We must now regard money as the retransformation of value, posited as money, into value-in-process. That is, money is the retransformation of capital into the material conditions of production.[24] In this respect, Marx calls money the realization of capital *par excellence*; money is the pure form of value (N 638, MEW 537). It is value in and for itself, and it is objectified labor (N 671). With the realization of capital in money, capital now appears as presupposed to its own circulation. Marx states: "Capital, in its reality, therefore now appears as a series of turnovers. It is no longer merely one turnover, one circulation; but rather the positing of turnovers; positing of the whole process."

---

[1] *Diese Voraussetzungen, die ursprünglich als Bedingungen seines Werdens erschienen—und daher noch nicht von seiner Aktion als Kapital entspringen konnten—erscheinen jetzt als Resultate seiner eignen Verwicklichung, Wirklichkeit, als gesetzt von ihm—nicht als Bedingungen seines Entstehens, sondern als Resultate seines Daseins* (N 460, MEW 372).

[2] *Ursprünglich schien die Produktion jenseits der Zirkulation und die Zirkulation jenseits der Produktion zu liegen. Der Kreislauf des Kapitals—die Zirkulation als Zirkulation des Kapitals gesetz—umfaßt beide Momente. In ihr erscheint die Produktion als End—und Anfangspunkt der Zirkulation und vice versa. Die Selbständigkeit der Zirkulation ist jetzt zu einem bloßen Schein herabgesetzt, ebenso wie die Jenseitigkeit der Produktion* (N 514, MEW 421).

[3] "But this self-relation of the determinateness as the union of itself with itself is equally the negation of the determinateness, and the Notion as this equality with itself is the universal. But this identity has equally the determination of negativity; it is the negation or determinateness which is self-related; thus the Notion is individual. Each of them, the

universal and the individual, is the totality, each contains within itself the determination of the other and therefore these totalities are one and only one" (SL 582).

[4] "If we now consider circulation, or the circulation of capital as a whole, then the two great differentiations within itself appears to be the production process and circulation itself, both as moments of its circulation" (*Betrachten wir nun die Zirkulation oder den Umlauf des Kapitals als Ganzes, so erscheinen als die beiden größen Unterscheidungen innerhalb derselben 2 Momente, der Produktionsprozeß und die Zirkulation selbst, beide als Momente seiner Zirkulation*) (N 517, MEW 424).

[5] "This much has now been said, that circulation is itself a moment of production, since capital becomes capital only through circulation; production is a moment of circulation only insofar as the latter is itself regarded as the totality of the production process" (*Soviel ist jetzt schon gesagt, daß die Zirkulation selbst ein Moment der Produktion ist, da erst durch diese das Kapital als Kapital wird; die Produktion nur Moment der Zirkulation ist, insofern diese selbst als Ganzes des Productions prozesses betrachet wird*) (N520, MEW 427).

[6] This appearance as a duality is a function of considering each of the moments as it is in its particularity, and as it is with reference to the other. Thus, the moments are said to be (1) the real production process and its duration; (2) the transformation of the product into money; (3) the transformation of the money into the elements of productive capital; and (4) the exchange between capital and living labor capacity (N 520, MEW 427).

[7] "The universal is thus the totality of the Notion, it is a concrete, and far from being empty, it has through its Notion a content, and a content in which it not only maintains itself but one which is its own and immanent in it" (*Das Allgemeine ist somit die Totalität des Begriffes, es ist Konkretes, ist nicht ein Leeres, sondern hat vielmehr durch seinen Begriff Inhalt—einen Inhalt, in dem es sich nicht nur erhält, sondern der ihm eigen und immanent ist*) (SL 603-4, STWII 277).

[8] *Das Geld verwandelte sich in seiner Zirkulation in Ware, und in dem Austausch von G-W endigte die Konsumtion den Prozess; oder die Ware tauschte sich aus gegen Geld—und in dem Austausch W-G entweder verschwindend, um selbst wieder gegen W ausgetauscht zu werden, wo der Prozeß wieder in der Konsumtion endete, oder das Geld zog sich aus der Zirkulation zurück und verwandelte sich in toten Schatz und nur gemeinten Reichtum. Nirgends entzündete sich der Prozeß an sich selbst, sondern die Voraussetzungen der Geldzirkulation lagen außer ihr und sie bedurfte beständig neuen Anstoß von außen. Soweit sich beide Momente austauschten, war, innerhalb der Zirkulation, die Formveränderung nur formell. Soweit sie aber inhaltlich wurde, fiel sie aus dem ökonomischen Prozeß heraus; der Inhalt gehörte nicht in ihn hinein. Weder erhielt sich der Ware als Geld noch das Geld als Ware; jedes war das eine oder das andere. Der Wert als solcher erhielt sich nicht in und durch die Zirkulation als übergreifend über seinen Verwandlungsprozeß, seine Formveränderung; noch wurde der Gebrauchswert selbst (was im Produktionsprozeß des Kapitals der Fall) von dem Tauschwert produziert* (N 535-36, MEW 442).

[9] *Beim Kapital ist die Konsumtion der Ware selbst nicht final; fällt in den Produktionsprozeß; erscheint selbst als Moment der Produktion, i.e. des Wertsetzens. Das Kapital aber ist jetzt gesetzt, aber in jedem der Momente, worin es bald als Geld, bald als Ware, bald als Tauschwert, bald als Gebrauchswert erscheint, gesetzt als sich in dieser Formveränderung nicht nur formell erhaltender, sondern verwertender Wert, sich auf sich selbst als Wert besiehender Wert. Das Übergehn aus einem Moment in das andre erscheint als besondrer Prozeß, aber jeder dieser Prozesses ist das Übergehn in den andren. Das Kapital is so gesetzt als prozessierender Wert, der in jedem Moment Kapital ist* (N 536, MEW 442).

[10] Marx returns to this particular subject, i.e., circulation, from the vantage point of "circulating capital," and examines the mediations between product, commodity, and money in more detail some hundred pages later. I will therefore also refer to this section, since it sheds light on the way in which Marx conceived of these form-determinations of capital and their relation to one another.

[11] *In der Zirkulation des Kapitals haben wir eine Reihe von Tauschoperationen, von Tauschakten, deren jede gegen die andre ein qualitatives moment vorstellt, ein Moment in der Reproduktion und Wachstum des Kapitals. Ein System von Austauschen, Stoffwechsel, soweit der Gebrauschswert betrachtet, Form wechsel, soweit der Wert als solcher betrachtet wir. Das Produkt verhält sich zur Ware wie Gebrauchswert zum Tauschwert; so die Ware zum Geld. Hier erreicht die eine Reihe ihre Höhe. Das Geld verhält sich zur Ware, in die es reckverwandelt wird, als Tauschwert zum Gebrauchswert; noch mehr so das Geld zur Arbeit* (N 637, MEW 537).

[12] *Insofern das Kapital in jedem Moment des Prozesses selbst die Möglichkeit des Übergehns in seine andre, nächste Phase und so die Möglichkeit des ganzen Prozesses ist, der den Lebenakt des Kapitals ausdrückt, so erscheint jedes der Momente potentialiter als Kapital—daher Warenkapital, Geldkapital—neben dem im Produktionsprozeß als Kapital sich setzenden Wert*(N 637, MEW 537).

[13] *1. Schöpfung des Mehrwerts oder unmittelbarer Produktionsprozeß. Sein Resultat das Produkt. 2. Bringen des Produkts auf den Markt. Verwandlung des Produkts in Ware. 3. a)Eingehn der Ware in die gewöhnliche Zirkulation. Zirkulation der Ware. Ihr Resultat: Verwandlung in Geld. Dieses erscheint als erstes Moment der gewöhnlichen Zirkulation. b) Rückverwandlung des Geldes in die Produktionsbedingungen: Geldzirkulation; in der gewöhnlichen Zirkulation erscheint die Warenzirkulation und Geldzirkulation stets an zwei verschiedne Subjekte verteilt. Das Kapital zirkuliert erst als Ware, dann als Geld und vice versa. 4. Erneuung des Produktionsprozesses, was hier als Reproduktion des ursprünglichen Kapitals und Produktionsprozeß des Surplus kapitals erscheint* (N 619, MEW 519).

[14] Marx characterizes this series of mediations as entailing a relation between use value and exchange value, where one serves as a mediating factor in different stages: One and the same relation appears sometimes in the form of use value and sometimes in that of exchange value, but at different stages and with a different meaning. To use is to consume, whether for production or consumption. Exchange is the mediation of this act through a social process. Use can be posited as, and be, a mere consequence of exchange; then again, exchange can appear as merely a moment of use, etc. From the standpoint of capital (in circulation), exchange appears as the positing of use value, while on the other side its use (in the act of production) appears as positing for exchange, as positing its exchange value. Likewise with production and consumption.

[15] "If we examine this movement, we find that the circulation of capital, through the operation of exchanges, opens up at one point to release the product into general circulation, and to constitute itself out of the latter as equivalent in money. . . . On the other side, capital throws its form as money out of its circulation process again . . . or, after having realized itself as value in ordinary circulation and at the same time posited itself as the measure of its own realization, it then moves in the money form only as medium of circulation, and thus sucks into itself out of general circulation and enters its own course, issuing into the production process. The circulation of capital thus contains a relation to general circulation, of which its own circulation forms a moment, while the latter likewise appears as posited by capital" (N 619-20).

[16] *Soweit das Geld als Zirkulationsmittel hier figuriert, ist es in der Tat nur als Vermittlung der Produktion einerseits mit der Konsumption, in dem exchange, wo das Kapital den*

Wert in der Form des Produkts von sich abstößt, und Vermittlung zwischen der Produktion und Produktion andrerseits, wo das Kapital sich in der Form des Geldes abstößt und die Ware in der Form der Produktionsgbedingung in seinen Kreislauf zieht (N 667, MEW 568).

In a very important passage that is an adumbration, Marx foreshadows what he explicitly details in this section. Marx summarizes the entire "series of mediations" as follows: "It is important to note that wealth as such, i.e., bourgeois wealth, is always expressed to the highest power as exchange value, where it is posited as mediator, as the mediation of the extremes of exchange value and use value themselves. This middle term always appears as the economic relation in its completeness, because it comprises the opposed poles, and ultimately always appears as a one-sidedly higher power vis-à-vis the extremes themselves; because the movement, or the relation, which originally appears as the middle term between the extremes necessarily develops dialectically to where it appears as mediation with itself, as the subject from whom the extremes are merely its moments, whose autonomous presuppositions it supersedes in order to posit itself through their supersession, as that which alone is autonomous. . . . Where it is posited as middle term, exchange value is always the total economic expression, itself one-sided against the extremes; e.g. money in simple circulation; capital itself as the mediator between production and circulation. Within capital itself, one form of it in turn takes up the position of use value against the other as exchange value. Thus, e.g., does industrial capital appear as producer as against the merchant, who appears as circulation. Thus the former represents the material, the latter the formal side, i.e., wealth as wealth. At the same time, mercantile capital is itself in turn the mediator between production (industrial capital) and circulation (the consuming public) or between exchange value and use value, where both sides are posited alternately, production as money and circulation as use value (consuming public) or the former as use value (product) and the latter as exchange value (money)" (N 332, MEW 250-51).

17 "Thus a moment enters into value-determination which indeed does not come out of the direct relation of labour to capital. The frequency with which the same capital can repeat the production process (creation of new value) in a given period of time is evidently a condition not posited directly by the production process itself. Thus, while circulation does not itself produce a moment of value-determination, for that lies exclusively in labour, its speed does determine the speed with which the production process is repeated, values are created—thus, if not values, at least to a certain extent the mass of values" (*Es kommt hier also in der Tat ein Moments der Wertbestimmung herein, das nicht vom direktem Verhältnis der Arbeit zum Kapital herrührt. Das Verhältnis, worin dasselbe Kapital, in einem gegebnen Zeitraum, den Produktionsprozeß [Schopfung von Neuwert] wiederholen kann, ist offenbar eine Bedingung, die nicht direkt durch den Produktionsprozeß selbst gesetzt ist. Wenn die Zirkulation daher kein Moment der Wertbestimmung selbst hervorbringt, das ausschließlich in der Arbeit liegt, so hängt von ihrer Geschwindigkeit, worin der Produktionsprozeß sich wiederholt, Werte geschaffen werden—also, wenn nicht die Werte, so die Masse der Werte zu einem gewissen Grade*) (N 538, MEW 443-44).

See also pp. 619-20 for a characterization of the relation between circulation and production as one of condition to conditioned. In addition, Marx elsewhere treats of the relation, when he states: "However, the movement of the metamorphosis through which it must pass now appears as a condition of the production process itself; just as much as its result. . . . Its (capital's) value-positing therefore appears as conditioned (and value is capital only as self-immortalizing and self-multiplying) qualitatively, in that it cannot renew the production phase without passing through the phases of circulation. . ." (*Aber die Bewegung der Metamorphosen, die es durchzumachen hat, erscheint jetzt als*

Bedingung des Produktionsprozesses selbst; ebensosehr wie als sein Resultat. . . . Sein Wertsetzen selbst erscheint daher bedingt [und nur als sich perennierender und vervielfältigender Wert ist der Wert kapital) 1. qualitativ; indem es, ohne die Phasen der Zirkulation zu durchlaufen, die Produktionsphase nicht erneuern kann . . .) (N 638, MEW 538).

[18] "Production based on capital originally came out of circulation; we now see that it posits circulation as its own condition, and likewise the production process in its immediacy as moment of the circulation process, as well as the circulation process as one phase of the production process in its totality" (*Ursprünglich ging die auf das Kapital gegründete Produktion von der Zirkulation aus; wir sehn jetzt, wie sie die Zirkulation als ihre eigne Bedingung setzt und ebensosehr den Produktionsprozeß in seiner Unmittelbarkeit als Moment des Zirkulationsprozesses, wie den Zirkulationsprozeß als eine Phase des Produktionsprozesses in seiner Totalität*) (N 543, MEW 448).

[19] "The continuity of production presupposes that circulation time has been superseded. If it has not been superseded, then time must pass between the different metamorphoses through which capital must travel; its circulation time must appear as deduction from its production time. On the other hand, the nature of capital presupposes that it travels through the different phases of circulation not as it does in the mind, where one concept turns into the next at the speed of thought, in no time, but rather as situations which are separate in time. It must spend some time as a cocoon before it can take off as a butterfly. Thus the conditions of production arising out of the nature of capital itself contradict each other. The contradiction can be superseded and overcome only in two ways. . . ." (*Die Kontinuität der Produktion unterstellt, dass die Zirkulationszeit aufgehoben ist. Ist sie nicht aufgehoben, so muss Zeit verlaufen zwischen den verschiednen Metamorphosen, die das Kapital durchlaufen muß; seine Zirkluationszeit muß als Abzug an seiner Produktionszeit erscheinen. Andrerseits unterstellt die Natur des Kapitals, daß es die verschiednen Phasen der Zirkulation durchläuft, und zwar nicht in der Vorstellung, wo der eine Begriff in den andren mit Gedankenschnelle, in no time, umschlägt, sondern als Zustände, die der Zeit nach auseinanderliegen. Es muß eine Zeitlang verpuppt sein, eh es als Schmetterling fliegen kann. Die aus der Natur des Kapitals selbst hervorgehnden Bedingungen seiner Produktion widersprechen sich also. Aufgehoben und überwunden werden kann der Widerspruch nur . . . auf zweierlei Weise. . .*) (N 548-49, MEW 453-54; see also pp. 619-20).

[20] *Der Gesamtproduktionsprozeß des Kapitals schließt ein sowohl den eigentlichen Zirkulationsprozeß wie den eigentlichen Produktionsprozeß. Sie bilden die 2 großen Abschnitte seiner Bewegung, die als Totalität dieser 2 Prozesse erscheint. Nach der einen Seite ist die Arbeitszeit, nach der andren die Zirkulationszeit. Und das Ganze der Bewegung erscheint als Einheit von Arbeitszeit und Zirkulationszeit, als Einheit von Produktion und Zirkulation. Diese Einheit selbst ist Bewegung, Prozeß. Das Kapital erscheint als diese prozessierende Einheit von Produktion und Zirkulation, eine Einheit, die sowohl als das Ganze seines Produktionsprozesses*) (N 620, MEW 521).

[21] *Das Kapital ist daher in jeder besondren Phase die Negation seiner als des Subjekts der verschiednen Wandlungen. Nicht-zirkulierendes Kapital. Fixes Kapital, eigentlich fixiertes Kapital, in einer der verschiednen Bestimmtheiten, Phasen fixiert, die es zu durchlaufen hat. . . . Das Kapital als das alle Phasen durchlaufende Subjekt, als die bewegte Einheit, prozessierende Einheit von Zirkulation und Produktion, ist zirkulierendes Kapital; das Kapital als selbst in jeder dieser Phasen eingebannt, als in seinen Unterschieden gesetzt, ist fixiertes Kapital, engagiertes Kapital. Als zirkulierendes Kapital selbst fixiert es sich, und als fixiertes Kapital zirkuliert es. Die Unterscheidung von capital circulant und capital fixe erscheint daher zunächst als Form-bestimmung des Kapital, je nachdem es als*

Einheit des Prozesses oder als bestimmtes Moment desselben erscheint (N 620-21, MEW 521).

[22] Errol E. Harris, *An Interpretation*, p. 250.

[23] *Aber es ist jetzt zugleich gesetzt, es ist jetzt Bedingung fur dies Geld geworden, wieder Kapital zu warden, sich durch Kauf von Arbeit, durch Durchgehn durch den Produktionsprozess vervielfaltigendes und erhaltendes Geld. Seine Form als Geld ist als blosse Form gesetzt; eine der veilen Formen, die es in seiner Metamorphose durchlauft* (N 626, MEW 526-27).

[24] "In the exchange of the commodity for money, the material and the formal changes coincide; for, in money, precisely the content itself is part of the economic form. . . To the extent that money figures here as medium of circulation, it does so indeed only as mediation of production, on one side with consumption, in the exchange where capital discharges value in the form of the product, and as mediation, on the other side, between production and production, where capital discharges itself in the form of money and draws the commodity in the form of the condition of production into its circulation" (*In Austausch der Ware gegen Geld fallt die stoffliche und Formveranderung zusammen; da im Geld eben der Inhalt selbst zur okonomischen Form bestimmung gehort. . . Soweit das Geld als Zirkulationsmittel hier figuriert, ist es in der Tat nur asl Vermittlung der Produktion einerseits mit der Konsumption, in dem echange, wo das Kapital den Wert in der Form des Produkts von sich abstosst, und Vermittlung zwischen der Production und Production andrerseits, wo das Kapital sich in der Form des Geldes abstosst und die Ware in der Form der Produktionsbedingung in seinem Kreislauf zieht*) (N 667, MEW 568).

CHAPTER 6

THE OBJECTIVITY OF FIXED CAPITAL

Capital does not "develop out of nothing, nor drop from the sky, nor from the womb of the self-positing Idea" (N 278, MEW 203). Once Marx has disclosed the formal structure of circulating capital as a unity of form-determinations, he then seeks to explicate the process of the "objectification of the productive forces of capital," or, capital in its "material presence." Marx has demonstrated that capital must be conceived of as a self-differentiated, integrated whole—an organic unity. He will now formulate an exposition of the process wherein capital becomes objectified.

This final section of the *Grundrisse* is the most concrete of the entire manuscript. Marx no long presents capital in the abstract determinateness of its self-movement. Rather, he presents capital as what is objectively real, as machinery, as a real process of the appropriation of living labor, and as profit. This development proceeds from a consideration of the relation between capital and the mode of production that had preceded capital (N 581 90, MEW 487-92). Capital does not "drop from the sky," or develop out of the "womb of the self-positing Idea;" but from within, and in distinction to, the existing forces and relations of production. Here Marx describes capital as appropriating the means of production in their "immediate form" (*unmittelbar Form*), and superseding this form by positing a form that is adequate to "the end" (*der Zweck*) of circulating capital (N 691, 710, MEW 605 624).

Marx's exposition of the initial relation of capital to the previous mode of production reflects the logical form and content of the first two chapters of "Objectivity." Here Hegel formulates what he terms the process of the objectification of the concept. The relation between concept and object is at first an immediate one. The initial process of objectification entails the supersession of the "immediate form" (*unmittelbar Form*) of objectivity, and the positing of a form that is adequate to "the end" (*der Zweck*) of the Concept. Once objectivity is posited in a form that is adequate to the purpose of the concept, it is shown to be a means to this end. In which case, objectivity is completely penetrable by the end. It therefore undergoes a series of transformations wherein its immediate nature is overcome, and it is posited in a form that is completely adequate. The end endows objectivity with a soul, or a self-moving principle.

Marx first describes how capital supersedes the means of production in their "immediate form," and then posits them in a form adequate to its end. Capital necessarily becomes fixed capital, or machinery. Machinery is the most adequate form for the realization of the end of capital. Machinery undergoes a series of transformations, wherein it is posited in a form that is most adequate to this end. Marx claims that capital endows machinery with a soul of its own, or a principle of self-movement. Marx then defines fixed capital as a "living organism" with its own "members." Fixed capital engages in a process of self-consumption in its process of reproduction. Its "life-process" consists in a movement wherein the production process relates to what is external to itself. Fixed capital "consumes coal, oil, etc. (*materies instrumentales*) just as the worker consumes food, to keep up its "perpetual motion."

The deep, logical structure of Marx's exposition of capital in its "material presence" as a "living organism," is indebted to Hegel's exposition of the objectification of the concept as "Life." In Hegel's description the living organism as consists of its own members engaging in a process of self-consumption in the process of reproduction. This living organism then relates itself to what is external to itself, and transforms this externality into an internality in the process of reproducing itself.

Finally, Hegel demonstrates that the concept realizes itself as an identity with itself, when it generates the "germ of the living individual." It distinguishes itself within itself from itself as individual moments of the living genus. It thereby generates an "infinite process" of the production and reproduction of the realized genus. Yet the realization of the genus is not solely the realization of the concept, it is also the making explicit of the idea itself. Here the idea relates to itself as idea, that is, as a simple universal.

As we have seen, when Marx exposes capital as an objective unity of production and circulation, capital is realized as capital; it is capital as capital. Capital as capital distinguishes itself within itself from itself, and relates itself to itself. In so doing, capital generates profit. It must thereby be conceived of as a process of the producing and reproducing of itself, that is, as a "self-reproducing being." Yet it is not merely the positing of "self-eternalizing value," but also the realization of capital as money. Interest-bearing capital is capital relating to itself as capital—the "pure abstract form" of profit-bearing capital.

1. CAPITAL AS *DAS ZENTRUM*

In the last chapter, we saw that capital must be conceived of as a unity of qualitatively distinct, *specific form-determinations*. It is a "unity-in-distinction" of both production and circulation. As such, capital is properly and formally characterized as "circulating capital." In contrast to the exposition of the form-determinations of capital, or the investigation into the formal nature of capital, Marx here presents what he terms the "particular modes of the existence of capital" (N 620-1, 690, MEW 534-35, 604). These modes are capital's "objective relations." They are the "objectification of the productive forces" of capital.

As stated previously, capital does not "develop from the womb of the self-positing Idea," but from within and in distinction to the existing forces and relations of production that it inherits.[1] Capital has its presuppositions, and its development consists in the supersession of these existing forces and relations of production under its own form (N 586, 620, 694, MEW 488, 534, 596). Marx here describes the mode of production that precedes capital as entailing an independent, scattered work force that is dispersed over the land (N 586, MEW 488). It entails the "independent fragmentation" (*selbständigen Zersplitterung*) of the labor of hand weavers, spinners, and farmers, who live independently of one another and have very little to do with each other (N 587, MEW 489).

Commercial capital, the incipient form of capital, finds these independent and indifferent workers, and exchanges money for their independently produced goods. Here, then, capital as money has served to unite the labor of the many, independent workers. The labor of the many workers thereby becomes coordinated through their mutual relations with capital as a point of unity.[2] The coordination of the labor of many workers exists only "in-itself" (*an sich*) (N 587, MEW 489). They continue to work as before, independently of one another.[3]

In formulating this process of the "objectification" of capital, Marx followed Hegel's exposition of the objectification of the concept. Once Hegel has treated the concept as a unity of form-determinations, he moves on to show how the concept "determines itself into objectivity" (*sich zur Objektivität bestimmt*) (SL 705, STWII 402). That is, he first presents the concept in its "immediate being," and then demonstrates how it structures objectivity in accordance with its end.

The concept as it is initially presented is a merely implicit being in what is an external relation of independently existing identities, which are isolated one from another and indifferent to one another. Each is completely self-subsistent but each nevertheless possesses a passivity. They are therefore able to enter into causal relations. In what is termed "the mechanical process," or "mechanism," each active object acquires "a form of universality," which is communicated to it by that which exists externally (SL 711-12, STWII 410-11). This "form of universality" then spreads among other such objects. The form or activity is particularized in the active objects, in a relation of causality.

While these objects may at this juncture enter into a causal relationship, they nevertheless maintain their self-subsistence and isolation from one another. Hegel is careful to note that the relation or coordination of such objects is merely "in-itself," because each remains indifferent to the other (SL 715, STWII 414). The relation is merely formal in nature. Further exposition demonstrates that this initial positing of the "form of universality" within independently self-subsisting objects, develops to the point where an "objective universal" (*objektive Allgemeinheit*) "gathers-together" (*versammelt*) into "objective individuality" (*objektive Einzelheit*) the many objects (SL 723, STWII 424). Here objective universality appears as "the center" (*das Zentrum*), insofar as it is an "immanent form, a self-determining principle in which the objects inhere and by which they are bound together into a genuine one" (*immanente Form, selbstbestimmendes Prinzip, welchem die Objekte inharieren und wodurch sie zu einem wahrhaften Eins verbunden sind*) (SL 723, STWII 424). Objective universality is the center around which the disparate objects are now joined.

Marx employs this logical formulation to characterize the relation that gradually emerges between capital as *capitalist* and the many independent, scattered workers. Upon the formal relation that emerges as a consequence of an exchange of capital as money for their products, capital then becomes what is termed "a center" (*ein Zentrum*) (N 586, MEW 488). Each of the independent workers now works for capital, without working together. The many independent workers thereby "possess a center" in capital. For, as Marx states: "The unification of their labors appears as a particular act alongside which the independent fragmentation of their labor continues" (*Das Vereinigen ihrer Arbeiten erscheint als ein besondrer Akt, neben dem die selbständige Zersplitterung ihrer Arbeiten fortdauert*) (N 586, MEW 489). Furthermore, he states:

> However, capital does indeed exist from the outset as the one or unity as opposed to the workers as many. And it thus appears as the concentration of workers as distinct from that of work, as a unity falling outside them. In this respect concentration is contained in the concept of capital—the concentration of many living labor capacities for one end. Centralizing effect of capital on labor as the independent and external unity of these many available existences.[4]

The emergence of capital as the center is the first condition necessary for money to be exchanged as capital for free labor. A second process then begins whereby the many laborers are further united. This second process entails "the supersession of the independent fragmentation of these many workers" (*die Aufhebung der selbständigen Zersplitterung*).[5] The process is the supersession of their relative independence because capital now acts so as to "gather them together" (*sie versammelt*) in one spot under its command. Thus, capital is no longer a mere center, or a concentration of many exchanges, but now "posits the concentration of the workers in production" (*setzt die Vereinigung der Arbeiter in der Production*) (N 587, MEW 489). Capital no longer merely acclimates itself to the existing conditions of production, but creates its own conditions as its own basis. Capital is the "supersession of individual isolation"; it "ties them together and hence as the unity which creates this productive force."[6]

Hegel's development of "Absolute Mechanism" provides Marx with the logical form of his exposition. Hegel demonstrates that once objective universality has emerged as "the center," whose self-determining principle acts on and determines the previously external objects, these objects are then superseded as external.[7] The center is not a body. It is rather the unity or the "one" (*Eins*) that is now an immanent form or a self-determining principle through which the many are bound together.

This supersession of the independent individuals entails a "gathering-together" into a unity. The relationship that obtains between them is no longer a mere composition. Rather, universality has particularized itself in these individualities. The latter now "strive toward" (*ein Streben*) the center. This striving toward the center is a function of the identity that now permeates the external objectivity of the objects. The concept is presented as a self-determining unity that has completely reduced external objectivity to its animating principle. Hegel cautions us, however, that the concept as this objective totality is but an inner (SL 724-25, STWII 426-27). It is determinate, but its law has not yet formed its object in accordance with itself. Its animating principle is said to be the law that is immanent in the objects.

Marx maintains at this point that capital is the "collective force, the social force, the supersession of individual isolation, first that of exchange with the workers, then that of the workers themselves" (N 587, MEW 489). This concentration or process of unification results in "regimentation, greater discipline, regularity and the posited dependence in production itself on capital" (*Einregimentierung, größre Disziplin, Stetigkeit und gesetzte Abhängigkeit in der Produktion selbst vom Kapital*) (N 587, MEW 489). It is, in short, the establishment of production based on the laws of surplus value.

Marx further maintains that this process takes a number of years and thus the relative independence of individual workers is only gradually superseded by capital. But once capital has brought about the complete dependence of the workers on capital, the ties between the workers and the conditions of production are completely dissolved. Production by capital begins with the "regroupment" (*Gruppierung*) of workers around individual capital. Marx states: "The detachment of the individual from the production conditions of labor = the regroupment of many around one capital" (*Die Loslösung des einzelnen von den Produktionsbedingungen der Arbeit = Gruppierung vieler um ein Kapital*) (N 589, MEW 491). In this case, capital has become the "exclusive base" (*ausschliesslichen Boden*) of the subsistence of the workers (N 589, MEW 491). There then exists the posited negative unity that must obtain between capital and wage-labor in the production of surplus value.

In "Chemism," Hegel explicates the process by which objective universality completely supersedes the remaining independence of self-subsistent objects. These objects contain within themselves a relative independence (SL 725-26, STWII 427-28). Each possesses, therefore, a contradiction between its externality and the law that is immanent within it. They thereby form an "external community" (*ausserliche Gemeinschaft*) (SL 729, STWII 431). Although they are grouped together by the self-determining principle of the concept, their unity has an existence independent of them. The concept is the medium through which they are grouped.

Each external object in relation to the other endures various processes in and through which its externality is superseded, until, their relative independence is completely superseded (SL 729-30, STWII 431-32). The concept then emerges as the "exclusive base" of the subsistence of the previously independently existing individuals. The concept no longer presupposes external independent objects; rather, its own activity posits its objective existence in a process of self-determination and self-realization. It is now completely liberated from externality and posits its conditions as its own (SL 731-33, STWII 434-36).

2. THE MECHANICAL OBJECT AS THE MOST ADEQUATE FORM OF FIXED CAPITAL

The "objectification" process of capital, whereby it posits itself in the "particular modes of its existence," begins then with the subjugation of the old mode of production under its own process (N 589, MEW 491). The "supersession of individual isolation" or the relative independence of workers, had entailed a "gathering-together" or a process of unification, wherein capital now "posits the concentration of the workers in production." Insofar as the many workers are united by the one capital in a common location, capital is described as ". . . proceeding out of itself as its own basis, it constantly posits itself ahead of itself in its various forms as consumable product, raw material and instrument of labor, in order constantly to reproduce itself in these forms. They appear initially as the conditions presupposed by it, and then as its results."[8]

Initially, however, with the advent of manufacturing and the rise of the mode of production of capital, Marx contends that the productive force of labor has "still to be brought to life" (N 588). The initial "gathering-together" of spinners, weavers, etc., under the command of capital entails the unification of workers only in a common location. Surplus value is here the result only of a great mass of workers. Necessary labor therefore takes up the great portion of the entire available labor time. Consequently, surplus labor time is relatively small.

Marx reiterates that the tendency of capital is to posit greater surplus labor time in relation to necessary labor time. This tendency entails that capital form the conditions of its own production to its own "end" (*der Zweck*) (N 589, MEW 591). As a consequence, there is an inner tendency within capital to "make special skill superfluous, and to make manual work directly physical labor, generally superfluous both as skill and as muscular exertion; to transfer skill, rather, into the dead forces of nature" (*das besondre Geschick überflüssig zu machen und die Handarbeit, die unmittelbar körperliche Arbeit überhaupt als geschickte Arbeit sowohl wie als Muskelanstrengung überflüssig zu machen; das Geschick vielmehr in die toten Naturkräfte zu legen*) (N 587, MEW 490).[9] In which case, the worker will no longer "insert a modified material thing as the middle term between the object and himself; rather, he inserts the process of nature, transformed into an industrial process, as a means between himself and inorganic nature, mastering it."[10] In short, in order to realize this necessary tendency, the means of labor must be superseded in this their "immediate form" (N 699, MEW 599).

Marx's exposition follows quite closely the transitions that Hegel formulated between mechanism and chemism, on the one hand, and teleology, on the other. The "gathering together" of formerly independent objects in a process of concentration or unification, results in the supersession of externality and the positing of the concept in objectivity. The concept emerges from its presuppositions to posit them as its own result (SL 742, STWII 447). By positing its own presuppositions, or that which it requires for an objective relation, the concept "unites with its reality."

It is yet the case, however, that the determination of externality by the concept is only an initial determining. As such the concept's objectivity has the shape of a presupposition. Because the external object possesses the determination of the concept only as an internality, the concept is not the realized "end" (*der Zweck*) (SL 743, STWII 449). Its first positing is but an initial step toward the end, and therefore the external object is merely a "means." To realize this "end-in-itself," the "means" must be superseded in its "immediate form" (SL 744-45, STWII 450-51).

Marx contends that to actualize or realize capital's "end-in-itself," the means of labor must be superseded in their "immediate form" (N 691, 710; MEW 591, 614). As long as the means of labor remain as presuppositions that are adopted historically by capital, they undergo only a formal modification.[11] They are then not only a means of labor in regard to its material side, but at the same time a "particular mode of the existence of capital determined by its total process" (*ein durch den Gesamtprozeß des Kapitals bestimmte besondre Daseinsweise desselben*) (N 691, MEW 592). They become fixed capital. Yet they remain the means of labor in its "immediate form" (N 699, MEW 599). It is only through the supersession of the means of labor in this "immediate form," that capital can bring the productive forces of labor to "life."

Marx characterizes "fixed capital" as the objectification of the productive force of society. He states that: "The productive force of society is measured in fixed capital, exists there in its objective form . . ." (*Die Produktivkraft der Gesellschaft ist gemessen an dem Capital fixe, existiert in ihm in gegenständlicher Form*) (N 694, MEW 595). It is the "power of knowledge objectified" (*vergegenständlichte Wissenkraft*) (N 706, MEW 602). It represents the "conquest of the forces of nature by the social intellect" (*die Unterwerfung der Naturkrafte unter den gesellschaftlichen Verstand*) (N 709, MEW 605). Capital absorbs the accumulation of the knowledge and skill of the general productive forces of the "social brain" (*gesellschaftlichen Hirns*) into itself (N 694, MEW 594). These in turn appear as particular modes of the existence of capital, that is, as fixed capital.

The supersession of the means of labor in its "immediate form" is a function of the employment of scientific knowledge, whereby the "communal spirit of labor" is transferred into fixed capital. Science then compels the "dead forces of nature" to "act purposefully" in the form of the means of production (N 693, MEW 594). It is thus the "inner tendency" of capital to transform the means of labor into machinery, through scientific knowledge.[12]

In this manner "the form in which it (the means of labor) was adopted in the production process of capital, the direct means of labor, is superseded by a form posited by capital itself and corresponding to it" (*es als unmittelbares Arbeitsmittel in den Produktionsprozess des Kapitals aufgenommen wurde, in eine durch das Kapital selbst gesetzte und ihm entsprechende Form aufgehoben*) (N 692, MEW 592). Thus the means of labor in their "immediate form" are superseded in and through the workings of the "social intellect," and thereby transformed into an existence that is adequate to "the end" of capital.

Hegel contends that the concept or end is at first only immediately united with externality. The means is in a limited sense subsumed under the end; nevertheless, the end remains in some sense external to the means. The means is thus a mere "mechanical object" (SL 744, STWII 450). In this way the end and means are separated, because the end is but one of many determinations that are possessed by the means. The means therefore lacks the development that is needed to adequately unite with the end.

The "mechanical object" is nevertheless penetrable by the activity of the end. Thus the end possesses the power or urge to form the means in accordance with its activity. The means is completely receptive of this activity, since it is in-itself identical with the end. Yet the means remains in its "immediate form." Through the activity of the end, a form adequate to the activity of the end supersedes the means in its "immediate form."[13] The "mechanical object" undergoes a process of transformation. In this manner the end gives itself a content, and the externality of the means and the objectivity of the end are then one and the same. The latter's self-determining activity posits the "mechanical object" as a determination of itself (SL 747, STWII 453). Its activity is the activity of the end. The "mechanical object" is endowed with a "soul" (*Seele*) (SL 745, STWII 451).

Marx maintains that once the means of labor has been absorbed into the production process of capital, it passes through a process of "metamorphosis," which culminates in the machine. Science compelled the "dead forces of nature" to "act purposefully" as an automaton. Machines become "a moving power that moves itself" (*bewegende Kraft, die sich selbst bewegt*) (N 692, MEW 592). Through the knowledge provided by the "social intellect," capital endows the machine "with a soul of its own in the mechanical laws acting through it" (*die ihre eigne Seele besitzt in den in ihr wirkenden mechanischen Gesetzen und zu ihrer beständigen Selbstbewegung*) (N 693, MEW 593). In this manner, capital transfers the skill of the laborer into the machine. The machine then displaces the worker because the machine now possesses the skill and strength that capital needs to generate surplus value. The production process becomes a process that is no longer dominated by living labor. Rather, as Marx states:

> Labor appears merely as a conscious organ, scattered among the individual living workers at numerous points of the mechanical system; subsumed under the total process of the machinery itself, as itself only a link of the system, whose unity exists not in living-workers, but rather in the living machinery, which confronts his individual insignificant doings as a mighty organism.[14]

The automatic system of machinery is the most adequate form of the realization of capital's "end-in-itself" (N 710, MEW 614). Marx states: "Machinery appears, then, as the most adequate form of fixed capital, and fixed capital, insofar as capital's relation with itself is concerned, appears as the most adequate form of capital as such" (*Die Maschinerie erscheint also als die adäquateste Form des Capital fixe, soweit das Kapital in seiner Beziehung auf sich selbst betrachtet wird, als die adäquateste Form des Kapitals überhaupt*) (N 694, MEW 594).

Marx is indebted to Hegel's exposition of "Teleology" for the logical form of his presentation of the objectification of capital in fixed capital—its "material presence." Hegel distinguishes between the form and content of the realized end. Though the relation between the end and the "mechanical object" is one in which the end "maintains itself" in the object, the self-determining activity of the concept must not be thought of as identical with its posited externality. It is not identical with the "mechanical object." Rather this objectivity has been posited by the activity of the end, and as such it possesses its existence in and through the activity of the end.

Marx likewise distinguishes between the objectification or objectivity of capital in fixed capital, and capital as such. The crass materialism of many classical political economists led them to identify the material presence of capital in fixed capital with capital itself. Marx distinguishes between the form and content of fixed capital. Fixed capital has indeed been posited by the activity of capital, yet it must not be identified with capital. Marx makes it perfectly clear that its material presence is not identical to the *Begriff* of capital. He states:

> In another respect, however, insofar as fixed capital is condemned to an existence within the confines of a specific use value, it does not correspond to the concept of capital, which, as value, is indifferent to every specific form of use value, and can adopt or shed any of them as equivalent incarnations.[15]

Capital may endow machinery with "a soul of its own"; it may "bring the forces of production to life," but it is not identical to these forces of production.

3. FIXED CAPITAL AS A LIVING ORGANISM

The supersession of the means of labor in its "immediate form" entails a transformation into a form that is adequate to the activity of capital. The inner tendency of capital—"value existing for-itself"—serves as the impetus to develop fixed capital in relation to living labor. Marx states: " . . . the form in which it was adopted in the production process of capital, the direct means of labor, is superseded by a form posited by capital itself and corresponding to it." That adequate form of fixed capital is the machine, the automaton.

With the emergence of fixed capital as the automaton, the productive forces of labor are "brought to life by capital." The automaton is variously described as endowed by capital with "its own soul," as a "living organism," as a "moving power that moves itself," as "self-activating objectified labor," and as "objectified labor endowed with apparent life." In fact, in a number of instances Marx describes the forces of production that are adequate to the activity of capital as "living." Indeed, Marx sometimes suggests an analogy between fixed capital and the human body (N 639, 640, 661, 670). Capital possesses its own "inner organic movement" (*innre organische Bewegung*) (N 680, MEW 581). It possesses its own "body" in machinery. Marx further suggests that as a "living organism," the machine possesses "members" (*Gliedern*); it consists of "numerous mechanical and intellectual organs" (*zahlreichen mechanischen und intellektuellen Organen*); and, finally, labor is the machine's "conscious organ" (*bewußtes Organ*) (N 691, MEW 591).

Such a formulation or presentation of the nature of machinery betrays indebtedness to Hegel's exposition of "Life." The supersession of the means in its immediate form results in a unity between it and the concept, such that the former is now adequate to the activity of the latter. The concept has completely subordinated externality to its own end and created the material conditions for its own objectification. This unity of the concept and reality is "the idea." This unity, however, is the idea in its immediacy. It has not yet developed the moments that will give it concrete existence. As such the idea is initially "Life."

The objectivity that is posited by the activity of the concept as one of its moments is variously described as a "living individual" (*lebendige Individuum*), endowed with a "soul," and therefore possessing a "self-moving principle" (*selbst bewegende Prinzip*) (SL 765, STWII 475). Because the concept is immanent in it, the living being possesses a purpose or a constituting principle. Hegel describes this living being as follows:

> This objectivity of the living being is the organism, it is the means and instrument of the end, perfect in its purposiveness since the concept constitutes its substance; but for that reason this means and instrument is itself the realized end, in which the subjective end is thus immediately brought into unity with itself. In respect of its externality the organism is a manifold, not of parts but of members. . . .[16]

Thus this living being endowed with its own soul is an organism that possesses its own members. They are its members precisely because their existence and activity are subordinated to, and posited by, the activity of the concept.

Hegel further defines the relation of concept to organism as a process of production to product (SL 767, STWII 477). The two are not, however, to be thought of as really distinct from each other. Rather, the concept produces itself in and through its inner tendencies, such that the product itself is the producing agent; or, the product is product only by being the process of production. Thus, the product is not distinct from the end as the act of production; rather, the act of production is the end as product.

The three moments of the concept, universality, particularity, and individuality form the basis of an elaboration of this process (SL 768, STWII 478). As an individual, the living organism relates to its objectivity as something external, something that the organism uses as its own "means and instrument" (*Mittel und Werkzeug*). The external relation to itself is then superseded in its immediacy or abstract moment. This supersession of immediacy is a movement from externality to the supersession of externality—a "reflection-into-self." Thus, the living organism relates to itself as a means or instrument, but then supersedes this external relation. This negative unity is the vitality of the organism. The movement is an exposition of the self-consumption and reproduction of its own vital organs. The movement from externality to the supersession of externality is thus a process of renewal, whereby the organism reproduces its own means and instruments for maintenance.

When Marx outlined the logical development of fixed capital, he also considered "the inner organic movement of capital, its relation to itself" (*die innre organische Bewegung des Kapitals, seine Beziehung auf sich*) (N 680, MEW 581). This "inner organic movement" is the reproduction of the production process. Marx contrasts this reproductive process with the renewal of circulation capital as such, that is, with the commodity and money. Marx compares fixed capital with the skeleton of the body. He contends that the reproduction process of fixed capital takes much longer than that of circulating capital. He states:

> The simultaneity of the process of capital in different phases of the process is possible only through its division and break-up into parts, each of which is capital, but capital in a different determination. This change of form and matter is like that in the organic body. If one says, e.g., the body reproduces itself in 24 hours, this does not mean it does it all at once, but rather the shedding in one form and renewal in the other is distributed, takes place simultaneously. Incidentally, in the body the skeleton is fixed capital; it does not reproduce itself in the same period of time as flesh, blood. There are different degrees of speed of consumption (self-consumption) and hence of reproduction.[17]

Thus the "inner organic movement of capital, its relation to itself," entails the self-consumption of fixed capital, which is at once a process of its reproduction. The use value of the machinery passes into the product. Yet in the present context of the exposition, capital must be seen as not only a unity of form-determinations, but also as possessing "particular modes of existence" as "self-eternalizing value." Each moment of capital, each particular mode of its existence, exists as value. Thus in the "inner organic movement" of capital, the "living organism" that is the machine endowed with a "soul" of its own, passes the "self-eternalizing value" that it possesses from its form into the form of product.[18]

Because the dissolution of the use value of machinery is a moment in capital's own circulation as "self-eternalizing value," it is at the same time the reproduction of fixed capital. The value of the machinery is passed along in increments into the commodities that issue from the production process. The commodities then enter circulation and are sold as compared to fixed capital, which realizes its value only by remaining in the hands of the capitalist as use value. Marx states:

> Fixed capital, by contrast, realizes itself as value only as long as it remains in the capitalist's hand as use value, or, expressed as an objective relation, as long as it remains in the production process, which may by regarded as the inner organic movement of capital, its relation to itself, as opposed to its animal movement, its presence for another.[19]

The total reproduction of capital in its "relation to itself" occurs upon the complete dissolution of the use value of fixed capital. In this manner the total value of the machinery returns via the circulation of commodities. The old use value is replaced by a new use value of the same kind, that is, it is reproduced.[20]

Marx summarizes the entire process of the reproduction of fixed capital through its own self-consumption as follows:

> A part of use value ejected by capital as the product, a result of the production process, becomes an object of consumption and thus drops out of circulation of capital altogether; another part enters into another capital as a condition of production. This is itself posited in the circulation as such, since it ejects itself from itself in the first half of circulation as commodity, i.e., as use value; i.e. dismisses itself with respect to itself in this form from its own circulation as use value, article of consumption, but exchanges itself as money for commodity as condition of production, in the second half of its circulation.[21]

Here then we see that reproduction, or "the inner organic movement of capital, its relation to itself" entails a negative unity. It is first a process of self-consumption, then a process wherein the product of the production process in turn becomes a condition for it, through the medium of money. Reproduction, then, may be seen as a constant movement of self-consumption and regeneration.

4. THE LIFE-PROCESS OF CAPITAL

In a number of instances Marx refers to the process of production and reproduction as "the life-process" (*der Lebensprozeß*) of capital (N 638, 646, 658, 660, 701, 706, 879). He distinguishes this "life-process" of capital from the "inner organic movement of capital, its relation to itself," that is, capital as a "living organism," or fixed capital. The "life-process" of capital includes fixed capital as one of its moments. The self-consumption and reproduction of the production process is merely one moment in the "metabolism of capital." Whenever Marx refers to "the life-process" of capital in this section of the *Grundrisse,* he refers to the relation of the production process to circulation. Where the discussion of the "inner organic movement" of capital had focused on the reproduction of fixed capital, the discussion of "the life-process" of capital focuses on what is external to the production process, in its relation to circulation. The exposition of the reproduction process of capital is thus broadened to include both production and circulation.

There are two phases in the "metabolism" of circulating capital. In the first phase, the product of the production process is exchanged for money. The second phase consists of an exchange of money for commodities that are the conditions of production. This second phase is "the life-process" of capital. Here the transformation of money into commodity presupposes production. Marx states:

> But in the second phase of circulation, capital exchanges money for commodity, and its transformation into commodity now itself appears as a moment of value-positing, because the commodity is accepted as such into the circulation process of capital. While it presupposes consumption in the first phase, in the second it presupposes production, production for production; for value in the form of the commodity is here taken into the circulation of capital from the outside, or, the inverse process is undertaken in the first phase. The commodity, as use value for capital itself, can only be the commodity as an element, use value, for its production process.[22]

Here, then, this value or commodity is taken as external to the production process, and transformed into a moment of it.

Marx gives two examples of that which is first external to the production process, then transformed into a moment of it. The first example is the *matiéres instrumentales.* These instruments are circulating capital, which becomes fixed capital only by being consumed in the production process. They are consumed "but do not have, like fixed capital proper, a material substance determined purely by their formal presence" (*haben aber nicht, wie das eigentliche capital fixe, ein rein durch ihr Formdasein bestimmtes Stoffliches*) (N 732, MEW 627). Fixed capital is said to "consume coal, oil, etc. (*matiéres instrumentales*), just as the worker consumes food, to keep up its perpetual motion" (*wie der Arbeiter Nahrungsmittel, so Kohlen, öl etc. konsumiert [matiéres instrumentales]*) (N 693, MEW 593).

The second example is, of course, living labor itself. At this point, Marx employs rather graphic metaphors to underline the relation of capital as fixed capital to living labor. The context of the relation of living labor capacity to machinery is the context in which the real appropriation of labor by capital occurs. The appropriation of labor within the context of the reproduction of fixed capital is of a qualitatively different nature than was the case with capital in its incipient form. Marx therefore employs terms that are commensurate with this qualitative difference.

Capital as fixed capital "absorbs labor into itself—'as though its body were by love possessed'" (*die lebendige Arbeit in sich absorbierend—'als hatt' es Lieb'*) (N 704, MEW 600). The exchange between living labor and capital "appears not as an exchange of substances between the simultaneous labor powers, but as the metabolism of capital" (*erscheint nicht als Stoffwechsel der gleichzeitigen Arbeitskrafte, sondern als Stoffwechsel des Kapitals*) (N 701, MEW 597). Moreover, Marx states: "In machinery, objectified labor materially confronts living labor as a ruling power and as an active subsumption of the latter under itself, not only by appropriating it, but in the real production process itself. . . ."[23]

Living labor is "absorbed" into the production process and transformed into a "member," a "conscious organ" (N 693, MEW 593). In the circulation that constitutes the payment of wages, capital expels itself as objectified labor, "in order to assimilate living labor power, its life's breath" (*um die lebendige Arbeitskraft, seine Lebensluft, sich zu assimilieren*) (N 676, MEW 576-77). Living labor "sells himself as an effect," while he is "absorbed into the body of capital as cause, as activity" (*als Ursache, als Tätigkeit, wird er absorbiert vom und inkarniert in das Kapital*) (N 674, MEW 575). Capital sucks "its living soul out of labor" (*seine Lebensseele aus der Arbeit*) (N 660, MEW 561). It can exist as fixed capital "only by constantly sucking in living labor as its soul, vampire-like" (*nur, indem es als ein Vampyr die lebendige Arbeit beständig als Seele einsaugt*) (N 646, MEW 545). Fixed capital is a "living organism" that literally devours living labor—"it sucks its living soul out of labor."

Marx's exposition of capital's "life-process" is indebted to Hegel's exposition of the "Life-Process." Marx perceives that the extreme reality of the appropriation of living labor by fixed capital can be exposed in and through the logical progression of Hegel's exposition. For Hegel, "the life-process" follows upon the development of "life" in general. The latter had focused on the living organism and "its relation to itself." The living organism is presented in all its concrete vitality in a process of its own self-consumption and reproduction.[24] Thus, reproduction in the first instance consists in the self-consumption and reproduction of the organism's various members.

In the reproduction of itself, the living organism is an actual individuality, a self-related being for-itself. Insofar as it is now a concrete organism, it is related to an objective world that confronts it. Hegel calls its assimilation of what is external "the life-process" (*der lebensprozeß*). The "life-process" thus presupposes a process of self-consumption and reproduction. Here the exposition focuses on the relation between the living organism and what is external to it.

This externality lacks in its mechanical and chemical presence the formal unity that is possessed by the organism (SL 771, STWII 482). Because of this lack of substantiality, that which is external to the organism cannot enter into relation with it except in terms of the universality that pervades the organism. The object is then inherently conformable to the universality that pervades the organism. The organism "absorbs" or "assimilates" the object in a process whereby the mechanical and chemical makeup of the organism transforms this externality into an internality (SL 771-72, STWII 482-83). The organism uses its own externality or instrumentality to act upon the object. Thus the external, mechanical and chemical processes pass over into an internal process, and the organism converts what had been external into a means for its own activity, and "gives its own subjectivity to it for substance" (SL 771-72). The process of assimilation or absorption coincides, therefore, with the organism's process of reproduction.[25]

For Marx, the "life-process" of circulating capital appears in a threefold manner (N 678ff, MEW 578ff). Circulating capital is first of all a total process, which includes all the different moments through which capital passes. It is a being in constant movement. It appears as both circulating and fixed. It is either commodity capital, money capital, or capital as conditions of production. In the second phase, however, it appears as small-scale circulation. Here it is the exchange between itself as money and labor capacity. This exchange accompanies the production process, and is presupposed by it. Third, and finally, it appears as large-scale circulation, that is, as movement outside the production process. Marx contrasts large-scale circulation with fixed capital as fluid. Moreover, large-scale circulation is capital's "animal movement, its presence for another" *(animalische Bewegung, gegen sein Dasein für andres)* (N 680, MEW 581).

Marx contends at the end of the development of this exposition that, whereas circulating and fixed capital had appeared earlier as merely different form-determinations of the same capital in the different phases of its turnover, they are now posited at the same time as "two different modes of the existence of capital" (2 *verschiedne Existenzarten des Kapitals*) (N 737, MEW 631). Here, where we are dealing with fixed capital in its highest development, the production of capital appears as the production in definite portions of circulating and fixed capital. Capital produces itself in this double way of circulating. It is both production and reproduction in the double form of fixed and circulating capital (N 737, MEW 631). Capital must therefore now be conceived as reproducing itself as "two different kinds of capital." Marx states: "Capital is now posited as the unity of production and circulation . . ." (*Das Kapital ist nun gesetzt als Einheit von Produktion und Zirkulation*. . . (N 745, MEW 637). Thus the "metabolism" of capital includes these two great sections of itself in its "life-process."

Hegel contends at this point that the result of the process of assimilation and absorption of the object is the reproduction of the organism. Yet it is not merely the reproduction of the organism, it is also the positing of itself as a self-identical unity of the particular moments of its existence (SL 772, STWII 483-84).

5. THE GENERATION OF PROFIT AND THE REPRODUCTION OF CAPITAL AS CAPITAL

With the completion of the exposition of both the internal and external moments of the reproduction of capital—the "metabolism" of capital—capital is posited as a unity of its two particular modes of existence, that is, as fixed and circulating capital. With the completion of the exposition of the "objectification" of capital, capital is posited as value that reproduces itself, and is therefore "perennial." Marx states:

> Capital is now posited as the unity of production and circulation.... Capital is now realized not only as value which reproduces itself and is hence perennial, but also value which posits value. Through the absorption of living labor time and through the movement of its own circulation (in which the movement of exchange is posited as its own, as the inherent process of objectified labor), it relates to itself as positing new value, as producer of value. It relates as the foundation to surplus value as that which it founded. Its movement consists of relating to itself, in which it produces itself, at the same time as the foundation of what it has founded, as value presupposed to itself as surplus value, or to the surplus value as posited by it.[26]

Capital is, then, a perennial movement that in relating to itself, produces and reproduces itself. Capital is further characterized as "proceeding from itself" as an "active subject," that is, as the "subject of the process" (N 746, MEW 639). In proceeding from itself, capital relates to itself as "self-increasing value." Capital "relates to surplus value as something posited and founded by it; it relates as well-spring of production, to itself as product; it relates as producing value to itself as produced value."[27]

Because a specific sum of value produces a specific surplus value in a specific amount of time, the newly produced value is not measured according to the real measure of produced value, which is the relation between surplus and necessary labor time. Rather the newly created value is measured in terms of a presupposed, specific sum of value; and surplus value measured solely in terms of this presupposed sum of capital is profit. Marx states: "Surplus value thus measured by the value of the presupposed capital, capital thus posited as self-realizing value — is profit; regarded not *sub specie aeternitatis*, but *sub specie-capitalis*, the surplus value is profit. . . ."[28]

This *sub specie capitalis*—capital as it relates to itself as a "self-reproducing being" or perennial value—is further described as follows: ". . . capital as capital, the producing and reproducing value, distinguishes itself within itself from itself as profit, the newly produced value" (*das Kapital unterscheidet sich in sich selbst als Kapital, dem produzierenden und reproduzierenden Wert, von sich als Profit, dem neuproduzierten Wert*) (N 746, MEW 638). Finally, after capital has distinguished itself within itself from itself as profit, and insofar as this newly produced value is itself "of the same nature as the capital" (*der derselben Natur ist wie das Kapital*), it "supersedes the separation again, and posits it in its identity to itself as capital which, grown by the amount of the profit, now begins the same process anew in larger dimensions."[29]

Once capital relates to itself and distinguishes itself within itself from itself as profit, and then supersedes this separation, it has described a circle, and thereby expands itself "as the subject of the circle" (*als Subjekt des Kreises*) (N 746, MEW 639). Capital as capital—*sub specie capitalis*—is therefore a "self-expanding circle" (*sich ausdehnenden Kreis*), a spiral.[30]

In so describing capital as this "self-reproducing being," Marx is indebted to Hegel's exposition of the "process of genus." The description of the logical moments of the reproduction of the organism entails an exposition of its relation to itself in a process of self-consumption, and its relation to what is external to it. In "the life-process" of the organism, its reproduction in relation to what is external to it leads to the positing of it as a self-identity of the particular moments of its existence. As self-identical, the organism raises itself from mere particularity to universality. It is no longer merely one among many, but it now contains in-itself the reality of a genus.

This self-identity is "the foundation of itself" (*die Grundlage seiner selbst*); it "brings itself forth out of actuality" (*aus der Wirklichkeit sich hervorbringt*) (SL 772, STWII 484). It is the foundation of what it founds. Whereas prior to this it had proceeded only from the concept, its "genesis which was an act of presupposing, now becomes its production" (*seine Entstehung, die ein Voraussetzen war, nun seine Produktion wird*) (SL 772-73, STWII 484). This production or "bringing itself forth out of actuality" is in fact a multiplication of this same individuality. Nevertheless it is as yet merely in-itself the genus, or self-reproducing individuality.

The becoming of genus entails that the concept relates itself to itself through self-reproducing individuality. The concept thus distinguishes itself within itself from itself as what are, at first, two simple individualities (SL 773, STWII 485). The latter, taken abstractly, are particular relative to one another. In themselves they are the genus, but they are not yet identical. Their realized identity is a function of the genus relating to itself through this individuality. The process of genus is thus described as one in which the genus distinguishes itself within itself from itself and relates to itself through self-reproducing individuality. Thus the genus relates itself to itself as a process of production, to itself as a product. Hegel describes this process as the supersession of what had been abstractly depicted as single individuals, and the production of "the actual concept—the germ of a living individual." Hegel states:

> "The reflection of the genus into itself is from this side the means whereby it obtains actuality, the moment of the negative unity and individuality being thereby posited in it—the reproduction of the living species" (*Die Reflexion der Gattung in sich ist nach dieser Seite dies, wodurch sie Wirklichkeit erhält, indem das Moment der negativen Einheit und Individualität in ihr gesetzt wird— die Fortpflanzung der lebenden Geschlechter*) (SL 774, STWII 486).

This "process of the genus," distinguishing itself within itself from itself, this relating itself to itself as a process of production to the product—the "germ of the living individual"—is an infinite process. Thus the genus distinguishes itself from itself as self-reproducing individuality, then supersedes the separation in its own process of self-reproduction and multiplication, only to begin the process again—*sub specie aeternitatis* (SL 774, STWII 486). The result is a "realized genus."

Marx claims that once capital is posited as this "self-reproducing being," it is posited as capital. Capital as it relates itself to itself, and thereby generates profit, is "real capital." Profit-bearing capital is "value posited as simultaneously self-reproducing and multiplying, and as constantly self-equivalent presupposition, distinguished from itself as surplus value posited by itself" (*der Wert, gesetzt als zugleich sich reproduzierend und vervielfältigend und als sich gleichbleibende Voraussetzung, von sich selbst als durch es gesetztem Mehrwert unterschieden*) (N 878, MEW 764). Real capital is furthermore described as realizing itself again as money. Thus the product of the production process that bears the property of surplus value is sold. The capitalist thereby realizes his profit in the form of money.

With the emergence of profit-bearing capital, or money as realized capital, there is posited the possibility that capital should attain a higher form of existence than previously observed. There now exists the possibility that capital itself may enter into circulation as a commodity. Prior to this point, capital posited itself both as commodity and as money. It appeared merely as the vanishing moments of its own circulation, alternating between itself as commodity and money. But capital had not itself entered into circulation as commodity. The commodity or money had not been sold as capital.

Now, however, with the emergence of money as realized, profit-bearing capital, capital itself becomes a commodity. This it does as interest-bearing capital. Here capital does not stand opposite labor in exchange; rather, interest-bearing capital stands opposite profit-bearing capital. As such, interest-bearing capital is said to be the "purely abstract form" (*rein abstrakte Form*)—the simple universal form—of profit-bearing capital; or, capital as it relates to itself as capital (N 878, MEW 764).

The result of the genus process is a "realized genus" (SL 774, STWII 486). Yet it is not merely the "realized genus"; in addition, the concept itself is now fully posited as identical with objectivity, in and through self-reproducing individuality. It too is thus "realized." In addition, because "life" is "the idea" in its immediacy, the idea too has been made explicit through the "realized concept." Thus, the infinite process of the self-reproduction and multiplication of the genus gives rise to a higher form of its existence. The Idea has emerged as Idea, in and through the process of its mediation. It has emerged as what Hegel terms "simple universality." The latter is the Idea as it relates to itself as Idea.

---

[1] "It must be kept in mind that the new forces of production and relations of production do not develop out of nothing, nor drop from the sky, nor from the womb of the self-positing Idea; but from within and in antithesis to the existing development of production and the inherited, traditional relations of property. While in the completed bourgeois system every economic relation presupposes every other in its bourgeois economic form, and everything posited is thus also a presupposition, this is the case with every organic system. This organic system itself, as a totality, has its presuppositions, and its development to its totality consists precisely in subordinating all elements of society to itself, or in creating out of it the organs which it still lacks. This is historically how it becomes a totality. The process of becoming this totality forms a moment of its process, of its development" (*Es ist zu bedenken, daß die neuen Produktivkräfte und Produktionsverhältnisse sich nicht aus Nichts entwickeln noch aus der Luft, noch aus dem Schoß der sich selbst setzenden Idee; sondern innerhalb und gegensätzlich gegen vorhandne Entwicklung der Produktion und überlieferte, traditionelle Eigentumsverhältnisse. Wenn im vollendeten bürgerlichen System jedes ökonomische Verhältnis das andre in der bürgerlich-ökonomischen Form voraussetzt und so jedes Gesetzte zugleich Voraussetzung ist, so ist das mit jedem organischen System der Fall. Dies organische System selbst als Totalität hat seine Voraussetzungen, und seine Entwicklung zur Totalität besteht eben darin, alle Elemente der Gesellschaft sich unterzuordnen oder die ihm noch fehlenden Organe aus ihr heraus*

zu schaffen. Es wird so historisch zur Totalität. Das Werden zu dieser Totalität bildet ein Moment seines Prozesses, seiner Entwicklung) (N 278, MEW 203).

Marx will discuss the "becoming" of capital in relation to the prior existing mode of production at a number of points in the text. The section that we will concentrate on is one wherein it is clear that he is employing Hegel's exposition of "Objectivity." This particular section appears between the pages of 584-90 in the Nicolaus translation.

[2] "The simplest form, a form independent of the division of labour, is that capital employs different hand weavers, spinners etc. who live independently and are dispersed over the land. (This form still exists alongside industry.) Here, then, the mode of production is not yet determined by capital, but rather found on hand by it. The point of unity of all these scattered workers lies only in their mutual relation with capital, which accumulates the product of their production in its hand and, likewise, the surplus values which they created above and beyond their revenue" (*Die einfachste und von der Teilung der Arbeit unabhängigste Form ist, daß das Kapital verschiedne selbständig und zerstreut wohnende Handweber, Spinner etc. beschäftigt. [Diese Form existiert noch immer neben der Industrie.) Hier ist also die Produktionsweise selbst noch nicht von ihm bestimmt, sondern von ihm vorgegunden. Der Einheitspunkt dieser zerstreuten Arbeiter liegt nur in ihrer wechselseitigen Beziehung zum Kapital, daß das Produkt ihrer Produktion in seiner Hand akkumuliert wird und so die Surpluswerte, die sie über ihre eigne Revenu hinaus geschaffen*) (N 586, MEW 488).

[3] "Their unification by capital is thus merely formal, and concerns only the product of labour, and not labour itself. Instead of exchanging with many, they exchange only with the one capitalist. This is therefore a concentration of exchanges by capital" (*Ihre Vereinigung durch das Kapital ist daher nur formell und betrifft nur das Produkt der Arbeit, nicht die Arbeit selbst. Statt mit vielen auszutauschen, tauschen sie mit dem einen Kapitalisten aus. Es ist daher eine Konzentration der Exchanges durch das Kapital*) (N 586, MEW 488).

[4] *Wohl aber steht das Kapital von vornherein als eins oder Einheit den Arbeitern als vielen gegenüber. Und so erscheint es als die Konzentration der Arbeiter gegenüber die Arbeit als außer ihnen fallende Einheit. Nach dieser Seite ist die Konzentration im Begriff des Kapitals enthalten — die Konzentration vieler lebendigen Arbeitsvermöigen zu einem Zweck; eine Konzentration, die sich ursprünglich keines wegs schon in der Produktionsweise selbst durchgeführt, sie durchdrungen zu haben braucht. Zentralisierende Wirkung des Kapitals auf die Arbeitsvermögen oder Setzen seiner als der selbständig außer diesen vielen existierenden einheit derselben* (N 590, MEW 492).

[5] ". . . the supersession of the independent fragmentation of these many workers, so that the individual capital no longer appears towards them merely as social collective power in the act of exchange, uniting many exchanges, but rather gathers them in one spot under its command. . . ." (. . . *die Aufhebung der selbständigen Zersplitterung dieser vielen Arbeiter, wo das eine Kapital ihnen gegenüber nicht mehr nur als gesellschaftliche Kollektivkraft im Akt des Austauschs erscheint, so daß in ihm viele Austausche vereinigt sind, sondern sie an einem Ort unter sein Kommando, in eine Manufaktur versammelt*) (N 587, MEW 489).

[6] "Now capital appears as the collective force of the workers, their social force, as well as that which ties them together, and hence as the unity which creates this force" (*Jetzt erscheint das Kapital sowohl als die Kollektivkraft der Arbeiter, ihre gesellschaftliche Kraft, wie als die sie zusammenbindende und diese Kraft daher schaffende Einheit*) (N 587, MEW 489).

Capital is the "collective force, the social force, the supersession of individual isolation, first that of exchange with the workers, then that of the workers themselves" (*Kollektivkraft, gesellschaftliche Kraft und Aufhebung der Vereinzelung, zuerst des Austauschs mit den Arbeitern, dann der Arbeiter selbst erscheint*) (N 589, MEW 491).

[7] "In the first place then the empty manifoldness of objects is gathered into objective individuality, into the simple self-determining center. Secondly, insofar as the object as an immediate totality retains its indifference to determinateness, the latter is present in it also as unessential or as a mutual externality of many objects. Universality exhibited itself as first in the relationship of communication as present only through positing; but as objective universality it is the pervading immanent essence of the objects" (*Die leere Mannigfaltigkeit des Objekts ist nun erstens in die objektive Einzelheit, in den einfachen selbstbestimmenden Mittelpunkt gesammelt. Insofern zweitens das Objekt als unmittelbare Totalität seine Gleichgültigkeit gegen die Bestimmtheit behält, so ist diese an ihm auch als unwesentliche oder als ein Außereinander von vielen Objekten vorhanden. . . . Die Allgemeinheit zeigte sich zuerst im Verhältnisse der Mitteilung als eine nur durchs Setzen vorhandene; als objective aber ist sie das durchdringende, immanente Wesen der Objekte*) (SL 721-22, STWII 423).

[8] *. . . von sich selbst ausgehend, setzt es sich beständig in seinen verschiednen Formen als konsumierbares Produkt, Rohstoff und Arbeitsinstruments voraus, um sich in diesen Formen beständig zu reproduzieren. Sie erscheinen einmal als die von ihm selbst vorausgesetzten Bedingungen und dann als sein Resultat. Es produziert in seiner Reproduktion seine eignen Bedingungen* (N 675, MEW 576).

[9] See also N 690ff, MEW 592ff.

[10] *Es ist nicht mehr der Arbeiter, der modifizierten Naturgegenstand als Mittelglied zwischen das Objekt und sich einschiebt; sondern den Naturprozeß, den er in einen industriellen umwandelt, schiebt er als Mittel zwischen sich und die unorganische Natur, deren er sich bemeistert* (N 705, MEW 601).

[11] "As long as the means of labour remains a means of labour in the proper sense of the term, such as it is directly, historically, adopted by capital and included in its realization process, it undergoes a merely formal modification, by appearing now as a means of labour not only in regard to its material side, but also at the same time as a particular mode of the presence of capital, determined by the total process—as fixed capital. But, once adopted into the production process of capital, the means of labour passes through different metamorphoses, whose culmination is the machine. . ." (*Solange das Arbeitsmittel im eigentlichen Sinn des Wortes Arbeitsmittle bleibt, so wie es unmittelbar, historisch, vom Kapital in seinen Verwertungsprozess hereingenommen ist, erliedet es nur eine formelle Veranderung dadurch, dass es jetzt nicht nur seiner stofflichen Seite nach als Mittel der Arbeit erscheint, sondern zugleich als eine durch den Gesamtprozess des Kapitals bestimmte besondre Daseinsweise desselben—als Capital fixe. In den Produktionsprozess des Kapitals aufgenommen, durchlauft das Arbeitsmittel aber verschiedne Metamorphosen, deren letzte die Maschine ist. . .*) (N 692, MEW 592).

Marx recalls his initial treatment of the labor process that had preceded the exchange between capital and wage-labor. There the "material presuppositions" of the production process, i.e., the material of labor, the means of labor, and living labor, appeared merely as the essential moments of the labor process which capital appropriates. This material side, however, did not at all coincide with its formal side, i.e., the formal side as capital (N 691, MEW 591). As regards this formal side, the material presuppositions appear only as quantitative subdivisions of capital. Elsewhere in this section, Marx states: ". . . within the process itself, as regards the form, the elements of labor and the two others were specified as constant values, and the former as value-positing. But as far as their distinctness as use values, their content was concerned, this fell entirely outside capital's specific character as form" (N 619-20, MEW 519-20).

[12] "The increase of the productive force of labour and the greatest possible negation of necessary labour is the necessary tendency of capital, as we have seen. The transformation

of the means of labour into machinery is the realization of this tendency" (*Die Vermehrung der Produktivkraft der Arbeit und die größte Negation der notwendigen Arbeit ist die notwendige Tendenz des Kapitals, wie wir gesehn. Die Verwirklichung dieser Tendenz ist die Verwandlung des Arbeitsmittels in Maschinerie*) (N 693, MEW 594).

Furthermore, he states: "It is, hence the tendency of capital to give production a scientific character; direct labour is reduced to a mere moment of this process. As with the transformation of value into capital, so does it appear in the further development of capital, that it presupposes a certain given historical development of the productive forces on one side—science too among these particular forces—and, on the other, drives and forces them further onwards" (*Der Produktion wissenschaftlichen Charakter zu geben, daher die Tendenz des Kapitals, und die unmittelbare Arbeit herabgesetzt zu einem bloßen Moment dieses Prozesses. Wie bei der Verwanlung des Werts in Kapital, so zeigt sich beit der nähern Entwicklung der Produktivkräfte voraussetzt — unter diesen Produktivkräf ten auch die Wissenschaft — andrerseits sie vorantreibt und forciert*) (N 699, MEW 595).

[13] "The activity of the end through the means is for that reason still directed against this presupposition, and the end is activity and no longer merely an urge and a striving, precisely because the moment of objectivity is posited in the means in its determinateness as something external, and the simple unity of the Concept now has this objectivity as such in itself" (*Die Tätigkeit, nicht mehr bloß Trieb und Streben, als im Mittel das Moment der Objektivität in seiner bestimmtheit als Außerliches gesetzt ist und die einfache Einheit des Begriffs sie als solche nun an sich hat*) (SL 795, STWII 451).

[14] *Sie erscheint vielmehr nur als bewußtes Organ, an vielen Punkten des mechanischen Systems in einzelnen lebendigen Arbeitern; zerstreut, subsumiert unter den Gesamtprozeß der Maschinerie selbst, selbst nur ein Glied des Systems, dessen Einheit nicht in den lebendigen Arbeitern, sondern in der lebendigen [activen] Maschinerie existiert, die seinem einzelnen, unbedeutenden Tun gegenüber als gewaltiger Organismus ihm gegenuber erscheint* (N 693, MEW 593).

[15] *Andrerseits, soweit das Capital fixe in seinem Dasein als bestimmter Gebrauchswert festgebannt, entspricht es nicht dem Begriff des Kapitals, das als Wert gleichgültig gegen jede bestimmte Form des Gebrauchswerts und jede derselben als gleichgültige Inkarnation annehmen oder abstreifen kann* (N 694, MEW 594).

Furthermore he states in this section: "However, while capital gives itself its adequate form as use value within the production process only in the form of machinery and other material manifestations of fixed capital, such as railways, etc., this in no way means that this use value—machinery as such—is capital, or that its existence as machinery is identical with its existence as capital. . . ." (*Wenn aber das Kapital in der Maschinerie und andren stofflichen Daseinsformen des capital fixe, wie Eisenbahnen, etc. [worauf wir spater kommen warden] sich erst seine adäquate Gestalt als Gebrauchswert innerhalb des Productionsprozesses gibt, so heißt das keineswegs, daß dieser Gebrauchswert—die Maschinerie an sich—Kapital ist oder daß ihr Bestehen als Maschinerie identisch ist mit ihren Bestehn als Kapital. . .*) (N 699, MEW 595-96).

[16] *Diese Objektivitat des Lebendigen ist Organismus; sie ist das Mittel und Werkzeug des Zwecks, vollkommen zweckmäßig, da der Begriff ihre Substanz ausmacht; aber eben deswegen ist dies Mittel und Werkzeug selbst der ausgefuhrte Zweck, in welchem der subjektive Zweck insofern unmittelbar mit sich selbst zusammengeschlossen ist. Nach der Außerlichkeit des Organismus ist er ein Vielfaches nicht von Teilen, sondern von Gliedern. . .* (SL 766, STWII 476).

[17] *Die Gleichzeitigkeit des Prozesses des Kapitals in verschiednen Phasen des Prozessess ist nur möglich durch Teilung desselben und Abstoßen in Portionen, wovon jede Kapital ist, aber Kapital in einer verschiednen Bestimmung. Dieser Form- und Stoffwechsel wie im*

organischen Leib. Sagt man z.B., der Korper reproduziert sich in 24 Stunden, so tut er das nicht auf einmal, sondern das Abstoßen in der einen Form und Erneuern in der andren ist verteilt, geht gleichzeitig vor sich. Übrigens im Korper der Knochenbau das Kapital fixe erneuert sich nicht in derselben Zeit, wie Fleisch, Blut. Es finden verschiedne Grade in der Geschwindigkeit der Konsumption [der Selbstkonsumtion] und daher der Reproduktion statt (N 661, MEW 562-63).

[18] "Fixed capital can enter into circulation as value, however, only to the extent that it passes away as use value in the production process. It passes, as value, into the product—i.e., as labour time worked up or superseded in it—insofar as it passes away in its independent form as use value. In being used, it is used up, but in such a way that its value is carried over from its form into the form of the product. . . . Its total value is completely reproduced, i.e., is fully returned via circulation only when it has been completely consumed as use value in the production process. As soon as it is completely dissolved into value, and hence completely absorbed into circulation, it has completely passed away as use value and hence must be replaced, as a necessary moment of production, by a new use value of the same kind, i.e. must be reproduced. The necessity of reproducing it, i.e. its reproduction time, is determined by the time in which it is used up, consumed within the production process" (*Das Capital fixe kann aber nur als Wert in die Zirkulation treten, soweit es als Gebrauchswert im Produktionsprozeß vergeht. Es geht als Wert in das Produkt ein — d.h. als in ihm aufgearbeitete oder in ihm aufgehobne Arbeitszeit — insofern es in seiner selbständigen Gestalt als Gebrauchswert vergeht. Durch seinen Gebrauch wird es abgenutzt, aber so, dass sein Wert aus seiner Form in die des Produkts übertragen wird . . . Vollständig reproduziert, d.h. aus der Zirkulation zurückkehren, wird sein totaler Wert nur, sobald es vollständig als Gebrauchwert im Produktionsprozeß verzehrt ist. Sobald es vollständig in Wert aufgegangen und daher vollständig in die Zirkulation eingegangen, ist es vollständig als Gebrauchswert vergangen und muß daher als notwendiges Moment der Produktion durch einen neuen Gebrauchswert derselben Art ersetzt, d.h. reproduziert werden. Die Notwendigkeit, es zu reproduzieren, d.h. seine Reproduktionszeit, ist bestimmt durch die Zeit, in der es innerhalb des Produktionsprozesses aufgezehrt, konsumiert wird*) (N 681-82, MEW 58-82).

[19] *Das Capital fixe dagegen realisiert sich nur als Wert, solang es als Gebrauchswert in der Hand des Kapitalisten bleibt, oder, als sachliche Beziehung ausgedrückt, solang es im Produktionsprozeß bleibt, was als die innre organische Bewegung des Kapitals, seine Beziehung auf sich, gegen seine animalische Bewegung, gegen sein Dasein für andres betrachtet werden kann* (N 680, MEW 580-81).

[20] This reproduction occurs, however, only in successive parts. Unlike the circulation of commodities, which reproduce their value upon exchange, the reproduction of fixed capital requires the sale of a great many commodities through successive phases of the production process. Its reproduction in no way corresponds to the reproduction of value that occurs in an average turnover of commodities. Rather, the reproduction of the value of fixed capital requires the sale of a mass of commodities in successive turnovers. It would follow, therefore, as Marx states: "Hence, the larger is the part of capital consisting of fixed capital—i.e., the more capital acts in the mode of production corresponding to it, with great employment of produced productive force—and the more durable the fixed capital is, i.e., the longer its reproduction time, the more its use value corresponds to its specific economic role—the more often must the part of capital which is determined as circulating repeat the period of its turnover, and the longer is the total time the capital requires for the achievement of its total circulation. Hence the continuity of production becomes an external necessity for capital with the development of that portion of it which is determined as fixed capital" (N 719).

[21] *Ein Teil des vom Kapitals als Produkt, als Resultat des produktionsprozesses abgestoßnen Gebrauchswerts wird Gegenstand der Konsumtion und fällt so aus der Zirkulation des Kapitals überhaupt heraus; ein andrer Teil geht ein in ein andres Kapital als Produktionsbedingung. Dies ist in der Zirkulation des Kapitals selbst gesetzt, da es in der ersten Halfte der Zirkulation als Ware, d.h. als Gebrauchswert sich von sich abstoßt, also mit Bezug auf es selbst in dieser Form aus seiner eignen zirkulation sich als Gebrauchswert, Konsumtionsartikel entläßt; in der zweiten Halfte seiner Zirkulation aber sich als Geld gegen Ware als Produktionsbedingung umtauscht* (N 729, MEW 624).

[22] *In der zweiten Phase der Zirkulation aber tauscht das Kapital Geld aus gegen Ware, und seine Verwandlung in Ware erscheint jetzt selbst als Moment der Wertsetzung, weil die Ware als solche in den Zirkulationsprozeß des Kapital hereingenommen wird. Wenn es in der ersten Phase die Konsumtion voraussetzt, setzt es in der zweiten die Produktion voraus, die Produktion fur die Produktion; denn der Wert in der Form der Ware wird hier von außen in die Zirkulation des Kapitals hereingenommen oder der umgekehrte Prozeß wie in der ersten Phase vorgenommen. Die Ware als Gebrauchswert fur das Kapital selbst kann nur die Ware als Element, Gebrauchswert fur seinen Produktionsprozeß sein* (N 730, MEW 626).

[23] *In der Maschinerie triit die vergegenständlichte Arbeit stofflich der lebendigen als die beherrschende Macht entgegen und als aktive Subsumtion derselben unter sich, nicht nur durch Aneignung derselben, sondern im realen Produktionsprozeß selbst. . .* (N 694, MEW 594).

[24] As Hegel states, in the process of reproduction "the individual in the first instance draws upon itself in making its own objectivity its object" (SL 772).

[25] "Since life is the truth of these processes, and therefore as a living being is the concrete existence of this truth and the power dominating these processes, it takes them within its embrace, pervades them as their universality, and their product is completely determined by it. This conversion of them into the living individuality constitutes the return of this latter into itself, so the production, which as such would be transition into an other, becomes reproduction, in which the living being posits itself as self-identical for itself" (SL 772).

[26] *Das Kapital ist nun gesetzt als Einheit von Produktion und Zirkulation. . . . Das Kapital is jetzt realisiert nicht nur als sich reproduzierender und daher perennierender, sondern auch als wertsetzender Wert. Durch die Absorption in sich der lebendigen Arbeitszeit einerseits und die ihm selbst angehörige Bewegung der Zirkulation (worin die Bewegung des Austauschs als seine eigene gesetzt wird, als immanenter Prozeß der vergegenstänlichten Arbeit), verhalt es sich zu sich selbst, als Neuwert setzend, Wert produzierend. Es verhält sich als Grund zum Mehrwert als dem von ihm Begrundeten. Seine Bewegung besteht darin, indem es sich produziert, sich zugleich als Grund von sich als Begrundetem, als vorausgesetzter Wert zu sich selbst als Mehrwert oder zu dem Mehrwert als von ihm gesetztem zu verhalten* (N 745, MEW 637-38).

[27] "Proceeding from itself as the active subject, the subject of the process—and, in the turnover, the direct production process indeed appears determined by its movement as capital, independent of its relation to labour—capital relates to itself as self-increasing value; i.e., it relates to surplus value as something posited and founded by it; it relates as well-spring of production, to itself as product; it relates as producing value to itself as produced value" (*Das Kapital, von sich als dem aktiven Subject ausgehend — dem Subjekt des Prozesses — und in dem Urnschlag erscheint der unmittelbare Produktionsprozeß in der Tat bestimmt durch seine Bewegung als Kapital unabhängig von seinem Verhältnis zur Arbeit — verhalt sich zu sich als sich vermehrendem Wert, d.h., es verhalt sich zu dem Mehrwert als von ihm Gesetztem und Begrundetem; sich als Produktionsquelle zu sich*

selbst als Produkt; als produzierender Wert zu sich selbst als produziertem Wert) (N 746, MEW 638).

[28] *Der Mehrwert, so gemessen an dem Wert des vorausgesetzten Kapitals, das Kapital, so gesetzt als sich verwertender Wert — ist der Profit; unter dieser specie — nicht aeterni, sonder capitalis betrachtet, ist der Mehrwert Profit* (N 747, MEW 638).

[29] "After it has distinguished the profit, as newly reproduced value, from itself as presupposed, self-realizing value, and has posited profit as the measure of its realization, it supersedes the separation again, and posits it in its identity to itself as capital which, grown by the amount of the profit, now begins the same process anew in larger dimensions" (*Nachdem es den Profit als neureproduzierten Wert von sich als vorausgesetztem sich verwertenden wert unterschieden und den Profit als das Maß seiner Verwertung gesetzt hat, hebt es die Trennung wieder auf, und setzt ihn in seiner Identität mit sich als Kapital, das nun, angewachsen um den Profit, denselben Prozeß von neuem beginnt in größeren Dimensionen*) (N 746, MEW 639).

[30] Furthermore, Marx states: "Hence capital appears as capital, as presupposed value relating to itself, through the mediation of its own process, as posited, produced value, and the value posited by it is called profit" (*Es erscheint daher das Kapital als Kapital, als vorausgesetzter Wert, durch die Vermittlung seines eignen Prozesses sich auf sich beziehend, als gesetzter, produzierter Wert, und der von ihm gesetzte Wert heißt Profit*) (N 762, MEW 654).

CHAPTER 7

CONCLUSION

The Introduction Revisited

In the final section of the SL, Hegel engages in a metalogical consideration of the nature of scientific method. A necessary development in the advance of logical categories has progressed to the point that a formal consideration of the procedures of science itself is necessary. This metalogical consideration of scientific method is, at the same time, Hegel's critique of the methods of science and philosophy, and, in particular, of the empiricist methodologies formulated in the seventeenth and eighteenth centuries. Hegel distinguishes between the methods of the understanding and a properly rational method. He claims that those who would restrict method to the former fail to see that the methods of understanding are moments, or stages, in the process of scientific investigation.[1] The acquisition of knowledge, or cognition, involves three distinct moments. Each moment approximates more or less closely to the *Begriff* or concept of a subject matter. The first two moments are analytic and synthetic cognition. Together they comprise the "cognition of inquiry." The final moment in cognition is the complete presentation of the concept of the subject matter. The latter is knowledge in the true sense, or comprehension.

Hegel accomplishes two things in presenting the methods of the understanding as moments in the process of comprehension. He provides us with a critique of empiricist methodologies, and he establishes the claim that they are nevertheless essential components of cognition. The analytic and synthetic methods are the initial stages in the scientific investigation of the concept of a subject matter. They cannot be neglected or presented as the only methods that are adequate to the object. The cognition of inquiry entails analysis and then synthesis; or, cognition must be inductive and then deductive. The final moment of cognition, or comprehension per se, is at once analytic and synthetic. It is, properly speaking, based upon synthetic a priori principles.[2]

The logical structure and content of Marx's introduction reflects an identical approach to the nature of scientific method. Marx is critical of empiricist methodologies, though he includes them as moments, or stages, of scientific method. He is critical of those classical political economists who restricted method to analysis, though he maintains that analysis is an essential moment in a "method of inquiry." The method of inquiry initially must be inductive in nature. He is also critical of the classical political economists' version of synthetic method because it leads to a conception of the whole as comprised of "accidental relations." Nevertheless synthesis was the second moment or stage in the method of inquiry. The method of inquiry is inductive, then deductive. Marx claims, however, that analysis and synthesis fail to lead to the comprehension of capital as an organic system. They do not lead to a "speculative grasp" of the proper object. Instead, the proper grasp of a subject matter was, for Marx as it had been for Hegel, a result of synthetic a priori principles.

1. ANALYTIC AND SYNTHETIC COGNITION IN HEGEL AND MARX

In H. Uchida's work on Marx's *Grundrisse*, Uchida draws attention to the fact that Marx and Hegel used identical conceptions of the method of analysis.[3] Both Marx and Hegel describe analysis as *Anschauung*, or mere perceptual intuition, a *begifflos Vorstellung*. Cognition begins from a presupposed, concrete whole. While the presupposed whole is a concrete whole in and for itself, to investigators it initially appears as chaotic. Scientific exposition must reduce the chaotic conception of this whole to the simple determinations that comprise its essential nature. This process of analysis, or abstraction, proceeds until the investigator successfully isolates the most "simple determinations," or the "abstract, highest essence," of the object.

Uchida rightly points out that, for Marx, the first political economists began with the "living whole," and initially had a "chaotic conception" of that whole. Progress in economics consisted of moving analytically toward ever more "simple concepts." Adam Smith, for example, had abstracted from every limiting determination and arrived at the "abstract universality" of wealth-creating activity. Uchida's consideration, however, again falls short of an adequate account of the nature of the scientific method as conceived by both Hegel and by Marx. In fact, Uchida does not understand that the analytic method is merely the first of three moments, or stages, in scientific investigation. In addition, though he correctly points out that Marx's description of the analytic method in his introduction to the *Grundrisse* mirrors Hegel's own, he does not see that the entire introduction is indebted for its logical structure to the final chapters of Hegel's SL.

That analysis is merely the first of three moments of scientific method for Marx is shown by the fact that it is *aufgehoben*, transformed yet preserved, in the introductory paragraphs of his presentation of the proper object of investigation. Marx begins his introduction with a presentation of the object to be defined: material production. The fact that Marx could begin with such an abstraction, or universal, and not with the concrete "living whole" that he would then submit to analysis, shows that he believed that the hard work of abstraction had largely been completed by the classical political economists.

Marx is able to begin, therefore, with the next moment, or logical stage, of scientific investigation. He begins with the object to be defined and its definition. Most classical political economists used the synthetic method in their exposition of the system of capitalist production. According to this conception of the synthetic method, one ought to begin with the logical universal or "production in general," and move then to the particular determinations or the conditions of production, and from there to an exposition of capitalist production. Proven propositions about the system of capitalist production would then comprise the content of the exposition.

Marx does not, however, merely adopt the synthetic method of empiricism and employ it in the manner of the classical political economists. Rather, he uses it in such a way that it is at the same time a critique of the empiricists' version of the synthetic method. In fact, the manner in which he uses it indicates that for him Hegel's critical account of this method must be employed as the proper logical procedure of scientific investigation.

Hegel describes the movement of the synthetic method as the reverse of the analytic method. The analytic method starts from the individual, and proceeds to the general. In the application of the synthetic method, the investigator begins with a definition, from which he or she proceeds by classification to a theorem. The synthetic method is the development of the moments of the concept on the object of scientific investigation. While analytic cognition is the *apprehension* of what is, synthetic cognition aims at the *comprehension* of what is. It seeks to grasp the multiplicity of determinations in a unity, as a totality.

Thus, the first stage of the synthetic method is definition. Hegel characterizes definition as the transformation of a given objectivity into the simple form of the concept, that is, into universality, particularity, and individuality. In the transformation of the object into the simple form of individuality, the investigator presents the object as that which he or she will define, as an abstract representation. In the simple form of universality, the investigator presents the object according to the determinations of the judgment of necessity. Here, one isolates the genus, and to be more specific, the proximate genus of the object. In the simple form of particularity, the investigator presents the object according to its specific differences. Once the proximate genus and the specific difference have been isolated, the investigator moves to the particular conditions that give rise to the universal.

Division consists in the isolation of those particular elements that constitute the conditions through which the universal is actualized.

Hegel demonstrates how an investigator must first order the different elements according to an assumed basis of division. The different elements of the object are "set over and against each other" in an order that is established by the understanding. In the completed process of division, however, the investigator discerns the relationship among these particular elements according to the moments of the concept: universality, particularity, and individuality. The investigator may then express the relationship among the particular elements in a regular or formal syllogism.

Marx followed this exact procedure in his application of the synthetic method in the introduction. He moved from definition to division in his initial presentation of capitalism's mode of production. Of course, Adam Smith, Ricardo, and James Mill had also moved from a consideration of the definition of production in general to the conditions of production. This difference between an empiricist's conception and Hegel's critical version of synthetic method distinguishes the classical political economists' introductory presentation of the subject matter from Marx's own. The moments of the concept govern not only Marx's definition of production in general, but also his initial consideration of the relationship between the particular determinations or the conditions of production.

Marx begins his exposition by abstracting the logical universal of production in general and prescinding from historical conditions. He accuses the classical political economists of failing to follow even the most elementary of logical procedures. They failed to distinguish the logical universal of production in general from particular historical instantiations. They therefore confused this universal with a specific mode of production. He tells us that all epochs of production have certain common traits (*Merkmale*) and common characteristics (*Bestimmungen*). Production in general is an abstraction, but a "rational abstraction," because it "really brings out and fixes the common element." This universal is derived from a process of comparison (*Vergleichung*). Marx states: "There are characteristics which all stages of production have in common, and which are established as universal by the mind (N 88)."

Once Marx presents the object of definition, he then isolates the proximate genus of production in general in a series of judgments of necessity. For example, he states that all production is the appropriation of nature by an individual within and through a specific form of society; all forms of production presuppose stored up, past labor; production is always a particular branch of production and it is always a totality, that is, it is always a certain social body, a social subject, which is active in a greater or lesser extent in the particular branches of production; and all forms of production produce their own legal relations, forms of government, etc. Once Marx isolates the proximate genus of production in general, he then distinguishes it from the particular determinations, or conditions of production. He states that this universal "splits into different determinations." The universal of production in general had been abstracted from the actual conditions of the process of each mode of production. Each mode of production contains specific determinations that are involved in the process as a whole. Some of these determinations belong to all epochs of production, while others only to a few. No form of production can be properly conceived of without some of these particular determinations. The most modern and the most ancient modes of production share some determinations. The work of science must first abstract or isolate the particular conditions valid for production as such, and clearly distinguish them from actual historical conditions.

In Marx's criticisms of the classical political economists, we can detect the difference between the empiricist premises and Marx's Hegelian orientation. The classical political economists engaged in a "crude-tearing-apart" of production, and its particular conditions. They merely "set alongside it" its particular determinations; they neglected their "real relationship." By contrast, Marx maintains that when one moves in scientific investigation from a consideration of the universal in definition to the particular determinations of division, one must not neglect the fact that the particular conditions are individual moments in a complex unity.

Marx then follows Hegel's rules of synthetic method. He applies the form-determinations of the concept in a presentation of the relationship among the particular conditions of production in a regular or formal syllogism. He states: "Thus production appears as the point of departure, consumption as the conclusion, distribution and exchange as the middle, which is however itself twofold, since distribution is determined by society and exchange by individuals (N 89)." Moreover, he states: "Thus production, distribution, exchange and consumption form a regular syllogism: production is the universality, distribution and exchange the particularity, and consumption the individuality in which the whole is joined together (N 89)."

Marx began by presenting the object of definition, or material production. He then moved to isolate the universality of this abstract representation. Production in general splits into different determinations. In definition, Marx presented production in its abstract universality; in division, he presents it as the universality, or determining principle, of the relationship of its particular determinations.

At this point in the synthetic advance, Marx tells us that the possibility for misunderstanding exists. Production may be misconstrued as a transcendent principle that is not subject to the same historical conditions as its own particular determinations. A scientific exposition must demonstrate that the relationship of production to its conditions is an essential one. It must be proven that they are all moments of an organic whole, with production as the universal determining principle. When Marx presented production as a unity of distinct moments, and then moved to demonstrate that it is also an organic unity, he was again following closely the guidelines for the synthetic method that Hegel had outlined in the penultimate chapter of the SL.

Hegel proves that the synthetic method is the second moment in the cognition of inquiry. A synthetic advance from division to demonstration, or to a theorem, completes the cognition of inquiry. Demonstration begins with a definition, but a definition that consists of a formal relationship among the moments of the concept. In division, one merely presents the relationship of universality, particularity, and individuality as an immediate unity. Division does not consist in a proof that the moments are essentially related as an organic unity. In demonstration, the investigator proves that the moments of the concept are the mediated moments of a single process. He or she differentiates the subject matter into its essential real determinations, and then demonstrates that the subject matter is a unity within itself. The process of demonstration is brought to a close with a second definition that contains within it this mediated unity.

Marx follows this exact procedure in his synthetic advance from a formal "connection" among the various particular determinations of production, to a demonstration that the relationship among the many moments is not "accidental." For example, he states that distribution is distribution only in relation to production, and vice versa. He shows that each is identical to the other, mediates the other's existence, and is a necessary condition of the other. Likewise, he demonstrates that each of the other elements originally presented in "connection" with production are in fact moments of a single whole. But because production is the universal or the point of departure for the entire process, it is the predominate moment and therefore logically prior to the other particular determinations. Marx states: "The conclusion we reach is not that production, distribution, exchange and consumption are identical, but that they all form the members of a totality, distinctions within a unity. Production predominates not only over itself, in the antithetical definition of production, but over the other moments as well (N 99)."

The original, stipulated definition, in which Marx presented production in connection with its particular conditions, gave way to a demonstrated, second definition. Marx states: "A definite production thus determines a definite consumption, distribution and exchange as well as definite relations between these different moments." Mutual interaction takes place between the different moments, as is the case "with every organic whole."

2. SYNTHETIC A PRIORI PRINCIPLES AND MARX'S PLAN FOR THE ECONOMICS

For both Hegel and Marx, the cognition or method of inquiry consists of two moments, or stages, in scientific investigation. The first entails the reduction of a "living whole" from a *begrieflos Vorstellung*, to simple or essential concepts. By way of analysis, the mind moves from an abstract or immediate representation, the "imagined concrete," to abstract universality. The latter serves, in turn, as the basis for the second moment of the method of understanding. In Hegel's critical version of synthetic method, the investigator applies the simple form-determinations of the concept to the object of definition. Once the logical universal has been isolated, the investigator then moves from universality to particularity and there isolates the particular determinations or conditions of the universal. In division, the investigator no longer presents the universal in its abstract universality as a definition, but in "connection" with its own conditions. But because the relationship between the many determinations is a mediated one, the investigator must then demonstrate that the object is in fact a concrete unity of distinct moments. Then, once the process of the proof is complete, the investigator concludes the inquiry with a second or real definition that displays the object as a concrete, organic whole.

Although the synthetic method attains to the "self-related determinateness" of a concrete whole, this form of cognition is still an external one for both Hegel and Marx. Synthetic method presupposes analytic cognition, and therefore empirical universality as a starting point. The necessity that it comprehends is an abstract one. For example, Marx claims that the so-called general preconditions of all production "are nothing more than these abstract moments with which no real historical stage of production can be grasped." The synthetic component of the cognition of inquiry merely works the results of observation and abstraction into concepts. It in no way attains to an identity of thought and the "living whole" from which the investigation had originated. It is not the "speculative grasp" or the comprehension of the concept of the subject matter.

In the introduction, Marx states that the concrete is concrete because it is the result of the relation of many determinations. It is a unity in diversity, as a totality. As a consequence, it appears in the process of thinking as a process of concentration (*Zusammenfassung*), as a result. Once an investigator has isolated the abstract determinations of this organic unity, they must be ordered in such a fashion that the whole is reproduced in "the way of thought." Marx describes this "way of thought" in the form of a critique of Hegel.

Hegel had made the mistake of conceiving of the real "as the product of thought concentrating itself, probing its own depths, and unfolding itself out of itself, by itself." Marx maintains that this method of rising from the abstract to the concrete is merely "the way in which thought appropriates the concrete, reproduces it as the concrete in the mind." Furthermore, the concrete in the mind is a "totality of thoughts," and is a product of thought. As such, it results in comprehension (*Begreifens*). The comprehension of an organic unity is not "a product of the concept which thinks and generates itself outside or above observation and conception," but rather it is a product of the working-up of observation and conception into concepts. Marx terms this the speculative grasp of the object.

In the final chapter of the SL, Hegel characterizes the "absolute method" as a "product of thought concentrating itself, probing its own depths, and unfolding itself out of itself, by itself." It results in the comprehension of the subject matter, because it is the complete presentation of the *Begriff* of the latter. It is speculative cognition. In a consideration of this speculative or true cognition, Hegel reviews the entire course of the SL. Speculative cognition presupposes the moments of inquiry. It does not begin, therefore, with the empirically given or with empirical universality, but with a universality that is the "objective immanent form" of the organic unity. The beginning contains all the determinations that characterize the essential nature of the concrete totality. Progress in true cognition consists in cognizing the nature of the subject matter within this universality. Thus, the further determinations of the initial universal are found within the universal itself. To this extent, the absolute method is analytic. However, the complete nature of the concrete totality is not cognized in this initial universality. The absolute method is therefore just as much synthetic, because the advance is made from this simple universal to particular determinations or conditions of it. The true cognition of the concrete totality is a function of the explication of the many moments that relate to each other in constituting the whole.

True cognition is a synthetic method, but one that must be clearly distinguished from the synthetic component of inquiry. It is enough merely to state that the method is analytic to distinguish it from the latter. The analysis of the subject matter takes place entirely within the *Begriff* of that subject matter. For this reason the absolute method must be characterized as synthetic a priori.

The concrete totality is, then, that from which the beginning is made. But because it is first presented in its immediacy and not as an organic, self-related whole, the first determinations are presented as mere diversity. The exposition proceeds from this initial immediacy or simple universality to a consideration of the relationship between particular determinations of the whole. I need not review the entire course of the SL, but suffice it to say that as the first part of the scentific exposition is concerned with universality, the second entails an explication of particular conditions, and the third demonstrates that the subject matter under investigation is an organic unity.

As I note in the introduction to the present work, the precise nature of the logical development of the categories is a function of the relationship between the subject matter itself, or the content, and the form of thinking that must be used to comprehend it. In and through correct inferences we come to see that the subject matter under consideration is not the whole that we desire to know, but part of it. These partial insights are superseded until we arrive at an insight into the whole. At each level of the development the form of thinking determines the nature of the content. But, likewise, the content determines the form of thinking. Because the form and content are inseparable, the nature of the development is absolutely necessary. Each transition is inexorably linked to the prior development and, in turn, form and content determine subsequent developments.

All this must be kept in mind in our assessment of Marx's scientific method. As the "speculative grasp," or comprehension of the concept of capital, the method of presentation that governs the entire *Grundrisse* must not be characterized as synthetic in the usual sense of the term, that is, not with the same meaning that characterized the classical political economist approach to the capitalist economic system. Rather, the method of presentation was for Marx as it was for Hegel synthetic a priori.

This characterization can be clearly discerned in Marx's outline or plan of his exposition. In the "Chapter on Capital," Marx presents the entire development of the systematic exposition of capital as a movement from universality to particularity and finally to individuality. The full presentation of the organic whole of capital in a "totality of thoughts" is a function of the intimate relation between form and content that characterized Hegel's conception of *Wissenshaft*. Thus, as Marx states at the end of his discussion of method in the introduction, it is the subject matter itself, or capital, that determines the form of thinking, or category, that must be used to explicate it. But likewise, it is the form of thinking or category that determines the order in which the whole or content must be presented. In this way the simple universality of the commodity form of the product, the "germ" of the entire development, of necessity gives way to the exposition of the particular "moments" of capitalist production. And finally, capital is presented as a self-reproducing whole of many determinations, an organic unity in difference. We should not be at all surprised, therefore, to learn that Marx used the entire SL to order the material found in the *Grundrisse*.

In fact, chapters 2 through 6 of the present work have demonstrated that Marx's use of Hegel's concept of scientific method was by no means a haphazard affair. Rather, because Marx sought the complete exposition of the entire nature of the organic unity of capital, and, to be more specific, of capital in general in the *Grundrisse,* he simply would not have treated Hegel's ordering of the categories lightly. He saw the necessity of the ordering of the categories, and therefore, understood that a scientific dialectical exposition of capital as an organic unity must respect that ordering.

We have seen that the *Grundrisse* can be divided into three sections, or stages, based on its logical form. The first, most abstract stage of the exposition of capital in general is structured according to the logic of being; the second according to the logic of essence; while the third, most concrete stage is structured according to the logic of concept. Each section, or stage in exposition, is distinguished from the others based on the peculiar logic used in the exposition of the particular subject matter treated in that section. What this has entailed is as follows.

Hegel begins his exposition of the idea with the immediate content of knowledge, and with thought in its merely conceptual phase. The categories employed provide us with a view of the immediate forms of existence of an organic whole. The exposition of the content of the logic of being is, as a consequence, an exposition of the external relations between things, or the objects of sense. This section is the most abstract section of the entire SL because the subject matter under consideration are objects that are isolated and separated from the concrete, organic unity within which they are embedded.

Because this section is concerned to expose the external relations between objects of sense, or the immediate forms of existence as they superficially appear, the categories themselves are externally related. The relation between categories within the logic of being is a mere "passing over into," as a "transition," or a "vanishing of one into the other." The logical form is a relation between categories, rather than a relation *of* categories. So for example, quality "passes over into" the category of quantity. Here Hegel shows that a qualitatively determined, immediate being is potentially quantifiable because it is the result of activity. The exposition of quantity results in a transition into measure. In measure, a quantitative, spurious infinite generates an exponent, which is the rule or standard of comparison between related quanta. The entire exposition of the logic of being is then submerged in the emergence of the material substrate.

In chapter 2, I demonstrated that the relation between economic categories in Marx's exposition of "simple circulation" reflects precisely the logical form of being, or the relation between categories as a "passing over into," a "vanishing of one into the other." Marx begins his exposition of capital as organic unity in the precise manner that Hegel recommends as logically proper. He begins with capital's immediate forms of existence as they superficially appear. Such forms of existence are things, or objects of sense; and, as such, they are externally related. So for example, a qualitatively determined, immediate product is shown to be potentially quantifiable, because it is the result of a laboring activity. Its quantitative determination results in infinite computations that relate like determined objects. Such a relation between products produces an exponent, which, in turn, becomes money as a measure. Marx brings to a close the entire exposition of simple circulation, or capital as it appears, with the emergence of money as a universal material representative of wealth.

I have drawn attention to the fact that Marx frequently refers to the relation between the product/commodity and money within the context of "simple circulation," as a mere "passing over into," or a "vanishing of one into the other." The commodity is exchanged for money, and money for commodity; which, in turn, is exchanged for money, in a virtual "infinite series" of exchanges. In this context, the commodity drops out of circulation only to be consumed, while money is hoarded as dead treasure.

Simple circulation is in no way productive of capital. As Marx states, it cannot "ignite itself from within," and its "immediate being" is therefore "pure illusion." Simple circulation is the "mediation of extremes," which it itself does not "posit." Marx proves decisively that capital cannot be defined in terms of an external relation between things. His careful scientific exposition distinguishes between "simple circulation" and an underlying reality, which it presupposes. A careful scientific exposition distinguishes between capital as it appears, and the essence of capitalist production.

In the second stage in the development of the SL, Hegel demonstrates that reflection on the immediate content of knowledge reveals an underlying reality in terms of which the immediate being of that which appears is to be explained. Reflection on external relations reveals an inner essence that is presupposed by them. Things are not as they appear, but they exist in and through internal and external relation.

In the exposition of the logic of being, Hegel showed that objects of immediate experience are constituted in external relations. In the exposition of the logic of essence, he demonstrates that constitutive relations are not solely external. Essence is an exposition of relational properties *of* things, rather than an exposition of the external relations *between* things.[4] Because the logic of essence is an exposition of the essential relations within things, Hegel defines the categories relationally. In being, categories vanished into each other; in essence, categories are constituted in dyadic relations. Moreover, in being the relation between categories was one of transition; in essence, the relation between categories is "intro-reflection."[5]

The complete exposition of a particular category demonstrates that it "implies" or "posits" another. The second category is different from, or "in opposition to," the first one. Though each is different from or in opposition to the other, each is constituted in the relation. This relation is a new, essential unity. The exposition of the content of the new unity, in turn, gives rise to another relation in a movement from the more abstract to the more concrete essential relations of organic unity. So for example, the illusory or unessential and the essential are interdependent; as are identity and difference; the ground and the grounded; the thing and its properties; the whole and the parts; force and its expression; the inner and the outer, and so on. Essence is complete when the matter under consideration has proven itself to be an essential, organic unity of different, interdependent aspects.

I have demonstrated in chapters 3 and 4 that Marx's exposition of the essence of capitalist production reflects the logical form of essence. Once Marx had exposed capital's appearance in simple circulation, he then moves to distinguish between that appearance and an essential, underlying reality. The underlying reality is not an external relation among things, but a system of internal, interdependent relations.

Because the second stage is an exposition of internal, essential relations, Marx defines economic categories relationally. The exposition of a particular aspect begins with a relatively simple identity, for example, money, the commodity, or the whole of the working day. Marx then demonstrates that the simple identity "implies" or "posits" contradictory sides, which are nevertheless correlated aspects of an individual series. They are phases in the development of a single, more concrete whole. The more concrete whole, in turn, serves as the basis for further development, which likewise entails two phases that are superseded in a single whole. Thus, for example, the illusory nature of simple circulation and the return-movement of production are interdependent; the return-movement of production is dependent upon the contradiction between capital and its "non being," or living labor; production based on capital is the ground of the product/commodity; the product/commodity contains surplus value as its property; surplus value depends on a relation between the whole of the working day and its fractional parts; the relationship and tension between the parts within the whole is exposed as the natural force of capital to constantly reduce necessary labor time; and production depends on the outer barrier of circulation or consumption capacity.

Marx shows that these twofold relations are superseded in an essential, organic unity of the different, interdependent "moments" of production and circulation. He thereby defines capital as a "totality" of inseparable moments, that is, as circulating capital.

In the third, and final and most concrete section of the SL, Hegel scrutinizes the completed, complex organic whole itself. It was of course immanent within the entire development and as such was the foundation of the many categories of the two preceding parts. Organic unity was implicit in its appearance in being; posited or set-out as what it essentially is in essence; and, in the final development, organic unity proved to be a unity of being and essence, the universal organizing principle of the whole. In the final section, its own development is the focus of exposition.

Because the content of the exposition of the logic of the concept differs essentially from that of the two preceding sections, the logical form, or relation between categories, differs as well. In being, the categories had passed over into each other. Because the whole was merely implicit, the transition of one category into the next had characterized their ordering. In essence, Hegel shows how each category is essentially related to, or reflected in, the next. The nature of the development of the categories in concept is not a transition, or a reflection. The development is an explication of what is immanent in what has come before.[6] Each category represents the whole of organic unity, when viewed from a certain perspective. Each is therefore both the whole of the system, and one of its a specific "moments."

The logic of the concept divides into subjectivity and objectivity. The final section is concerned to expose, not the becoming of the concept, but the concept as it "proceeds from itself." In subjectivity, therefore, the many categories that had been used in the exposition of the concept's becoming are reexamined at a higher level, that is, as "form-determinations" of its own self-movement. Once Hegel has demonstrated that organic unity must be conceived of as a concrete universal, he can show that it is what is objectively real. Objectivity deals with the concept as objectified.

In chapters 5 and 6 of this work, I demonstrated that Marx's exposition of capital as it "proceeds from itself" reflects the logic of the concept. In the third, final, and most concrete stage in the exposition, Marx examines capital as a complete, complex organic unity. Capital as such had been immanent in the entire development. It was implicit in its mere appearance as simple circulation; it was posited or setout as what it essentially is in the second stage; and, in the final development, it proved itself to be an organic unity of circulation and production. As such, it is the universal organizing principle. In the final stage, it is the focus of the exposition.

Because the content of the concept of capital as such differs essentially from capital as it appears and the essence of capitalist production, the logical form, or relation between economic categories, differs as well. In its appearance, transition had characterized the ordering of economic categories. In the exposition of its essential, component parts, reflection had characterized the relation between categories. In this final section, the relation between economic categories is neither transition nor reflection, but development. It is rather an explication of what was immanent in the preceding stages. As a consequence, each economic category represents the whole, when viewed from a certain perspective. Each is therefore the whole of the organic unity of capital, and a specific "moment" of it.

According to the logic of the concept, the logic of development proper, Marx divides the final stage in the exposition into two sections, or stages. In the first, he reexamines all the many economic categories that served to expose the becoming of capital at a higher level of exposition. Rather than "moments" in the "becoming" of capital, Marx presents them here as "form-determinations" of capital as it "proceeds from itself." Finally, once he has demonstrated that capital as such must be conceived of as a concrete universal, he shows it as the objectively real, the objectification of fixed capital.

In demonstrating that the *Grundrisse* manuscripts are indebted for their logical form to the SL, this work has sought to understand the relation of Marx's critique of the political economy of bourgeois society to Hegel's system. Further, the work sought to improve on the outstanding contributions of H. Uchida, specifically by demonstrating that Marx's employment of the SL involved more than a piecemeal use of logical categories. As this work demonstrates, Marx was keenly aware of the reciprocal relation between form and content in Hegel's presentation of the logical development of the categories of science. Marx sought the complete exposition of the organic unity of capital in general. He recognized the scientific nature of such an exposition based on Hegel's method. He therefore respected Hegel's ordering of the logical categories in the SL.

---

[1] Hegel. SL, pp. 816-817.
[2] Hegel, SL, pp. 830-831.
[3] H. Uchida, *Marx's Grundrisse and Hegel's Logic*, pp. 18-20.
[4] Errol E. Harris, *An Interpretation* pp. 155-59.
[5] *Ibid.*, p. 214.
[6] *Ibid.*, pp. 220-22.

SELECT BIBLIOGRAPHY

1. G. W. F. HEGEL

Enzykopädie der philosophischen Wissenschaften, vol. 1. Frankfurt: Suhrkamp Verlag, 1970.

Science of Logic. trans. A. V. Miller. London: George Allen and Unwin, 1965.

Wissenschaft der Logik, vol. I-II. Frankfurt: Suhrkamp Taschenbuch Wissenschaft, 1969.

Philosophy of Right. trans. T. M. Knox. London: Clarendon Press, 1965.

Phenomenology of Spirit. trans. A. V. Miller. Oxford: Oxford University Press, 1977.

2. KARL MARX

Economic and Philosophic Manuscripts (1844). trans. Martin Milligan. ed. with intro. by Dirk J. Struik. New York: International Press, 1986.

The Critique of Hegel's 'Philosophy of Right'. ed. with intro. by J. J. O'Malley. Cambridge: Cambridge University Press, 1973.

"Theses on Feuerbach," in Marx and Engels: *Basic Writings on Politics and Philosophy*. ed. by Louis Feuer. New York: Doubleday, 1959.

The Poverty of Philosophy. New York: International Publishers, 1969.

Grundrisse: Foundations of the Critique of Political Economy (Rough Draft). trans. Martin Nicolaus. New York: Penguin Books, 1973.

Grundrisse der Kritik der politischen Ökonomie (Rohentwurf), Werke, vol. 42. Berlin: Dietz Verlag, 1983.

Ökonomische Manuskripte 1857/58, 1-2, Marx-Engels Gesamtausgabe (MEGA), 11/1.1, 1.2. Berlin: Dietz Verlag, 1976, 1981.

A Contribution to the Critique of Political Economy. trans. by S. W. Ryazanskaya. New York: International Publishers Press, 1970.

Capital: A Critique of Political Economy, vol. 1: *A Critical Analysis of Capitalist Production.* trans. by Samuel Moore and Edward Aveling. New York: International Publishers, 1968.

3. OTHER WORKS

Backhaus, Hans-Georg. "Zur Dialektik der Wertform," in *Beiträge zur marxistischen Erkenntnestheorie*, pp. 128-52. ed. by Alfred Schmidt. Frankfurt: VSA-Verlag, 1969.

Burbidge, John. *On Hegel's Logic.* New Jersey: Humanities Press, 1981.

Carver, T. *Karl Marx: Texts on Method.* Oxford: Blackwell, 1975.

———. "Marx—and Hegel's Logic," *Political Studies*, vol. 24:57-88.

Colletti, Lucio. "Marxismus und Dialektic," pp. 5-41 in *Marxismus und Dialektic.* Frankfurt, 1977. English translation, *Marxism and Hegel.* trans. and ed. by Lawrence Garner. London: Verso, 1979.

Duquette, David A. "Methodology and Development in Marx and Hegel," *The Owl of Minerva* 19 (Spring 1988): 131-48.

Findlay, J. N.. *Hegel, A Reexamination.* London: Clarendon Press, 1958.

———. *The Philosophy of Hegel.* New York: Coller Books, 1966.

Fulda, H. F. "Dialektik als Darstellungsmethode im 'Kapital' von Marx," in *Yearbook of the Philosophical Society of Finland* 37 (Winter 1978): 180-216.

Furth, Peter. "Arbeit und Reflexion," in Arbeit und Reflexion. ed. by Peter Furth. Köln: Peter-Rugensten, Verlag, 1980.

———. "Arbeit, Teleologie, Hegelianismus," pp. 99-121, in *Dialektik, Beiträge zu Philosophie und Wissenschaft.* Köln, 1981.

Gould, C. C. *Marx's Social Ontology: Individuality and Community in Marx's Theory of Social Reality*. Cambridge: MIT Press, 1978.

Harris, Errol. *An Interpretation of the Logic of Hegel*. New York: University Press of America, 1983.

Hartmann, Klaus. *Die Marxsche Theorie* Berlin: Gruyter, 1970.

Hartnack, Justus. *An Introduction to Hegel's Logic*, trans. by Lars Aagaard-Mogensen. New York: Hackett, 1998.

Henrich, Dieter. "Karl Marx als Schüler Hegels," in *Hegel in Kontext*. Frankfurt: VSA-Verlag, 1972.

Henrich, Dieter, editor. *Hegels Wissenschaft der Logik*. Stuttgart: Klett-Cotta, 1986.

Howard, Dick. *The Marxian Dialectic*. Cambridge: Southern Illinois University Press, 1972.

Inwood, Michael, editor. *Hegel*. New York: Oxford University Press, 1985.

Kain, Philip. *Marx's Method, Epistemology, and Humanism: A Study in the Development of His Thought*. The Netherlands: Reidel Publishing, 1986.

Krahl, H. J. "Bemerkungen zum Verhältnis von Kapital und Hegelscher Wesenlogik," in *Aktualität und Folgen der Philosophie Hegels*. ed. by 0. von Negt. Frankfurt: Suhrkamp Verlag, 1970.

Lukács, Georg. *History and Class Consciousness*. trans. and ed. by Rodney Livingstone. Boston: MIT Press, 1971.

MacGregor, David. *The Communist Ideal in Hegel and Marx*. Toronto: University of Toronto Press, 1984.

McCarthy, George F. *Marx's Critique of Science and Positivism: The Methodological Foundations of Political Economy*. The Netherlands: Kluwer Academic Publishers, 1988.

———. *Marx and the Ancients*. Maryland: Rowman and Littlefield, 1990.

McTaggart, J. *A Commentary on Hegel's Logic*. Cambridge: Cambridge University Press, 1931.

Mepham, J. "From the Grundrisse to Capital: The Making of Marx's Method," in *Issues in Marxist Philosophy*, vol. 1, *Dialectics and Method*. ed. by J. Mepham and D. H. Ruben. Brighton: Harvester Press, 1979.

Murray, Patrick. *Marx's Theory of Scientific Knowledge*. New Jersey: Humanities Press, 1981.

Norman, Richard, and Sean Sayers. *Hegel, Marx, and Dialectic: A Debate*. New Jersey: Humanities Press, 1980.

Oakley, Allen. *The Making of Marx's Critical Theory*. London: Routledge, 1983.

———. *Marx's Critique of Political Economy*. Vol.1.London: Routledge & Kegan Paul, Inc., 1984.

Ollman, Bertell. *Alienation*. NewYork: Cambridge University Press, 1971.

O'Malley, J., K. W. Algozin, H. P. Kainz, and L. C. Rice, editors. *The Legacy of Hegel*. The Hague: Martins Nijhoff, 1973.

O'Malley, J., "Marx's 'Economics' and Hegel's 'Philosophy of Right': An Essay on Marx's Hegelianism," *Political Studies* 24:43-56.

Pinkard, Terry. "The Logic of Hegel's Logic," in Michael Inwood, editor. *Hegel*. New York: Oxford University Press, 1985.

Reichelt, Helmut.*Zur logischen Struktur des Kapital —Begriff bei Karl Marx*. Frankfurt: VSA-Verlag, 1970.

Rosdolsky, Roman. *The Making of Marx's 'Capital'*. trans. by P. Burgess. London: Pluto Press, 1977.

Rubel, M., "A History of Marx's 'Economics'," in *Rubel on Karl Marx*. ed. by J. J. O'Malley and K. W. Algozin. Cambridge: Cambridge University Press, 1981.

———. "The Plan and Method of the 'Economics'," in *Rubel on Karl Mårx*. ed. by J. J. O'Malley and K. W. Algozin. Cambridge: Cambridge University Press, 1981.

Sayer, Derek. *Marx's Method: Ideology, Science, and Criticism in 'Capital'*. New Jersey: Humanities Press, 1979.

Smith, Tony. *The Logic of Marx's Capital*. New York: SUNY Press, 1990.

Theunissen, Michael. *Sein und Schein*. Frankfurt: Suhrkamp Verlag, 1978.

Uchida, H. *Marx's Grundrisse and Hegel's Logic*. ed. by Terrell Carver. New York: Routledge, 1988.

Winfield, R. D. "The Logic of Marx's Capital," *Telos* 27 (Spring 1976).

Wolf, Dieter. *Hegel und Marx: Zur Bewegungstruktur des Absoluten Geistes und des Kapital*. Hamburg: VSA-Verlag, 1979.

———. *Ware und Geld: der Dialektische Widerspruche im "Kap ital."* Hamburg: VSA-Verlag, 1985.

Zelèny, Jindrich. *Die Wissenschaftslogik und "Das Kapital."* Frankfurt: VSA-Verlag, 1968.

INDEX

Philosophical Studies in Contemporary Culture

H. Tristram Engelhardt, Jr., Series Editor

Kevin William Wildes, S.J., Associate Editor

1. G. Motzkin: *Time and Transcendence.* Secular History, the Catholic Reaction and the Rediscovery of the Future. 1992 ISBN 0-7923-1773-4
2. H. Tristram Engelhardt, Jr. and T. Pinkard (eds.): *Hegel Reconsidered.* Beyond Metaphysics and the Authoritarian State. 1994 ISBN 0-7923-2629-6
3. L.B. McCullough: *Leibniz on Individuals and Individuation.* The Persistence of Premodern Ideas in Modern Philosophy. 1996 ISBN 0-7923-3864-2
4. N. Capaldi: *The Enlightenment Project in the Analytic Conversation.* 1998 ISBN 0-7923-5014-6
5. K. Bayertz (ed): *Solidarity.* 1999 ISBN 0-7923-5475-3
6. S.A. Erickson (ed.): *The (Coming) Age of Thresholding.* 1999 ISBN 0-7923-5938-0
7. D.T. Schwartz: *Art, Education, and the Democratic Commitment.* A Defense of State Support for the Arts. 2000 ISBN 0-7923-6292-6
8. M.F. Carr: *Passionate Deliberation.* Emotion, Temperance, and the Care Ethic in Clinical Moral Deliberation. 2001 ISBN 1-4020-0143-6
9. M.E. Meaney, Ph.D. *Capital as Organic Unity.* The Role of Hegel's *Science of Logic* in Marx's *Grundrisse.* 2002 ISBN 1-4020-1037-0

KLUWER ACADEMIC PUBLISHERS – BOSTON / DORDRECHT / LONDON

GPSR Compliance

The European Union's (EU) General Product Safety Regulation (GPSR) is a set of rules that requires consumer products to be safe and our obligations to ensure this.

If you have any concerns about our products, you can contact us on ProductSafety@springernature.com

In case Publisher is established outside the EU, the EU authorized representative is:

Springer Nature Customer Service Center GmbH
Europaplatz 3
69115 Heidelberg, Germany

Batch number: 10823959

Printed by Printforce, the Netherlands